The Devil's Dominion examines the use of folk magic by ordinary men and women in early New England, despite clerical opposition to such practices. It shows that layfolk were generally far less consistent in their beliefs and actions than their ministers would have liked, and that there were significant affinities between Puritanism and magic that enabled even church members to switch from one to the other without any sense of wrongdoing. Godbeer also argues that the controversy surrounding astrology in early New England paralleled clerical condemnation of magical practice, and that the different perspectives on witchcraft engendered by magical tradition and Puritan doctrine often caused confusion and disagreement when New Englanders sought legal punishment of witches.

THE DEVIL'S DOMINION

THE DEVIL'S DOMINION

MAGIC AND RELIGION IN EARLY NEW ENGLAND

RICHARD GODBEER

Published by the Press Syndicate of the University of Cambridge
The Pitt Building, Trumpington Street, Cambridge CB2
40 West 20th Street, New York, NY 10011-4211, USA
10 Stamford Road, Oakleigh, Melborne 3166, Australia

First published 1992
First paperback edition 1993
Reprinted 1994

Printed in the United States of America

Library of Congress Cataloging-in-Publication Data is available

A catalogue record for this book is available from the British Library

ISBN 0-521-40329-4 hardback
ISBN 0-521-46670-9 paperback

In Memory of My Father
1936–1991

CONTENTS

ACKNOWLEDGMENTS

During the course of the last few years, I have had the good fortune to incur many debts of gratitude. In Massachusetts, my friends gave me the love and support without which the dissertation out of which this book grew would never have reached completion. Of those friends, my housemate Mary Francis deserves special mention. That Mary lived with this project for so long is no small tribute to her powers of endurance. When I think of the countless occasions on which we discussed my ideas and their often tortured expression, I remember her generosity of time and energy, her unwavering support, and, perhaps most precious of all, her sense of humor.

At Brandeis University, James Kloppenberg had a lasting influence on my work. I valued his rigor as a teacher and appreciated his encouragement throughout my time in the graduate program there. John Demos, my initial advisor, introduced me to the occult wonders of colonial history: he was an inspiring guide. And so to my principal advisor. To my mind, a dissertation advisor should combine the professional subtlety of a Whitehall Mandarin, the fighting spirit of a Valkyrie, the incisiveness of a rapier, the patience of a saint, and the benevolence of a fairy godmother. Christine Leigh Heyrman possesses all these qualities and more. She has my abiding respect, gratitude, and affection.

Since arriving in California, my work has been supported by fellowships from the National Endowment for the Humanities, the Center for Ideas and Society at the University of California at Riverside, the Academic Senate of the University of California at Riverside, and the University of California Regents. My colleagues in the History Department at UC Riverside have been supportive as friends and critics; especially Piotr Gorecki, Louis Masur, Sharon Salinger, Brian Smith, and Charles Wetherell. Elinor Abbot, Charles Lloyd Cohen, David D. Hall, Charles Hambrick-Stowe, Michael McGiffert, Carla Gardina Pestana, Elizabeth Reis, Benson Saler, Harry Stout, and Fredrika Teute have provided invaluable advice and innumerable insights. I am especially grateful to Frank

Smith, Katharita Lamoza, and the staff at Cambridge University Press for their careful preparation of the book for publication.

I owe many thanks to the staff of the Brandeis Farber/Goldfarb Library and UC Riverside's Tomas Rivera Library for the enthusiasm with which they helped to track down many of my sources. I am also extremely grateful to the staff of the Massachusetts Historical Society, whose expertise, efficiency, and good cheer did much to expedite my research there. The American Antiquarian Society, the Andover Historical Society, the Annmary Brown Memorial at Brown University Library, the Connecticut State Library, the Essex Institute, the Huntington Library, the Massachusetts Archives, and the New England Historical and Genealogical Society have also provided valuable assistance. In addition, I am indebted to John Demos for his generosity in lending documents and providing many citations.

PROLOGUE

When English colonists first crossed the Atlantic in the early seventeenth century, they directed their fragile vessels toward the southern reaches of North America, specifically the Chesapeake Bay. New England, the land north and east of the Hudson River, seemed much less inviting. Indeed, the first group of English migrants to arrive in New England landed at Plymouth in 1620 by mistake: they had intended to settle in Virginia. The landscape that greeted these hapless travelers was not encouraging: the New England coastline was rocky and austere; inland, as one colonist put it, "the whole country, full of woods and thickets, represented a wild and savage hue."[1] All in all, wrote another, it was a "remote, rocky, barren, bushy, wild-woody wilderness."[2] The climate was equally inhospitable: long and harsh winters punctuated by short and humid summers. By the end of their first winter in New England, half the Plymouth settlers had perished.

Yet New England had its possibilities. The region was abundant in timber, fish, waterfowl, and other wildlife. The forests that dominated the landscape were not difficult to penetrate, since the native Americans set fire to the underbrush each spring in order to facilitate traveling and hunting. The English set about adapting the landscape to suit their own way of life. As they cleared vast tracts of woodland to make way for a network of settled agricultural communities, New England was transformed into a land of fields and fences.[3] Supported initially by supplies from England and the generosity of native Americans, the colonists soon established themselves as a viable outpost of English culture. Contrary to initial expectations, the New England climate proved to be much healthier than in the south and the English flourished there: The first gen-

1 William Bradford, *Of Plymouth Plantation, 1620–1647*, ed. Francis Murphy (New York, 1981), p. 70.

2 Edward Johnson, *Johnson's Wonder-Working Providence*, ed. J. Franklin Jameson (New York, 1910), p. 210.

3 William Cronon, *Changes in the Land: Indians, Colonists, and the Ecology of New England* (New York, 1983).

eration of settlers lived an average of seventy years, ten years longer than their counterparts across the Atlantic.[4]

Most immigrants to seventeenth-century New England arrived as part of the "Great Migration," a Puritan-led exodus from Stuart England that began in 1630 and ended in 1642 with the outbreak of the English Civil War.[5] Puritan colonists were determined to establish in the northern colonies a New-English Israel, "New" in its exemplary godliness. In other respects, the settlers sought to reconstruct in their new environment as much as possible of the world they had left behind. Migrant families often traveled and settled in concert with friends and acquaintances from the same congregation, town, or county back in England. These groups established settlements that closely resembled the communities in which they had lived before migrating to New England.[6] Typically, each family received a plot of land in the town or village center, along with strips of farmland on the periphery of the community tract. Most families lived in close proximity to each other, their dwellings huddled around the meetinghouse. The quality of life in a typical New England community left little room for privacy of any kind. Indeed, townsfolk were encouraged to watch over their

4 For an overview of early American demography, see Jim Potter, "Demographic Development and Family Structure," in Jack P. Greene and J. R. Pole, eds., *Colonial British America: Essays in the New History of the Early Modern Era* (Baltimore, 1984), pp. 123–156.

5 Puritanism is defined here as a reform movement within the Church of England that called for a more rigorous exclusivity, including the strict limitation of access to the sacrament of the Lord's Supper. Puritans mounted a campaign for "moral reformation" throughout English society. Their attempts to suppress "ungodly" activities such as dancing and carousing provoked widespread opposition. In the context of seventeenth-century New England, I use the term to signify Congregationalist orthodoxy and those who considered themselves adherents of that orthodoxy.

The enterprise of defining Puritanism has given rise to much controversy. For contributions to this debate, see Basil Hall, "Puritanism: The Problem of Definition," in G. J. Cuming, ed., *Studies in Church History,* II (London, 1965), pp. 283–96; Charles George, "Puritanism as History and Historiography," *Past and Present,* 41 (1968): 77–104; William Lamont, "Puritanism as History and Historiography: Some Further Thoughts," *Past and Present,* 44 (1969): 133–46; Ian Breward, "The Abolition of Puritanism," *Journal of Religious History,* 7 (1972–3): 20–34; Thomas Clancy, "Papist–Protestant–Puritan: English Religious Taxonomy, 1565–1665," *Recusant History,* 13 (1976): 227–53; Paul Christianson, "Reformers and the Church of England under Elizabeth I and the Early Stuarts," *Journal of Ecclesiastical History,* 31 (1980): 463–84; and Patrick Collinson, "Comment," *Ibid.,* 485–7.

6 See David Grayson Allen, *In English Ways: The Movement of Societies and the Transferal of English Local Law and Custom to Massachusetts Bay in the Seventeenth Century* (Chapel Hill, 1981); and David Hackett Fischer, *Albion's Seed: Four British Folkways in America* (New York, 1989).

neighbors, so that they could report to the local authorities all "unseemly carriages."[7]

Most New England families supported themselves through subsistence farming, since neither the climate nor the soil would sustain commercial agriculture. But seventeenth-century New England was not self-sufficient. Along the coast, thriving mercantile communities were enmeshed in international trade, which enabled the purchase of manufactured goods from England. As the decades passed, a growing number of settlers became involved in trading networks that exported fur, fish, grain, and timber to England and the West Indies. During the second half of the century, seaports, already much more diverse and worldly in character than rural communities, became increasingly cosmopolitan and commercially oriented. Despite these changes, most New Englanders still pursued a predominantly agrarian and parochial way of life. The roads and pathways between towns and villages remained rudimentary and were often unpassable during the winter. A sizeable minority did travel back and forth from town to town, from colony to colony, and even across the Atlantic itself; but the majority of New Englanders, in common with the folk they had left behind in England, cared little for the world that lay beyond their own town or village and its adjacent communities.[8]

Within the local community, three institutions maintained order and stability: the family, the town meeting, and the church. The family household functioned as a microcosm of the larger society: its internal structure mirrored that of the community as a whole and prepared young people for their adult roles in colonial society. Once New Englanders reached adulthood, kinship played an important role in the choices they made as they formed friendships, initiated business relationships, made political alliances, and chose marriage partners. Kinship, both nuclear and extended, was a primary determinant of social action.[9] Beyond the family itself, the

7 John Demos evokes the social density of village life in *A Little Commonwealth: Family Life in Plymouth Colony* (New York, 1970) and *Entertaining Satan: Witchcraft and the Culture of Early New England* (New York, 1982), pp. 311–12. See also Richard Gildrie, *Salem, Massachusetts, 1626–1683: A Covenant Community* (Charlottesville, 1975); Kenneth Lockridge, *A New England Town, the First Hundred Years: Dedham, Massachusetts, 1636–1736* (New York, 1970); and Darrett Rutman, *Winthrop's Boston: A Portrait of a Puritan Town, 1630–1649* (Chapel Hill, 1965).

8 See T. H. Breen, "Persistent Localism: English Social Change and the Shaping of New England Institutions," *William and Mary Quarterly*, 32 (1975): 3–28. For an overview of the early American economy, see John J. McCusker and Russell R. Menard, *The Economy of British America, 1607–1789* (Chapel Hill, 1985).

9 See especially Edmund Morgan, *The Puritan Family: Religion and Domestic Relations in Seventeenth-Century New England* (1944; New York, 1966); John Demos, *A Little*

two most potent embodiments of corporate identity in New England were the town meeting and the church. The town meeting, from which women were excluded, provided a setting for the conduct of local affairs and the expression of common values. The only extra-familial institution to include both men and women was the church.

In matters of organized religion, the colonists deliberately forsook their English past. Each town congregation was an autonomous and self-governing body; there was no overarching ecclesiastical structure such as existed in the Church of England. Congregations acted independently of any higher authority, hiring and dismissing their ministers, admitting and expelling members, formulating church policy, and supervising public morality. Neither ministers nor their congregations dominated church affairs; clergy and laity worked together in a cooperative, although by no means always harmonious, spirit.[10] Civil governments did much to reinforce clerical influence within their jurisdictions: colonists were obliged by law to attend church on the sabbath and to pay taxes for the support of the ministry. In every northern colony except Rhode Island, Congregationalism was the only religious faith sanctioned by civil authority; outside Connecticut and Rhode Island, church membership was a prerequisite for the right to vote in colonial elections.

Congregationalist churches thus wielded great power, but their authority did not go unchallenged. Despite the formal hegemony of Puritanism in the northern colonies and the general success of Puritans in shaping New England culture, not all colonists adhered to Congregationalist orthodoxy. These dissidents included not only people who cared little for spiritual matters, but also godly New Englanders, including some church members, who dissented from the orthodox platform. The latter questioned official policy and sometimes refused to swallow their doubts in the face of disciplinary proceedings; such recalcitrants were excommunicated, in extreme cases even banished. Anne Hutchinson, for example, a skilled midwife who crossed the Atlantic to Massachusetts Bay in 1634, not only held heterodox views about salvation, but also dared to hold private meetings at which she explained her position to receptive

Commonwealth; Philip Greven, *The Protestant Temperament: Patterns of Child-Rearing, Religious Experience, and the Self in Early America* (New York, 1977); Gerald Moran and Maris Vinovskis, "The Puritan Family and Religion: A Critical Reappraisal," *William and Mary Quarterly,* 39 (1982): 29–63.

10 David D. Hall discusses this relationship in *Worlds of Wonder, Days of Judgment: Popular Religious Belief in Early New England* (New York, 1989), especially pp. 11–13.

neighbors. Hutchinson and several of her followers were exiled to Rhode Island. Other dissenters departed voluntarily. Thomas Hooker, the minister at Cambridge, opposed limiting the franchise to church members and favored less rigorous standards for church membership. In 1636, Hooker left Massachusetts along with part of his congregation and resettled in Connecticut. Other members of the covenanted community also became dissatisfied with Congregationalist orthodoxy, perhaps most notably Henry Dunster, the President of Harvard College, who converted to Baptism in 1653.

In addition to dissent from within, churches had to face sectarian evangelism from without. In 1656, the first Quaker missionaries arrived in New England and began to proselytize among the colonists. The civil courts took immediate action against these unwanted visitors and their converts; draconian measures, including four executions, contained but did not crush the Quaker movement. Throughout the second half of the seventeenth century, converts to Quakerism and other sectarian groups were relatively few in number, but their controversial behavior assured them high visibility and magnified the threat they posed to Congregationalist authority.[11]

Despite the presence of dissenters and sectarians, the orthodox succeeded in maintaining close control over religious life in early New England. But supernatural belief in the northern colonies was not exclusively religious. Alongside Protestant Christianity there coexisted a tangled skein of magical beliefs and practices that the colonists brought with them from England. Puritan ministers condemned magic as blasphemous and diabolical. Magic had no place in their vision of New England and so they were appalled to discover that colonists were using magical techniques. "It is a sad thing," lamented one cleric, "that ever any person should dare to do thus in New England." "Tis horrible," declared another, "that in this land of Uprightness, there should be any such Pranks of Wickedness."[12] The ministers' greatest cause for alarm was that magic appealed not only to those who rejected Puritanism, but also to church members. The spiritual corruption implied by and consequent upon magical practice tainted even the covenanted community.

11 See David D. Hall, ed., *The Antinomian Controversy, 1636–1638: A Documentary History* (Middletown, Conn., 1968); Philip Gura, *A Glimpse of Sion's Glory: Puritan Radicalism in New England, 1630–1660* (Middletown, Conn., 1984); Jeremiah Chaplin, *Life of Henry Dunster: First President of Harvard College* (Boston, 1872), especially pp. 109–35; and Carla Gardina Pestana, *Quakers and Baptists in Colonial Massachusetts* (New York, 1991). See also Chapter 6, n14.

12 Increase Mather, *A Discourse Concerning the Uncertainty of the Times of Men* (Boston, 1697), p. 24; Cotton Mather, *A Discourse on Witchcraft* (Boston, 1689), p. 27.

New England ministers condemned the use of magical techniques and urged their congregations to shun such "vile Impieties."[13] But magic proved to be less susceptible than either dissent or sectarianism to control by the guardians of spiritual purity. Magical beliefs were essentially informal, and therefore elusive: they were part of no coherent doctrinal system; neither were they implemented through an organized institutional structure. Sometimes colonists would ask a magical expert in their local community to act on their behalf, but often they experimented with magical techniques on their own. Because magical belief was so amorphous, the threat it posed to Puritanism was much more insidious than that presented by dissent and sectarianism. Indeed, many of those who turned to magic did not realize that their behavior was heterodox. For all the emphasis Protestant theologians laid upon the dichotomy between religious faith and magical practice, there were significant affinities between reformed Christianity and magic that enabled layfolk to switch from one to the other without any sense of wrongdoing. In addition to those who did not grasp official objections to magic, other layfolk chose to ignore clerical injunctions when convenient. The vagueness of magical tradition and its links to Puritan belief made it easier for such people to sidestep the spiritual implications of their behavior. This book explores magical tradition in early New England, its ambivalent relationship to officially sanctioned supernatural belief, and the conflicts that arose within New England communities as a result of lay resort to magical techniques.

13 Cotton Mather, *Wonders of the Invisible World* (1693; Amherst, Wisc., 1862), p. 96.

INTRODUCTION

Seventeenth-century New Englanders used magic to predict the future, to heal the sick, to destroy their enemies, and to defend themselves against occult attack.

> Rebecca Johnson of Andover, Massachusetts, was worried about her brother, whom she feared was dead. Johnson had her daughter balance a sieve on a pair of shears and ask "if her brother Moses Haggat was alive or dead." If the sieve turned, they would know he was dead. And so it did.
>
> Dorcas Hoar of Beverly, Massachusetts, used palmistry to divine the future. She borrowed a book on the subject from one of her neighbors, a book with "many streaks and pictures in it."
>
> A healer in Boston provided one of his patients with a charm that he promised would cure the tooth-ache. It was apparently "a usual thing for People to cure Hurts with Spells."
>
> Goodwife Glover, a Bostonian charged with witchcraft, admitted that she tormented her enemies by stroking rag dolls that she made to represent them. Court officials were sent to her house and returned with several of these dolls.
>
> Henry Grey, a Connecticut farmer, was convinced that his ailing heifer had been bewitched and so flogged the beast in order to injure the person responsible. Sure enough, a neighbor whom he suspected collapsed in agony.
>
> When Michael Smith informed some of his neighbors in Boston that he feared he was under an evil hand, they took some of Smith's urine and closed it in a bottle. A local healer immediately appeared outside the house where the "urinary experiment" was taking place and did not leave until the urine was

poured away. Those inside the house concluded that the healer had bewitched Smith.[1]

Incidents such as these seem far removed from the religious ideals that inspired the settlement of New England. Puritan ideology denounced magic as part of the corrupt and compromised world that constituted Stuart England. Puritan leaders planned to establish in the New World a society that would conform, as far as humanly possible, with their spiritual ideals: not for them the gulf between principle and practice for which they condemned so many English Protestants. Aboard the flagship *Arbella* in 1630, between England and Massachusetts Bay, governor-elect John Winthrop had delivered a lay sermon to his fellow travelers, in which he affirmed their purpose in crossing the Atlantic:

> The end is to improve our lives to do more service to the Lord, the comfort and increase of the body of Christ whereof we are members, that ourselves and posterity may be the better preserved from the common corruptions of this evil world, to serve the Lord and work out our salvation under the power and purity of His holy ordinances.

Once cut off from the malign influence of a society in which faith was all too often perfunctory, the colonists would find themselves better able to pursue a godly life. "That," declared Winthrop, "which the most in their churches maintain as a truth in profession only, we must bring into familiar and constant practice."[2]

As it turned out, many New Englanders were less consistent in the "practice" of their faith than Winthrop had hoped. Their use of magic bears testimony to the gulf between "profession" and "practice" of religion in early New England. Historian David Hall has recently warned against "the assumption that the people of New England exemplified a total or perfect faith." A small minority of layfolk were unswerving in their commitment and became deeply

1 Paul Boyer and Stephen Nissenbaum, *The Salem Witchcraft Papers: Verbatim Transcripts of the Legal Documents of the Salem Witchcraft Outbreak*, 3 vols. (New York, 1977), II: 507; *Salem Witchcraft Papers,* II: 398; Increase Mather, *An Essay for the Recording of Illustrious Providences* (Boston, 1684), p. 261; Cotton Mather, *Memorable Providences* (Boston, 1689), pp. 7–8; Willys Papers: Records of Trials for Witchcraft in Connecticut (Annmary Brown Memorial, Brown University Library, Providence, R.I.), W–33, 6 June 1692, testimony of Henry Grey and Ann Godfrey; Suffolk County Court Files: Original Depositions and Other Materials from the Proceedings of the Quarterly Courts of Suffolk County, Massachusetts (Massachusetts Archives, Columbia Point, Boston, Mass.), vol. 24, #1972, testimony of Hannah Weacome.

2 John Winthrop, "A Model of Christian Charity," in Perry Miller, ed., *The American Puritans: Their Prose and Poetry* (Garden City, N.Y., 1956), p. 82.

troubled whenever they fell short of their ideals; but the rest embodied their principles only intermittently. Hall emphasizes that such behavior did not necessarily signify "fundamental disaffection from religion." Many of those who applied their faith only sporadically nonetheless honored religious ideals; their principles were sincere, although they often neglected to judge their own behavior by the standards they espoused. These people were not cynical hypocrites; nor had they self-consciously lapsed from a commitment to active faith. Without explicitly rejecting their beliefs, they managed to set them aside from time to time.[3] In a similar vein, Laurence Veysey has suggested that New Englanders "were perfectly able to compartmentalize their thinking." Thus, they could believe quite sincerely in the doctrines and moral precepts laid down by Puritanism, and yet sometimes behave quite differently.[4] This mentality, a far cry from the rigorous consistency demanded by Puritan ministers, helps to explain the widespread currency of magical beliefs and techniques in seventeenth-century New England, despite the settlers' apparent commitment to a religious system that condemned and repudiated magic.

Before addressing in detail this split between clerical injunctions and lay practice, I should explain what I mean by two crucial terms. *Magic* and *religion* are used here to signify different ways of relating to supernatural power. Magical belief rests on the assumption that human beings can control occult forces (whether personal or impersonal) through ritual techniques. Magical skill enables people to harness supernatural power and use it for their own purposes: they can predict the future, protect themselves against harm, heal the sick, and strike down their enemies. Religious belief assumes the existence of a supernatural authority (usually personified) that controls the world in accordance with its own will; people can attempt to influence this divine power through prayer and other devotional exercises, but there is no guarantee that their desires will be fulfilled or their requests granted. Religious figures who perform miracles and prophesy do so as the instruments or conduits of divine puissance: supernatural power acts through them. Religion thus empowers the supernatural, whereas magic empowers human beings through their command of the supernatural. Religion is supplicative, magic manipulative.[5]

3 David D. Hall, *Worlds of Wonder, Days of Judgment: Popular Religious Belief in Early New England* (New York, 1989), especially pp. 14–17.

4 Laurence Veysey, "Intellectual History and the New Social History," in John Higham and Paul Conkin, eds., *New Directions in American Intellectual History* (Baltimore, 1979), p. 16.

5 For similar formulations, see William A. Lessa and Evon Z. Vogt, eds., *Reader in*

In making this clear-cut theoretical distinction between religious and magical strategies, I do not mean to suggest that the two are always treated as dichotomous or mutually exclusive. More often than not, people combine the two strategies: either they adhere to a system of beliefs that includes both magical and religious elements – usually on the grounds that divine authority does not exclude human power as a subordinate agency – or they ascribe simultaneously to two separate traditions, one magical and the other religious, switching back and forth between them as convenient. Often they do not even articulate the distinction. Most human cultures are, to use an anthropological term, *magico-religious*.[6] Yet using magic and religion as distinct analytical categories is doubly useful in the context of seventeenth-century New England. First, Puritan theology made a clear distinction between supplicative and coercive ritual; it insisted that they were incompatible and repudiated the latter. Second, these two categories of supernatural belief existed in New England culture as relatively pure types: Puritan devotional ritual was strictly supplicative, whereas the folk techniques I describe below were clearly coercive in that they were assumed to produce an automatic effect. In adopting a theoretical distinction close to that made by Puritan theologians, I do not mean to suggest that such a distinction made sense to all colonists. New Englanders cannot be divided into two opposed camps, one magical and the other religious. But a distinction can be made between colonists who restricted themselves to religious forms of behavior, in accordance with the rigorous demands of Puritan theology, and those who also used folk magic. The former may be characterized as exclusive, the latter inclusive.[7]

Comparative Religion: An Anthropological Approach, 3d ed. (New York, 1972), p. 413; John Middleton, ed., *Magic, Witchcraft, and Curing* (Austin, 1967), p. ix; and Melford Spiro, *Burmese Supernaturalism: A Study in the Explanation and Reduction of Suffering* (Englewood Cliffs, N.J., 1967), p. 270.

6 When analyzing nonwestern cultures, anthropologists now try to avoid using *magic* as a separate category of belief or practice. Some use the label *magico-religious.* Others define *religion* in extremely broad terms so as to incorporate all aspects of supernatural belief. Dorothy Hammond, for example, defines religion simply as "belief in superordinate agencies" (Dorothy Hammond, "Magic: A Problem in Semantics," *American Anthropologist,* 72 [1970]: 1355). Mischa Titiev has suggested "a fresh start toward a workable dichotomy" based on the distinction between regular, or "calendrical," practices and "critical" practices used only in time of "emergency or crisis" (William A. Lessa and Evon Z. Vogt, eds., *Reader in Comparative Religion: An Anthropological Approach,* 4th ed. [New York, 1979], pp. 335–7). As I argue below, the distinction between magic and religion remains useful for discussion of early modern western culture, especially when considering the ideas disseminated by Protestant propagandists.

7 Social anthropologists have often defined religion as group-oriented and magic as individual-oriented. According to Emile Durkheim, the former binds community members within a church, whereas the latter consists of individual rela-

When Protestant theologians in early modern England insisted that magical and religious beliefs were incompatible, they challenged attitudes and practices that were deeply embedded in English culture. Prior to the Reformation, not only had the Catholic church credited human beings with a degree of supernatural power, but English men and women had blended Christianity with traditional folk beliefs that were essentially magical. Supernatural belief and practice in medieval England was, for the most part, magico-religious. Sixteenth-century Protestant evangelists, however, rejected the notion that human beings could wield supernatural power and condemned magic as an attempt to coerce God. Protestant thinkers emphasized God's absolute sovereignty: all events in the world, they argued, were determined by God and expressed his omnipotent will; men and women should submit to divine providence. From this perspective, any attempt to manipulate the world through magical ritual exhibited a lack of proper humility. In Protestant thought, magic emerged as a category opposed to that of "true" religion; it embodied rebellion against God's will. Protestant reformers accordingly set out to purge Christianity of its magical accretions and to suppress folk magic.

That campaign is described by Keith Thomas in his monumental work, *Religion and the Decline of Magic* (1971). Thomas argues that Protestant propaganda was ultimately effective: by the end of the seventeenth century, not only had the reformist view of magic and religion as irreconcilable principles been generally accepted, but a growing number of people relinquished magical aids and turned instead to "a combination of self-help and prayer to God."[8] According to Thomas, Protestantism succeeded not only in dissociating itself from magic, but also in triumphing over it. Thomas's work has been profoundly influential, and any investigation of this subject, including my own, owes an incalculable debt to his achievement. Yet the thesis advanced by Thomas is controversial in several respects.[9] I will mention here a few of the questions raised by his

tionships between a magician and his clientele (Emile Durkheim, *The Elementary Forms of the Religious Life* [1915; New York, 1965], pp. 59–60). At least in the case of early New England, the distinction does not seem applicable, since colonists sometimes gathered in small groups of neighbors, friends, or relatives in order to engage in magical experiments; some people sought expert assistance, but others did not. Magic certainly had no church, as Durkheim points out, and it was less formal a realm of activity than religion, but it was often enacted in a group and did unite people, whether in hope or fear.

8 Keith Thomas, *Religion and the Decline of Magic* (1971; Middlesex, England, 1973), p. 331.

9 See especially reviews by Hildred Geertz, "An Anthropology of Religion and Magic, I," *Journal of Interdisciplinary History*, 6 (1975): 71–89; E. P. Thompson, "Anthropology and the Discipline of Historical Context," *Midland History*, 1

critics, since these will serve to clarify my own position and the ways in which it differs from that of Thomas.

Critics have accused Thomas of imposing his perception of a dichotomy between magic and religion onto early modern English culture. Thomas does recognize that the two traditions overlapped. Indeed, he gives many examples of Protestants from all levels of English society who resorted to magic.[10] Nevertheless, the rhetorical framework of his book treats magic and religion as rightfully separate and antagonistic entities. Several critics have accused Thomas of taking a perspective voiced by one segment of the population – namely, Protestant propagandists – and treating it as a generality. These critics argue that reformist propaganda was less successful than Thomas would have us believe and that the examples of overlap between magic and religion that he provides are much more representative of general attitudes than are the clear-cut categorical distinctions formulated by Protestant theologians.[11] Like Thomas, I find it useful to distinguish between magical and religious strategies, but I agree with his critics that the Protestant campaign to differentiate between magic and religion was only partially successful: by the end of the seventeenth century, some people did believe that magic and religion were incompatible; but others did not.[12] It would be perverse to attempt a historical analysis of this subject without reference to magic and religion as categories of supernatural belief; after all, some members of English society did distinguish between the two.[13] But we should view magic and re-

(1972): 41–55; and Stanley Jeyaraja Tambiah, *Magic, Science, Religion, and the Scope of Rationality* (New York, 1990), chap 2.

10 Thomas's interpretation is thus more nuanced than that exemplified by Robert Muchembled's *Culture populaire et culture des elites dans la France moderne* (Paris, 1978). Muchembled and a number of other French historians posit a sharp division between "elite" Christianity and "popular" folk culture; they portray the two traditions as relatively autonomous and self-contained. Stuart Clark discusses these studies in "French Historians and Early Modern Popular Culture," *Past and Present,* 100 (1983): 62–99. Nor does Thomas go so far as two of his reviewers: Lawrence Stone refers to "the official culture of Protestant Christianity" and "the counterculture of magic"; E. P. Thompson suggests the existence of a popular "anti-culture" (Lawrence Stone, "The Disenchantment of the World," *New York Review of Books,* 2 December 1971; E. P. Thompson, "Anthropology and the Discipline of Historical Context," p. 51).

11 See especially Stanley Jeyaraja Tambiah, *Magic, Science, Religion, and the Scope of Rationality,* p. 23; and Hildred Geertz, "An Anthropology of Religion and Magic, I," pp. 76–7.

12 Michael MacDonald's *Mystical Bedlam: Madness, Anxiety and Healing in Seventeenth-Century England* (New York, 1981) shows that ordinary people in early modern England continued to incorporate into their mental world a diffuse array of traditions and beliefs. This loose weave of attitudes and practices was far removed from the spirit of Protestant reformism.

13 Evangelical determination, however thwarted, to transform popular belief remains at the center of recent historical analysis. See, for example, Stuart Clark,

ligion as perspectives that may or may not be compatible, depending on the attitudes of those involved, instead of seeing them as necessarily antagonistic principles. We should also bear in mind that the distinction itself was not meaningful to all participants in early modern English culture. Changing the terms of discourse in this way enables us to recognize magic and religion as useful analytical categories without locking them into an inflexible relationship, or implying that all actors in a specific historical context treat them in a particular way.

Critics have also expressed misgivings about Thomas's claim that magical tradition was incoherent and fragmentary. Thomas recognizes "the interrelatedness of the main magical beliefs," but nevertheless sees magic as "a collection of miscellaneous recipes, not a comprehensive body of doctrine."[14] Critics believe that magic was much more integrated in its view of the world than Thomas suggests. One reviewer declares that magical belief constituted "a historically particular view of the nature of reality, a culturally unique image of the way in which the universe works, that provides a hidden conceptual foundation for all of the specific diagnoses, prescriptions, and recipes that Thomas describes."[15] I agree that magical techniques reflected an underlying mental structure, an unarticulated but nonetheless consistent view of reality. In the chapters that follow, I try to explicate that mental structure and its relationship to Protestant thought. However, I would not go so far as to characterize magical beliefs as comprehensive or systematic. There is a world of difference between a series of traditions that cohere through shared assumptions and an actual system of ideas. Magic in seventeenth-century England and New England belonged to the former, not the latter, category.[16]

"Protestant Demonology: Sin, Superstition, and Society," in Bengt Ankarloo and Gustav Henningsen, eds., *Early Modern European Witchcraft: Centres and Peripheries* (Oxford, 1990), especially pp. 72–4.

14 Keith Thomas, *Religion and the Decline of Magic,* p. 755 and p. 761.

15 Hildred Geertz, "An Anthropology of Religion and Magic, I," p. 83. See also E. P. Thompson, "Anthropology and the Discipline of Historical Context," pp 51, 52. In his response to Geertz, Thomas admits that he may have paid insufficient attention to underlying connections, but he questions, as do I, "whether magic always had the 'philosophical underpinnings' with which Geertz credits it" (Keith Thomas, "An Anthropology of Religion and Magic, II," *Journal of Interdisciplinary History,* 6 [1975]: 104. See also Laurence Veysey, "Intellectual History and the New Social History," p. 21.)

16 A number of scholars, most notoriously Margaret Murray, have argued for an unbroken pagan tradition in medieval and early modern Europe. They claim that surviving references to magic and witchcraft can be pieced together to show the persistence of an organized pagan network, united by a coherent set of beliefs and rituals. Murray's influential book, *The Witch Cult in Western Europe* (Oxford, 1921), describes a pre-Christian fertility cult, centered on the worship

Historians of seventeenth-century New England have only recently begun to take an interest in magical beliefs and practices. This growing interest stems from a transformation in the way that scholars perceive religious culture in the northern colonies. Over the past thirty years, historians have distanced themselves from the model of spiritual life in early New England associated, sometimes unfairly, with the work of Perry Miller. This paradigm focused exclusively on Puritanism and portrayed New Englanders as a monolithic community of thinking men (women making only occasional appearances) characterized by their intellectual commitment and united by their notion of covenant.[17] Recent historians have criticized this model on several fronts, including its stress on intellectual over experiential content in Puritanism and its notion of a largely homogeneous New England community. These revisionists emphasize instead the importance of emotional piety within the Puritan movement and the pluralism of early New England culture. Historians now recognize that some people were much less committed than others to Congregationalist orthodoxy; that alternative faiths attracted support from a small but vocal minority of colonists; and that layfolk did not merely receive their ministers' teachings as passive vessels, but adapted those teachings according to their own needs and priorities, influencing as active participants the substance and tone of their faith.[18]

Recent discussion of magic in early New England has further broadened our perception of supernatural culture in the northern colonies, as well as shed new light on the relationship between

of a two-faced and horned god, which flourished throughout western Europe until the seventeenth century, when Christian authorities used witch trials as the instrument of a bloody campaign against the rival religion. Murray's theory has been subjected to a series of blistering attacks, most notably by Norman Cohn, who has exposed in graphic detail Murray's flagrant abuse of her sources (Norman Cohn, *Europe's Inner Demons* [London, 1975], chapter 6). Most historians now dismiss the Murray thesis, although it has experienced something of a resurrection in Carlo Ginzburg's *I Benandanti* (Turin, 1966; trans. John and Anne Tedeschi as *The Night Battles: Witchcraft and Agrarian Cults in the Sixteenth and Seventeenth Centuries*, Baltimore, 1983).

17 See especially Perry Miller, *The New England Mind: The Seventeenth Century* (New York, 1939); *The New England Mind: From Colony to Province* (Cambridge, Mass., 1953); and *Errand into the Wilderness* (Cambridge, Mass., 1956).

18 The enormous body of scholarship to which I allude briefly in this paragraph is reviewed in detail by Michael McGiffert, "American Puritan Studies in the 1960s," *William and Mary Quarterly*, 27 (1970): 36–67; David D. Hall, "Understanding the Puritans," in Herbert Bass, ed., *The State of American History* (Chicago, 1970), pp. 330–49; Laura Ricard, "New England Puritan Studies in the 1970s," *Fides et Historia*, 15 (1982): 6–27; the bibliographic essay in Charles Lloyd Cohen, *God's Caress: The Psychology of Puritan Religious Experience* (New York, 1986), 275–89; and David D. Hall, "On Common Ground: The Coherence of American Puritan Studies," *William and Mary Quarterly*, 44 (1987): 193–229.

clerical and lay spirituality. Three scholars have considered the place magic occupied in the minds of seventeenth-century New Englanders. Richard Weisman posits a fundamental antipathy between two "competing cosmologies." He emphasizes the "rift between magic and religion" and sees "the proponents of magic" as engaged in a direct confrontation with the clergy.[19] In sharp contrast, David Hall rejects altogether the notion of two distinct traditions. Hall argues that the English men and women who settled in New England were literate, informed people of middling status who eschewed the "folk ways of thinking" which characterized European peasants. "Emigration," he tells us, "simplified the cultural system by making it more uniform." Hall emphasizes that the colonists did not abandon all folk traditions: ministers and layfolk combined formal theology with fragmentary pagan and folk beliefs in a syncretic worldview that was remarkably inclusive and tolerant. Hall also concedes that some colonists did use magic to predict the future and to protect themselves against witchcraft. But there was no "war . . . between magic and religion, in part because the clergy also were attracted to occult ideas . . . [and] relied on older lore as much as any layman." Instead, there was "an accommodation" between the two; interpretive disagreements did occur, but these took place within an overall framework of consensus.[20]

Jon Butler offers a third interpretation, which mediates between these two extremes. On the one hand, Butler treats magical beliefs as distinct from Christianity and emphasizes clerical hostility toward magical practices. On the other hand, he points out that people who used magic tended not to see their behavior as antagonistic to Christian faith. Instead, they saw the two as complementary: in order to "satisfy their spiritual needs," they turned sometimes to one, sometimes to the other. This "spiritual eclecticism" frustrated attempts by church officials on both sides of the Atlantic to secure "exclusive loyalty" from layfolk. Magic was less prevalent in early New England than across the Atlantic, Butler tells us: the strength of official opposition and the character of the initial migrant population "retarded magical practice." Even so, magic soon emerged in New England, as elsewhere in North America, giving rise to clerical concern and condemnation.[21]

The argument presented here is closest to the third of these

19 Richard Weisman, *Witchcraft, Magic, and Religion in Seventeenth-Century Massachusetts* (Amherst, Mass., 1984), pp. 53, 54, 66.
20 David D. Hall, *Worlds of Wonder, Days of Judgment*, pp. 5–7.
21 Jon Butler, *Awash in a Sea of Faith: Christianizing the American People* (Cambridge, Mass., 1990), pp. 1, 10, 20, 67–8, 70–3.

approaches.[22] Magical tradition and Puritan doctrine posited two different kinds of relationship between human beings and supernatural power, but there was no fundamental breach in early New England between magical and religious constituencies. Instead, as I remarked above, New Englanders may be divided into those who eschewed magic and those who did not; some were inclusive, others exclusive. We need to distinguish between the folkloric beliefs incorporated into religious culture by clergymen and layfolk and those specific magical traditions that ministers and the more exclusivist of their flock condemned as contradicting reformed theology. For this latter group, the tolerance to which David Hall has drawn our attention operated within carefully defined parameters. But not all layfolk were that discriminating: although ministers insisted that religious faith should preclude magical practice, some of their flock thought differently. Or perhaps it would be more accurate to say, behaved differently. In general, those who used magic do not appear to have analyzed their actions: they did not consciously repudiate religious doctrine; nor did they try to reconcile the two patterns of belief. To use Laurence Veysey's formulation, they compartmentalized. Of course, there were exceptions: we know of one healer who believed that his magical power was a gift from God; there were doubtless others who thought along similar lines.[23] But most layfolk who practiced magic seem to have lacked the intellectual self-consciousness that prompted their ministers to contrast magical assumptions with those underlying Puritan theology; or, if they were aware that their actions were heterodox, they feigned ignorance so as to explain away their use of magical techniques, should they be challenged by a minister for their behavior. Layfolk used magic because it was embedded in their cultural heritage and because it seemed useful.[24]

22 Jon Butler's book spans three centuries of religious and cultural history. The chapter in which he discusses early American "Magic and Occultism" encompasses the northern, middle, and southern colonies; it also extends through the eighteenth century. Necessarily, therefore, Butler alludes to magical practice in seventeenth-century New England only briefly. This study explores in detail the interpretative approach suggested by his remarks; it also draws on the many insights provided by David D. Hall, whose influence on my thinking is acknowledged in footnotes throughout this book.

23 John Hale, *A Modest Enquiry into the Nature of Witchcraft* (1702; Bainbridge, N.Y., 1973), pp. 131–2.

24 David Sabean points out that whereas early modern officials and intellectuals emphasized "right belief," ordinary folk "were more apt to see belief as a kind of matrix from which different sorts of action could flow" (David Sabean, *Power in the Blood: Popular Culture and Village Discourse in Early Modern Germany* [New York, 1984], p. 198). I should emphasize here that I do not ascribe to a narrowly functionalist view of supernatural belief. I argue below that New Englanders turned to magic in part because it served practical ends and answered specific

The very informality of magical tradition made it easier for layfolk to accommodate magical and religious strategies. Because folk magic rested upon nothing more than a series of implicit assumptions, people could avoid possibly unsettling comparisons with Puritan doctrine and thus adhere to both, switching from one to the other as seemed appropriate. Laurence Veysey has pointed out that simultaneous adherence to two different ways of thinking becomes easier if only one is "formalized and systematic, the other a matter of broad collective mentality." So long as one set of values or beliefs remains implicit and unspoken, the potential contradictions can lie dormant.[25] Equally significant in facilitating this dual allegiance were affinities between magical belief and possible interpretations of Puritan doctrine. As David Hall has pointed out, much of clerical teaching was vague and open-ended: ministers provided a range of interpretative possibilities from which individuals could choose as they saw fit.[26] I argue below that the ambiguity of Puritan teaching on certain issues may well have encouraged layfolk to see religious faith and magical practice as compatible.

But this willingness to accommodate and harmonize was by no means universal. Not surprisingly, magical practice sometimes antagonized those colonists whose faith was more self-consciously exclusive. Magical beliefs and actions became problematic in three kinds of situation. The first was explicit condemnation of magical practice by a clergyman, whether from the pulpit or in a personal confrontation with somebody known to have used magic. The second possible scenario involved a disagreement between layfolk about the use of magic in a particular situation. Ministers were not alone in their objections to magic: some layfolk repudiated all such

psychological needs. But in doing so, I do not mean to suggest that utilitarian factors alone can explain recourse to magic. People believe because they have been raised to do so, and because their beliefs make sense of the world; both inherited tradition and cognitive value are crucial factors in the persistence of a belief. The exchange between Thomas and Geertz in *Journal of Interdisciplinary History*, 6 (1975), includes a useful discussion of this subject. See especially pp. 77–9, 83–4, 98–103.

25 Laurence Veysey, "Intellectual History and the New Social History," pp. 16–17. Veysey argues that a "formal system of thought" differs from "collective mentality" in (a) its "degree of explicitness," and (b) its "self-conscious aspiration to be comprehensive or systematic in treating whatever realm of discourse it addresses" (p. 13). Also useful in this regard is Mary Douglas's notion of implicit and explicit knowledge, which Carol Karlsen applies in the context of attitudes toward women in early New England. See Mary Douglas, *Implicit Meanings: Essays in Anthropology* (London, 1975), especially pp. ix–xxi, 3–8; and Carol Karlsen, *The Devil in the Shape of a Woman: Witchcraft in Colonial New England* (New York, 1987), p. 154.

26 David D. Hall, *Worlds of Wonder, Days of Judgment*, especially p. 12. See also David D. Hall, "Towards a History of Popular Religion in Early New England," *William and Mary Quarterly*, 41 (1984), especially pp. 53–5.

practices and were not slow to criticize their neighbors and acquaintances for using magical techniques. Quarrels of this kind pitched colonists who insisted on "constant practice" of faith, in Winthrop's words, against those whose application of religious principle was more selective and intermittent, as well as against those who rejected Puritanism altogether.

The third context in which magical belief caused disharmony was at a trial for witchcraft, but here the confrontation between the two traditions was more insidious. Puritan and magical interpretations of witchcraft differed in ways that became significant when attempting to prove guilt in a court of law. Both saw witches as malevolent creatures who used occult means to harm their enemies, but where that occult power came from and how it should be proven were matters on which they diverged. Theologians believed that no human being could wield supernatural power and that witchcraft was brought about by the Devil on a witch's behalf. Magical tradition, on the other hand, endowed human beings with the ability to manipulate occult forces; it saw witchcraft as the abuse of magical skill. The laws against witchcraft in seventeenth-century New England embodied the theological view of witchcraft and demanded proof of direct contact between the accused and the Devil. Yet layfolk tended to think in magical rather than religious terms when confronted by witchcraft. Most lay New Englanders believed in the Devil and may have recognized on some abstract level that witchcraft and diabolism were connected. But in seeking to prove a witch's guilt, they focused on the suspect's malevolence and occult skill; witnesses in witchcraft cases rarely made any mention of the Devil.

The disjunction between legal conceptions of witchcraft and popular testimony about witchcraft made conviction extremely difficult. New England courts often acquitted witch suspects because there was no evidence of diabolical involvement, despite popular conviction that the testimony against the accused was sufficient to establish guilt. When a witch escaped punishment, those who had brought charges against the suspect were naturally disappointed and often extremely angry, not least of all because they feared retribution by the accused. *Witchcraft* was a multivalent term in seventeenth-century Anglo-American culture: its ambiguity enabled two different interpretations of the phenomenon to coexist for most of the time. But in the courtroom, that very flexibility became suddenly divisive, since participants in the legal process expected and yet regularly failed to communicate effectively. In this specific context, the discrepancy between magical and religious belief gave rise to tension and conflict between New Englanders.[27]

27 Recent studies of New England witchcraft by Paul Boyer and Stephen Nissen-

Writing this book has been like constructing a jigsaw puzzle for which many of the pieces are missing. Evidence for magical practice in early New England is scattered and fragmentary. This is hardly surprising, since folk magic did not operate through any institutional structure that would leave behind formal records; nor were magical techniques based upon any explicit doctrine that invited or required written exposition. The people who used magic were ordinary men and women about whom we know little. For the most part, we cannot approach these layfolk directly through personal testaments such as diaries or letters. Instead, we have to use sources that mediate between the historian and ordinary people.[28]

Almost all surviving information about magic comes from two kinds of source: court records and clerical writings. If townsfolk believed that a magical expert was using his or her skill for malevolent purposes, they might decide to bring formal charges of witchcraft against the practitioner. When such accusations came before a court of law, witnesses would sometimes describe healing and divining services that had been provided by the accused; the purpose of such evidence was to prove that the suspect did indeed possess occult skills. Once removed from their negative legal context, these depositions provide valuable clues about the positive role that magic played in some people's lives. By focusing on what Clive Holmes has called the "dissonances" between lay depositions and theological prescription, we can learn much about popular belief as a distinct tradition.[29] New England court records are fairly reliable as reports of what deponents said. Lengthy testimony was often abbreviated, unfortunately for us, but the substance of testimony does not appear to have been distorted. The very fact that

baum, John Demos, and Carol Karlsen focus on witch accusations and the social tensions they expressed. These scholars identify the kinds of people who were accused of witchcraft and the processes through which they were identified as witches. They show how New Englanders used witch accusations to attack women who challenged the expectations placed on them by gender norms, neighbors and acquaintances with whom accusers had quarreled, and the members of rival factions (Carol Karlsen, *The Devil in the Shape of a Woman;* John Demos, *Entertaining Satan: Witchcraft and the Culture of Early New England* [New York, 1982]; Paul Boyer and Stephen Nissenbaum, *Salem Possessed: The Social Origins of Witchcraft* [Cambridge, Mass., 1974]. Richard Weisman's study of witchcraft applies sociological theories of deviance to the New England setting. It also examines the disjunction between magical and religious interpretations of witchcraft. Weisman's view of the difficulties involved in trying New England witches is similar to my own, although the overall thesis of his book runs counter to mine (Richard Weisman, *Witchcraft, Magic, and Religion*).

28 For a valuable discussion of the opportunities and pitfalls presented by "oblique approaches" to popular culture, see Peter Burke, *Popular Culture in Early Modern Europe* (London, 1978), pp. 65–87.

29 Clive Holmes, "Popular Culture? Witches, Magistrates, and Divines in Early Modern England," in Steven L. Kaplan, ed., *Understanding Popular Culture: Europe from the Middle Ages to the Nineteenth Century* (New York, 1984), p. 94.

lay depositions so consistently failed to meet legal and theological expectations argues against their having been "doctored" significantly by court officials. Church records contain occasional references to disciplinary proceedings against members whose use of magic had reached the attention of church elders, but record-keeping in most local communities was irregular; moreover, many such records have not survived. New England ministers did, however, describe, analyze, and denounce magical traditions in sermons, treatises, journals, and correspondence. Clerical writings are clearly hostile toward magic and so must be treated with great caution. But there is no reason to question their actual descriptions of magical techniques, particularly since they are consistent with lay accounts of magical practice.

The nuggets of information contained in these legal and clerical sources frustrate as much as they inform. Clerical descriptions of specific incidents involving the use of magic often neglect to mention dates, names, and places. Layfolk who declared in legal depositions that they had consulted magical experts or used magic against witch suspects all too often surface in the records only as witnesses at a witch trial; they are otherwise invisible. Thus, many aspects of magical culture remain occult. Important questions about the social identity of those who turned to magic and the numbers involved are simply unanswerable.

Equally illusive is the issue of gender. Most of the magical experts mentioned in this book were women, but it would be rash to conclude that magical "cunning" was, in fact, a female preserve. Many of the references to specific "cunning folk" come from witch trials and so may not give a fair representation of who magical experts really were. Women in seventeenth-century New England were much more vulnerable than men to accusations of witchcraft; colonists perceived witchcraft as a primarily female phenomenon.[30] In early modern Europe, witch accusations were also directed, for the most part, against women. As Christina Larner puts it, witch-hunting was "to some degree a synonym for woman-hunting."[31]

30 Seventy-eight percent of the accused witches in early New England whose gender can be identified were women (Carol Karlsen, *The Devil in the Shape of a Woman,* p. 47). Moreover, half of the accused males were connected to female witches by kinship or friendship; these men became suspect "through a literal process of guilt by association" (John Demos, *Entertaining Satan,* pp. 60–2). Diabolical possession was also a largely female phenomenon; I discuss the disproportionate vulnerability of women to demonic attack in Chapter 3.

31 Christina Larner, *Enemies of God: The Witch-Hunt in Scotland* (Baltimore, 1981), p. 3. Larner argues that accusations of witchcraft reinforced male control at a time when the Reformation and Counter-Reformation gave women, along with men, full responsibility for their own souls, thus creating a new and uncomfortable ambiguity in the status of women. Vulnerability to accusations of witch-

Carol Karlsen has shown that New Englanders used witch accusations to attack women who violated gender-specific social norms, and that witchcraft cases reveal much about the articulation of gender in early modern society.[32] But they are much less useful as an indicator of who was practicing magic. Because witchcraft was seen as a female crime, male cunning folk who reputedly misused their occult skills were much less likely to end up in court. There may have been a substantial number of male practitioners whom colonists were disinclined to prosecute as witches simply because they were men. Clerical writings refer occasionally to men who specialized in magic and who do not appear to have ended up in court as accused witches; these individuals may have been exceptional, but perhaps not. Most of those experts who avoided prosecution are invisible to the historian, and so it seems reasonable to surmise that the predominance of women among magical practitioners of whose existence we know may be misleading. Women who practiced magic were certainly more vulnerable to legal prosecution than their male counterparts, but they were not necessarily practicing in greater numbers. The evidence for non-experts who used magic suggests that "amateur" experimentation did not attract one gender over another. Unfortunately, those people who used countermagic are often described simply as friends or neighbors of a bewitched individual, not as men or women. But a significant number of legal documents do refer to men employing magical techniques or consulting expert practitioners. Magical belief, it would seem, did not constitute a gender-specific view of the world.

For all their inadequacies, court records and clerical writings are invaluable for the glimpses they provide of magical tradition and its place in the lives of early New Englanders. The framework through which they allow us to peer is narratological: that is to say, when lay deponents and clerical commentators described magical practices, they did so by telling "stories." As far as possible, I have presented evidence in the context of these narrative frameworks, since the stories themselves more often than not elucidate effectively the assumptions underlying magical practice and the pur-

craft was an ironic consequence of this spiritual liberation, since "witchcraft as a choice was only possible for women who had free will and personal responsibility attached to them." Now that women had to be treated as spiritually autonomous, they could also be attacked as such. Witch-hunting was, then, "a rearguard action against the emergence of women as independent adults" (pp. 101–2). The predominance of women among accused witches is also discussed in H. C. Erik Midelfort, *Witch-Hunting in Southwestern Germany, 1562–1684* (Stanford, 1972), pp. 183–5; and Joseph Klaits, *Servants of Satan: The Age of the Witch-Hunts* (Bloomington, Ind., 1985), chap 3.

32 Carol Karlsen, *The Devil in the Shape of a Woman.*

poses it served.[33] I have tried not to remove the beliefs revealed in these narratives too far from the concrete situations in which they were expressed. In other words, I have sought to explicate magical tradition without doing undue violence to its informality; I hope to avoid reifying magical belief.

This book does not attempt a comprehensive survey of folklore in early New England. It examines one aspect of folk tradition: those beliefs and practices that assumed a human ability to control occult forces. Nor does it discuss "learned" magic, since the New England elite showed little interest in such matters.[34] John Winthrop, Jr., eldest son of the Massachusetts governor whose lay sermon I quoted above, owned an extensive alchemical library and may have authored a number of books on the subject. But Winthrop's interest was exceptional.[35] New England intellectuals did study and practice astrology, but, as I explain below, their attitude toward astral science was profoundly ambivalent.

The structure of this study is broadly topical, although the two chapters on witchcraft are divided chronologically. Chapter 1 describes attitudes toward magic in early modern England and then examines magical belief and activity in seventeenth-century New England; it suggests a linkage between magical practice and anxieties caused by Puritan theology. Chapter 2 focuses on opposition to magic and discusses the various situations in which magical practice gave rise to tension between New Englanders; it also asks why clerical criticism of magic became more vociferous during the last quarter of the century. Chapter 3 explores specific ambiguities in Puritan theology that may have encouraged layfolk to see religious

33 David D. Hall emphasizes the role played by "story frameworks" in the religious culture of seventeenth-century New England. He argues that people used a "well-charted" repertory of religious stories to make sense of their own experiences (David D. Hall, *Worlds Of Wonder, Days Of Judgment*, pp. 18, 245). There is an interesting parallel here: New Englanders appearing in court used "stories" about magic to explain and legitimize their hopes, convictions, and fears; clergymen used such stories for cautionary purposes. The time has surely come for a full-scale study of narratology in the culture of early New England.

34 Nor do I address the hazy relationship between magic and science in early modern thought. The magical ideas and activities of intellectuals in early modern England and Europe are examined in Frances Yates, *Giordano Bruno and the Hermetic Tradition* (London, 1964); Wayne Shumaker, *The Occult Sciences in the Renaissance: A Study in Intellectual Patterns* (Berkeley, 1972); Frances Yates, *The Rosicrucian Enlightenment* (London, 1973); Peter French, *John Dee: The World of an Elizabethan Magus* (London, 1973); Ingrid Merkel and Allen Debus, eds., *Hermeticism and the Renaissance: Intellectual History and the Occult in Early Modern Europe* (Cranbury, N.J., 1988). See also Stanley Jeyaraja Tambiah, *Magic, Science, Religion, and the Scope of Rationality*, chapters 1 and 2.

35 Jon Butler discusses seventeenth-century Virginia's "learned occult milieu" in *Awash in a Sea of Faith*, pp. 77–80.

and magical attitudes as compatible. Chapter 4 examines astrological belief and practice in the northern colonies; it argues that the assumptions underlying astrology and the controversy surrounding astrological prediction parallel in significant ways magical belief and clerical condemnation of magical practice. Chapters 5 and 6 center on witch trials and the problems caused by the discrepancy between popular and legal interpretations of witchcraft. Chapter 5 argues that these problems eventually undermined the credibility of the legal process as a medium for the punishment of witches; this led to a fall in witch prosecutions during the 1670s and 1680s. Chapter 6 asks why witch prosecutions revived in 1692 and shows that the collapse of the Salem witch trials was brought about by the same interpretative discrepancy that had plagued previous witch prosecutions. The book ends with an Epilogue in which I suggest that folk magic persisted throughout the eighteenth century.

In quoting the men and women of early New England, I have retained their idiosyncratic spelling and capitalization. Where the spelling is so erratic as to obscure meaning, I have clarified in parentheses. Some of these quotations are difficult to read; some will require more than one reading. I have resisted the temptation to modernize since adaptation of language can create an illusion of proximity. The presence of witches, healers, seers, and astrologers in late twentieth-century North America can all too easily mislead us into equating contemporary supernatural beliefs with those of early New England. The two mental worlds are really very different. I preserve seventeenth-century orthography in order to underline the "otherness" of the culture from which these words and their speakers originate.

1

MAGICAL EXPERIMENTS

DIVINING, HEALING, AND DESTROYING IN SEVENTEENTH-CENTURY NEW ENGLAND

> She acknowledged the turneing of the sieve, in her house by hir daughter, whom she Desyred to no [know] if her brother Moses Haggat was alive or dead. And that if the sieve turned he was dead, and so the sieve did turn.
>
> *Salem Witchcraft Papers*

> A man in Boston gave to one a Sealed Paper, as an effectual remedy against the tooth-ach[e], wherein were drawn several confused characters, and these words written, In Nomine Patris, Filii, et Spiritus Sancti, Preserve thy Servant, such an one.
>
> Increase Mather, *Essay for the Recording of Illustrious Providences*

The colonists brought with them from England a variety of magical beliefs and practices. These traditions had a lengthy and complicated pedigree, more often than not obscured in the mists of time. Throughout the medieval and early modern periods, most English men and women had access to local folk practitioners who provided magical services. These experts were known to contemporaries variously as "cunning" or "wise" folk, "conjurors," "white witches," and "wizards." Cunning folk were skilled artisans who practiced the mysteries of healing and divining; they performed a vital social service. Sixteenth- and seventeenth-century observers commented on the popularity of magical practitioners and the frequency with which people made use of their skills. Robert Burton, a don at Christ Church, Oxford, from 1599 to 1640, wrote that there were "cunning men, wizards, and white witches, as they call them, in every village, which, if they be sought unto, will help almost all infirmities of body and mind."[1] Anthony Burgess, a Puritan cleric, declared that "if men have lost anything, if they be in any pain or disease, then they presently run to such as they call wise men."[2] In

1 Robert Burton, *Anatomy of Melancholy,* 2 vols. (1621; New York, 1927), I: 382.

2 Anthony Burgess, *CXLV Expository Sermons upon the Whole Seventeenth Chapter of the Gospel According to Saint John* (London, 1656), p. 95.

addition to consulting experts, people also experimented with magic on their own: many healing and divining techniques needed no special training. Such techniques, transmitted by word and demonstration from generation to generation, were part of a common lore, accessible to anybody. Magic, then, whether in the hands of an expert or an amateur, was a vital resource in preindustrial English culture.

Folk magic had coexisted in England with Christianity, albeit uneasily, for over a thousand years.[3] The medieval church taught that human beings could wield supernatural power through sanctioned rituals: the performance of ecclesiastical ritual, if accompanied by sincere religious feeling, could heal sickness and protect against harm. This aspect of Christian teaching was vitally important as the church sought to establish itself in England, and as it competed with folk practitioners who did not hesitate to claim supernatural puissance. In campaigning to convert the people of England, evangelists emphasized the intercessory powers that priests could exercise on behalf of their flock and also the occult effects layfolk could bring about through the use of devotional ritual. The church appropriated certain kinds of non-Christian magic for its own use, incorporating these older traditions and practices into a sanctioned religious framework. Thus, church leaders hoped to tap the energies of their competition.[4] According to Christian propaganda, saintly men and women could predict the future, heal the sick, and perform other amazing feats. These "miracles" were publicized in order to demonstrate the power vested in Christianity and proved extremely effective as a tool of conversion.

But this strategy had its price, since many people confused Christian and non-Christian rituals. Instead of abandoning the latter in favor of the former, layfolk tended to use both. Theologians determined the legitimacy of a ritual act according to the power it invoked: from their perspective, ecclesiastical rites, which depended upon divine assistance, were acceptable; but nonecclesiastical rituals might rely, either implicitly or explicitly, upon demonic

3 The discussion that follows is indebted to Valerie Flint, *The Rise of Magic in Early Medieval Europe* (Princeton, 1991), Richard Kieckhefer, *Magic in the Middle Ages* (New York, 1990), and Keith Thomas, *Religion and the Decline of Magic* (1971; Middlesex, England, 1973), especially chaps. 2–9. See also Gabor Klaniczay, *The Uses of Supernatural Power: The Transformation of Popular Religion in Medieval and Early Modern Europe* (Princeton, 1990). Whereas Keith Thomas implies that churchmen compromised their faith in order to win popular support, I follow more recent scholarship in emphasizing the natural overlap as well as creative assimilation between the two traditions.

4 Valerie Flint discusses this process in *The Rise of Magic*.

power and so were reprehensible.[5] Churchmen stressed that men and women should seek to exercise supernatural power only through sanctioned channels and that the efficacy of such rituals depended upon spiritual sincerity. Yet ordinary people tended to focus on the effect of a ritual rather than the origin of its potency. For them, issues of causation had little or no significance. Church officials complained that many of their flock endowed religious objects and rituals with an automatic power that was independent of devotional effort. Prayers assumed a mechanical efficacy and were used in the manner of spells or charms. Holy water and holy relics were said to provide automatic protection against harm. Coins blessed as part of the offertory were credited with curative properties. Theologians repeatedly condemned the notion that ecclesiastical ritual was unconditionally efficacious, but their protestations were, for the most part, in vain.[6]

The loose compatibility of medieval Christianity and folk magic encouraged and sustained popular devotion, but it also created a situation in which the services offered by the church seemed remarkably similar to those provided by folk practitioners. Popular belief in the automatic potency of ecclesiastical ritual made it extremely difficult for priests to distinguish themselves from cunning folk. Instead of weaning people away from older traditions, church teachings and ritual structures were incorporated by layfolk into a preexisting array of supernatural beliefs and practices. Widespread confusion of church ritual and folk magic, as also of priests and cunning folk, testified to the pyrrhic nature of the church's victory in England.[7] Catholic theology may have further encouraged popular syncretism. Just as church ritual and folk magic empowered men and women through their ability to manipulate supernatural forces, so Catholic dogma laid emphasis on human capability. The church taught that God had endowed humans with the ability to earn and thus deserve salvation. The doctrine of salvation by works bespoke a faith in human potential that fit well with the occult powers claimed by both the church and cunning folk.

5 During the thirteenth century, some writers came to admit the possibility of "natural" magic, but the rise of necromancy, which involved the explicit invocation of demons, spirits, or the dead as agents of the magician, revived and intensified old fears of nonecclesiastical magic as inherently demonic (Richard Kieckhefer, *Magic in the Middle Ages,* pp. 16–17).

6 Richard Kieckhefer, *Magic in the Middle Ages,* chap. 4, and Keith Thomas, *Religion and the Decline of Magic,* chap. 2.

7 Kieckhefer emphasizes that "not only the converts but also the faith to which they were converted underwent a change, as elements of pre-Christian culture became grafted on to the new, medieval Christianity" (Richard Kieckhefer, *Magic in the Middle Ages,* p. 42).

Protestant reformers offered a direct challenge to this notion of human capability. Reformed theology taught that human beings could never earn or deserve salvation and that God bestowed grace as a gift of which men and women were utterly unworthy. God predestined some people to be saved and others to be damned; the bestowal of grace did not have any necessary connection with individual merit. Indeed, God's motives in giving salvation were completely beyond human comprehension, save that they testified to his infinite mercy and magnanimity. No one, not even the most irreproachable of believers, could be certain that he or she would be saved. According to Protestant theologians, grace was efficacious only if the individual to whom it was offered had complete faith, but the role played by men and women in the regenerative process did not compromise God's sovereignty: faith acted as a secondary cause; it operated within and was conditional upon a larger scheme of primary causation controlled by God. Thus, God "elected" only those whom he predestined to have faith.[8] Committed as they were to a theology which deemphasized human ability, it is hardly surprising that Protestant thinkers rejected the supernatural claims of the Catholic church. Indeed, it was they who first characterized magic and religion as inherently incompatible. Protestant theologians denounced as blasphemous the notion that priests could wield supernatural power on God's behalf and dismissed Catholic ritual as "conjuration."[9] They dedicated themselves to purging Christianity of its magical accretions.

The most significant practical distinction between Protestants and Catholics lay in their different attitudes toward ritual. The latter believed that they could use ritual to prevent or relieve misfortune. Catholic theologians insisted that ritual worked only if underpinned by true religious feeling, whereas many layfolk assumed that ritual efficacy was automatic. But there was general agreement among Catholics that the correct performance of a protective or curative ritual would bring about the desired effect. Protestant reformers, on the other hand, argued that all events in the world were controlled directly by God and expressed his omnipotent will; human beings had no access to ritual intervention. From this providentialist perspective, the only way to achieve safety or release from suffering

8 See William Stoever, *"A Fare and Easie Way to Heaven": Covenant Theology and Antinomianism in Early Massachusetts* (Middletown, Conn., 1978), pp. 109–111; and Ernest Benson Lowrie, *The Shape of the Puritan Mind: The Thought of Samuel Willard* (New Haven, Conn., 1974), pp. 71–73. David D. Hall describes recent studies of conditionality in "On Common Ground: The Coherence of American Puritan Studies," *William and Mary Quarterly,* 44 (1987): esp. pp. 201–2.

9 See Keith Thomas, *Religion and the Decline of Magic,* pp. 59–62.

was by appealing to God's mercy; even then, there was no guarantee that he would respond. Reformers insisted that human beings could not use ritual techniques to manipulate occult forces and that the only legitimate purpose of ritual was to provide a focus for spiritual effort. This is not to suggest that ritual did not play a significant role in Protestant culture. Even Puritans made constant use of ritual as a medium for individual and collective repentance. But Puritan ritual did nothing more than assist in creating an environment amicable to spiritual endeavor. It was compelling in the affective but not the effective sense.[10]

Protestants attacked the use of magic outside as well as inside the church. Christian leaders had long sought to discredit cunning folk as competitors, but the reformers of the sixteenth and seventeenth centuries were particularly vehement in their attacks. This was partly because they abhorred any kind of magic, whether church magic or folk magic. But Protestants also had especial reason to fear folk practitioners as professional rivals: when Catholic priests denounced folk magic, they knew that they could offer their own brand of supernatural empowerment as an alternative; Protestant ministers had no such advantage. In fact, Protestants had good reason to fear that as clergymen renounced all claim to supernatural power, people might well seek a substitute in folk magic. It is not possible to estimate whether recourse to folk magic did increase as Protestantism began to take hold throughout England. But several observers at the end of the sixteenth century did claim that the number of folk practitioners was roughly equal to that of parochial clergymen. This may not represent an increase, but it does suggest that folk magic at least retained its popular appeal.[11]

At the beginning of Elizabeth I's reign, the Church of England made clear its intention to root out folk magic. The Injunctions of 1559 forbade the use of "charms, sorcery, enchantments, invocations, circles, witchcrafts, soothsaying, or any such like crafts or imaginations," and prohibited recourse to cunning folk "for counsel or help."[12] Bishops and Archdeacons included questions about magic-related offenses in their visitation articles and expected local officials to produce suspects for trial in the ecclesiastical courts. None of this, however, resulted in large-scale prosecution or pun-

10 For detailed discussion of the role played by devotional ritual in New England culture, see David D. Hall, *Worlds of Wonder, Days of Judgment: Popular Religious Belief in Early New England* (New York, 1989), chap. 4, and Charles Hambrick-Stowe, *The Practice of Piety: Puritan Devotional Disciplines in Seventeenth-Century New England* (Chapel Hill, 1982).

11 Keith Thomas, *Religion and the Decline of Magic,* pp. 291–2.

12 Walter Frere and William Kennedy, eds., *Visitation Articles and Injunctions of the Period of the Reformation* (New York, 1910), III: 5.

ishment of cunning folk. Two factors may explain the relative immunity of magical practitioners from the agents of the Anglican church. First, as in all matters of Tudor government, officials were reliant upon local cooperation. Since cunning folk were generally valued by their communities, few people were willing to inform against them. Second, many church officials were no less "unreformed" in their spiritual beliefs and practices than the people whom they were supposed to be reforming. In 1583, for example, the churchwardens of Thatcham, Berkshire, consulted a cunning woman in an attempt to find out who had stolen the cloth from their communion table. Church officials often used magical practitioners to locate church property.[13] Miles Blomefield, who became churchwarden at Chelmsford in 1587, was himself an alchemist and cunning man.[14] The church occasionally took action against such offenders: Edmund Curteis, vicar of Cuckfield, Sussex, was deprived of his living in 1577 in part for seeking advice from a wise woman.[15] Such disciplinary cases were, however, unusual. So grave was the shortage of manpower within the Elizabethan church that a purge of the ministry was never a practical option.[16]

The changes that thoroughgoing Protestants called for, including the suppression of ecclesiastical and folk magic, were ambitious and far from universally welcome. Many officials within the church either doubted the wisdom of extreme measures or, as we have seen, were themselves "unreformed." Layfolk often resisted both the reforms themselves and the intrusion of authority that they represented. The Elizabethan government, by temperament extremely circumspect, insisted that reformation be gradual and cautious. Those who demanded a more rapid and thorough process of change were, then, generally unpopular. Contemporaries branded them as "Precisionists" and "Puritans."[17]

As extremists became increasingly frustrated by the patience and moderation that characterized Anglican reformism, a rift began to develop within the English Protestant movement. For much of Elizabeth I's reign, the Anglican leadership was broadly sympa-

13 George L. Kittredge, *Witchcraft in Old and New England* (1929; New York, 1956), pp. 197–8.

14 Irvine Gray, "Footnote to an Alchemist," *Cambridge Review*, 68 (1946): 172–4.

15 Henry Norbert Birt, *The Elizabethan Religious Settlement* (London, 1907), pp. 431–2. As well as being "a seeker to witches," Curteis was also purportedly "void of all learning and discretion, a scoffer at singing of psalms, a drunkard, [and] infected with a loathsome disease." For other examples of clergymen using magic, see Keith Thomas, *Religion and the Decline of Magic*, pp. 328–9.

16 Rosemary O'Day, *The English Clergy: The Emergence and Consolidation of a Profession, 1558–1642* (Leicester, England, 1979), esp. pp. 128–9.

17 For an example of Elizabethan satire at the expense of Puritans, see Shakespeare's characterization of Malvolio in *Twelfth Night* (c. 1600).

thetic to Puritan objectives, in theory if not in practice. But during the 1690s and increasingly under James I, a much more conservative air began to blow through the upper levels of the ecclesiastical hierarchy. The first two decades of the seventeenth century saw a revival of ceremony and the restoration of ritual furnishings in many parishes throughout the country. With the rise to power of an Arminian movement within the church during the 1620s, Puritans found themselves increasingly alienated from both the official religious hierarchy and the people at large.[18] Some eventually gave up on their fellow countrymen and departed across the seas, determined to establish a community that would be thoroughly godly in its way of life.

Ecclesiastical magic had no place in the religious life of seventeenth-century New England. But folk magic survived the journey across the Atlantic and flourished in the northern colonies. Cunning folk lived and provided magical services in every kind of New England town: in farming communities, seaports, and on the frontier. In Andover, Massachusetts, an agricultural community twenty miles northwest of Boston, townsfolk came to Samuel Wardwell to have their fortunes told.[19] In Easthampton, Connecticut, a small farming town on the eastern tip of Long Island, Elizabeth Garlick practiced as a healer.[20] Wethersfield, Connecticut, over thirty miles inland, was a chiefly agricultural community, but had a good harbor and developed a healthy trade in hemp, furs, and cattle. The people of Wethersfield could call on Katherine Harrison, a healer and fortune-teller.[21] Beverly, Massachusetts, a coastal town just north of Salem, had a fortune-teller named Dorcas Hoar.[22] Lynn, Mas-

18 Arminianism was a theological movement that began in the early seventeenth century as a reaction to the Calvinist doctrine of predestination. Arminians argued that divine sovereignty and human free will were compatible. See Nicholas Tyacke, "Puritanism, Arminianism, and Counter-Revolution," in Conrad Russell, ed., *The Origins of the English Civil War* (New York, 1973), pp. 119–43.
The foregoing overview of the Reformation in England and its popular limits owes much to the perspective offered by Christopher Haigh in *Reformation and Resistance in Tudor Lancashire* (New York, 1975); "Puritan Evangelism in the Reign of Elizabeth I," in *English Historical Review*, 92 (1977), 30–58; and *Church, State and Society in England, 1558–1642*, a lecture series given at Oxford in 1983 in which Haigh offered a much broader version of his earlier thesis. See also Christopher Haigh, ed., *The English Reformation Revised* (New York, 1987).

19 *Salem Witchcraft Papers: Verbatim Transcripts of the Legal Documents of the Salem Witchcraft Outbreak* (New York, 1977), III: 787.

20 *Records of the Town of Easthampton*, 5 vols. (Sag Harbor, N.Y., 1887–92), I: 134.

21 Willys Papers: Records of Trials for Witchcraft in Connecticut (Annmary Brown Memorial, Brown University Library, Providence, R.I.), W–11, 23 September 1668, testimony of Elizabeth Smith.

22 *Salem Witchcraft Papers*, II: 397.

sachusetts, site of a thriving shoemaking industry and the famous ironworks, had two healers, Anna Edmunds and Ann Burt.[23] In Boston itself, Jane Hawkins and Mary Hale were also known as healers.[24] Not all cunning folk were settled members of a community: Caleb Powell, a sailor who drifted into Newbury, Massachusetts, in the late 1670s, claimed to possess occult knowledge and offered his services to the townsfolk there.[25]

When New Englanders wanted to use magic in order to resolve problems and crises, they did not always turn to experts. Some magical techniques required no particular expertise; people could and did use such techniques independently of cunning folk. New Englanders used magic to surmount the barriers of time and space, to look into the future and across vast distances. Magic also enabled them to harness the world and adapt it to their own ends: to heal the sick, to protect against harm, and also to inflict harm. Through magic, men and women overcame their natural limitations: it made the world a more immediate and accessible place, giving new powers of perception and action to those who mastered its possibilities.

Unfortunately, there is no way to gauge the number of magical practitioners in seventeenth-century New England, or how many people actually consulted them. Nor is it possible to estimate how many New Englanders experimented with magic on their own. But it is clear that resort to magic was not uncommon. New England court records contain many references to magical activity. Legal testimony was often recorded in summarized form and so some of these entries are maddeningly compact, but others provide detailed descriptions of magical techniques and the contexts in which they were used. Puritan sermons, treatises, diaries, and correspondence also testify to the persistence of magical practices: in these writings, the godly reported and condemned popular recourse to magic. None of those describing magical experiments, whether in court testimony or elsewhere, ever suggested that such activities were in any way unusual. The ministers themselves were evidently convinced that magical practice was widespread.[26] This is not to suggest

23 *Records and Files of the Quarterly Courts of Essex County*, 9 vols. (Salem, Mass., 1911–78), II: 226–8; IV: 207–9.

24 John Winthrop, *Journal*, ed. James Hosmer, 2 vols. (New York, 1908), I: 266–8; Suffolk County Court Files: Original Depositions and Other Materials from the Proceedings of the Quarterly Courts of Suffolk County, Massachusetts (Massachusetts Archives, Columbia Point, Boston, Mass.), vol. 24, #1972.

25 *Records and Files of the Quarterly Courts of Essex County*, VII: 357.

26 I have found only one instance in which a New England clergyman expressed skepticism about the currency of magical rituals. In 1692, Francis Dane, pastor of Andover, Massachusetts, rejected "divers reports" of magical practice in his parish (*Salem Witchcraft Papers*, III: 881–2). However, since several of Dane's relatives and friends were among those accused of witchcraft, his statement is

that magic was ubiquitous in early New England, but those who did turn to magical techniques were clearly members of a sizeable constituency.

The extant sources reveal nothing about magical practice during the initial period of settlement. As noted above, most evidence relating to magic originates in clerical sources or legal depositions in which witnesses described the activities of cunning folk whom they suspected of witchcraft: few clerical writings survive from this early period and there were no witch trials before 1647. The absence of witch trials during the early years of settlement is not surprising: a formal accusation was unlikely to take place until there had been time for a gradual build-up of public hostility toward a suspect individual within the new community; townsfolk rarely brought charges until they had accumulated a substantial body of evidence against the suspect witch.[27] Accounts of the first witch trials contain hints of magical activity. When Margaret Jones of Charlestown, Massachusetts, was tried for witchcraft in 1648, her neighbors admitted that they had used countermagic to identify Jones as the person responsible for "mischief" that had "befel" their livestock. But even in this instance, the only surviving record of the townsfolk having used countermagic is a brief mention of the incident in John Hale's treatise about witchcraft, written some fifty years after Margaret Jones's execution.[28] This experiment did not necessarily take place as late as 1648; witnesses in witchcraft cases often mentioned incriminating incidents that had occurred many years prior to the trial. Margaret Jones herself had a reputation for making predictions that "came to pass accordingly" and may well have been a fortune-teller.[29] If colonists were using countermagic in or before 1648, so too could they have experimented with other kinds of magic, although we will never know for sure.[30]

Magic enabled people to see through obstacles, across space and over time: they could locate lost or stolen possessions; they predicted future events. They became seers. Divining magic served

far from trustworthy. The evidence presented below suggests that a number of Andover townsfolk did experiment with magic.

27 See John Demos, *Entertaining Satan: Witchcraft and the Culture of Early New England* (New York, 1982), p. 371.

28 John Hale, *A Modest Enquiry into the Nature of Witchcraft* (1702; Bainbridge, N.Y., 1973), p. 17.

29 John Winthrop, *Journal,* II: 344.

30 Whereas Jon Butler argues that magic did not emerge in the northern colonies "as soon as settlers arrived," I suspect that the lack of evidence for magical practice in the 1630s and early 1640s merely reflects the sparsity of appropriate sources for that period (Jon Butler, *Awash in a Sea of Faith: Christianizing the American People* [Cambridge, Mass., 1990], pp. 67–8).

different purposes in Old and New England. In early modern England, divination was used not only to predict the future, but also to locate stolen goods and to identify thieves. Theft was a major problem throughout the country, and there was no reliable official mechanism for the recovery of goods.[31] John Selden, a legal scholar and prominent parliamentarian during the first half of the seventeenth century, wrote that the presence of conjurors "kept thieves in awe, and did as much good in a country as a justice of peace."[32] In New England, on the other hand, people used divination principally to predict the future. Cotton Mather, minister of Boston's First Church, knew "a Person who missing anything, would use to sitt down and mutter a certain Charm, and then immediately, by an Invisible Hand be directly led unto the place where the Thing was to be found."[33] But there is little evidence to suggest that other cunning folk engaged in similar activities.[34] The use of divination to recover stolen property may have been rendered unnecessary by the informal but effective system of surveillance that New Englanders exercised over each other and that facilitated the detection of criminal activity.

New England diviners operated primarily as fortune-tellers. Katherine Harrison of Wethersfield, Connecticut, was "one that tould fortunes." Before coming to Wethersfield, Harrison had lived and worked in Hartford as servant to John Cullick, a merchant. One of her fellow servants, Elizabeth Bateman, was being courted by a young man called William Chapman, but her master disapproved of the match. Harrison predicted that Elizabeth would never marry a man named William and that her husband would be called Simon. Sure enough, Elizabeth eventually married a man named Simon Smith. There could be any number of explanations for Harrison's accuracy: she may have realized that their master's opposition to the marriage was unshakeable; she may have been

31 See Keith Thomas, *Religion and the Decline of Magic*, pp. 252–64. According to Alan Macfarlane, the location of lost or stolen property constituted 3/10 of magical activity by cunning folk in early modern Essex, as reported in legal depositions. Fortune-telling also accounted for 3/10; countermagic for 1/4; and healing for 3/20 (Alan Macfarlane, *Witchcraft in Tudor and Stuart England* [London, 1970], pp. 121–2).

32 Samuel Harvey Reynolds, ed., *The Table Talk of John Selden* (Oxford, 1892), p. 130.

33 Cotton Mather, "Paper on Witchcraft," in *Proceedings of the Massachusetts Historical Society*, 47 (1914): 265.

34 In 1692, Francis Dane of Andover reported the circulation of rumors that members of his parish had employed "ways to find their cattle" (*Salem Witchcraft Papers*, III: 882). Cotton Mather and John Hale referred briefly to the use of divination in locating lost or stolen goods in Mather, *A Discourse on Witchcraft* (Boston, 1689), p. 27, and Hale, *A Modest Enquiry*, p. 165.

using the medium of fortune-telling to lobby on Simon Smith's behalf. What matters for our purpose here is that townsfolk not privy to such explanations automatically assumed that Harrison had occult powers.[35]

Those who consulted fortune-tellers often treated their predictions as indisputable fact. Far north in Maine, Elizabeth Staples heard Alice Metherill, mother of a black bastard child, say that one "peter wittem had Read her forten [fortune] in a buck [book]... that shee shoulld mex sead [seed] with another nason [nation] and that was trou." The circumstances in which "peter wittem" made this prediction are utterly obscure: the fortune-teller may, for example, have known that Metherill was being courted by a man of "another nasion." But either Alice Metherill did not know that the fortune-teller possessed such information, or she ignored it in the face of her overriding belief in the credibility of the fortune-teller's art. For Alice Metherill and many others like her, such predictions were inherently "trou."[36]

Unquestioning faith in the accuracy of fortune-tellers' predictions sometimes resulted in tragedy. When William Adams, a Harvard graduate soon to be ordained as minister of Dedham, visited the town of Wenham in August 1672, he heard about the recent "strange death" of Thomas Whitteridge's wife. A fortune-teller had told Goody Whitteridge "that she should meet with great trouble, if she escaped with her life." This aroused "great horror" in Goody Whitteridge, who told her son that night "that it would be as the fortune teller had said." The boy tried to calm his mother, but she panicked and left the house "with great violence." The next morning, she was found nearby, dead from unknown causes.[37] Twenty years later, during the winter of 1691–92, a girl who belonged to a fortune-telling group in Salem Village, Massachusetts, fashioned a primitive crystal ball by suspending the white of an egg in a glass. She hoped to identify "her future Husbands Calling." To the girl's horror, there appeared in the glass "a Spectre in likeness of a Coffin." Soon afterward, several of those who belonged to the fortune-telling group fell ill and began to suffer strange fits. We will

35 Willys Papers, W–11, 23 September 1668, testimony of Elizabeth Smith; Samuel Willys Collection: Records of Trials for Witchcraft in Connecticut (Connecticut State Library, Hartford), #8, 8 August 1668, testimony of Mary Olcott. See also Samuel Willys Collection, #7, 11, and 12.

36 Neal Allen, ed., *Provincial and Court Records of Maine,* 4 vols. (Portland, Maine, 1931), IV: 49.

37 William Adams, "Memoirs," in *Collections of the Massachusetts Historical Society,* 1 (1852): 17–18.

never know exactly what occurred in the girls' minds, but it is clear that they took their experiment in divination all too seriously.[38]

Fortune-tellers used a number of different techniques. John Hale, the minister at Beverly, Massachusetts, had met diviners who claimed "to tell persons their Fortunes (as they call it) or future Condition by looking into their hands."[39] One of Hale's parishioners, Dorcas Hoar, "did pretend sum thing of fort[une] telling." She admitted to Hale that she "had borrowed a book of Palmistry" in which "their were rules to knoe what should come to pass."[40] Samuel Wardwell of Andover, Massachusetts, also used palmistry: Ephraim Foster had seen Wardwell telling fortunes and testified in court that "said Wardwell would look in their hand and then would Cast his Eyes down upon the ground allways before he told Eny thing."[41] In addition to reading palms, Dorcas Hoar could calculate a person's life expectancy by observing "veins abought [the] ey[e]s."[42] John Winthrop, the governor of Massachusetts, mentioned in a journal entry for 1644 a man recently arrived from Virginia "who professed himself to have skill in necromancy," the use of magical ritual to communicate with demons, spirits, or the dead in order to discover future events or locate stolen goods.[43]

The mastery of magical techniques such as palmistry and necromancy demanded training, and some practitioners learned their art from experts. Caleb Powell, a sailor who was staying in Newbury toward the end of 1679, claimed to have been instructed in the occult by Francis Norwood, a Quaker farmer from neighboring Gloucester.[44] Other cunning folk learned about divination from instruction manuals; these were the products of contemporary intellectual enquiry. There was a clear parallel between the fashionable doctrines of Neoplatonic philosophy and the assumptions underlying popular magic, although it was only through the occasional use of treatises and manuals by magical practitioners that intellectuals exercised any direct influence over folk magic.[45] Indeed, it was intellectual curiosity about folk traditions that stimulated the

38 John Hale, *A Modest Enquiry*, pp. 132–3.
39 Ibid., p. 144.
40 *Salem Witchcraft Papers*, II: 397, 400.
41 Ibid., III, 787.
42 Ibid., II, 400.
43 John Winthrop, *Journal*, II, 156.
44 *Records and Files of the Quarterly Courts of Essex County*, VII: 355–7.
45 Neoplatonism posited that there was no legitimate distinction between matter and spirit, that every component of the universe was animate and related to all other components by sympathetic correspondence. The doctrine of correspondence bore a close resemblance to the assumptions underlying image magic, for which see the following section.

codification of magical formulas and techniques. Scholars such as Agrippa and Paracelsus published treatises describing the philosophical principles that, they believed, underlay the ritual techniques of the village conjuror. These learned tomes and their less esoteric derivatives usually contained detailed descriptions of folk rituals, which conjurors could then use as a practical guide. In other words, these manuals acted as a conduit for the transmission of popular culture.[46]

People consulted instruction manuals in both Old and New England. Bearing in mind the unusually high rate of literacy in the northern colonies, there may have been a substantial constituency for such literature there.[47] Unfortunately, no manuals have survived from colonial New England, but it is clear that at least some were in circulation. Cotton Mather complained that such "books had stoln into the land, wherein fools were instructed how to become able fortune-tellers."[48] John Bradstreet of Rowley, Massachusetts, told his neighbors that he had "read in a book of magic."[49] According to John Hale, Dorcas Hoar was in possession of "a book of fortune telling . . . w[i]th streaks and pictures in it and that it was about the bigness of such a book poynting to a gramer, or book of like magnitude." Hoar had borrowed the book from a neighbor, John Samson, which suggests the existence of an informal network for the circulation of such material.[50] When Katherine Harrison was a maidservant in Hartford, Connecticut, she "would oft speake and boast, of her great familiaritie with mr Lilley," a famed English astrologer. Harrison claimed that she had read an astrological treatise by William Lilly while she was living in England. Perhaps she believed that this would enhance her credibility as a diviner in the eyes of her friends and neighbors.[51] Certainly, she was eager to publicize her "skill," of which she "boast[ed]" to her neighbours: Harrison was "a common and professed fortune teller."[52]

Other cunning folk also advertised their abilities.[53] Caleb Powell,

46 See Keith Thomas, *Religion and the Decline of Magic*, p. 272; and Katherine Briggs, "Some Seventeenth-Century Books of Magic," *British Journal of Folklore*, 64 (1953): 446–62.

47 See David D. Hall, *Worlds of Wonder, Days of Judgment*, chap. 1.

48 Cotton Mather, *Magnalia Christi Americana*, 2 vols. (1702; New York, 1967), I: 205.

49 *Records and Files of the Quarterly Courts of Essex County*, I: 265.

50 *Salem Witchcraft Papers*, II: 398.

51 Willys Papers, W–11, 23 September 1668, testimony of Elizabeth Smith; Samuel Willys Collection, #7, 7 August 1668, testimony of Thomas Waples.

52 Samuel Willys Collection, #7, 11, and 12; Willys Papers, W–11.

53 Here I part company with John Demos, who doubts that "individual persons achieved (or wanted) a public reputation" as cunning folk. In fact, Demos doubts that there were cunning folk in New England, although he concedes that "some

the sailor staying in Newbury, bragged of his "understanding in Astrology and Astronomy and the workings of the spirits." When the household of an elderly couple, William and Elizabeth Morse, was disrupted by the mysterious shaking, falling and throwing about of stones, bricks, and domestic utensils, Powell came forward and offered his services as a diviner to discover who was responsible.[54] Samuel Wardwell also made no secret of his abilities. A number of Andover townsfolk saw Wardwell telling people's fortunes. Thomas Chandler "often hard Samuel Wardle [Wardwell] of Andover till yung person their fortine." According to Chandler, Wardwell "was much addicted to that and mayd sport of it."[55]

Cunning folk did not have a monopoly on magical practice. There were ritual techniques that called for no expert knowledge, and some New Englanders experimented with these procedures on their own. One such technique involved balancing a sieve on opened scissors or shears and then asking a question; if the sieve trembled or turned, the answer to the question was affirmative. In a similar procedure, a key was placed inside a book, usually a bible or psalter, which was then held loosely while the diviner asked a question; if the book turned or fell, the answer was positive. Sometimes, the name of an individual mentioned in the question was written on a piece of paper, which was then placed in the hollow end of the key.[56] Neither of these techniques required particular expertise; anybody could master them. In 1692, Rebecca Johnson of Andover "acknowledged the turneing of the sieve, in her house by hir daughter."[57] Sarah Hawkes, daughter-in-law to fortune-teller Samuel Wardwell, also lived in Andover and also "turned the Sive and [Scissors]."[58] Henry Salter, yet another Andover citizen, apparently told a servant called Mary Warren that he had used both "the seive and seissors" and "the Key and bible."[59] Did these three Andover sieve-turners know of each other's experiments? Did they share information about the techniques they were using? Did one teach the others? Was Samuel Wardwell mixed up in any of their activities? There are, unfortunately, no answers to these questions in the surviving records, but it is clear that magic was not necessarily

of their ways . . . may have survived in at least attenuated forms" (John Demos, *Entertaining Satan*, p. 81).

54 *Records and Files of the Quarterly Courts of Essex County*, VII: 357.

55 *Salem Witchcraft Papers*, III: 787–8.

56 See George L. Kittredge, *Witchcraft in Old and New England*, pp. 196–9; and Keith Thomas, *Religion and the Decline of Magic*, pp. 253–4.

57 *Salem Witchcraft Papers*, II: 507.

58 Ibid., II: 387.

59 Ibid., III: 723.

esoteric, and that amateurs as well as experts could use it to divine the future.

Magic enabled New Englanders to change their world as well as to see it more clearly. Transformative magic was a double-edged weapon: people used it both to heal the sick and to hurt their enemies. This kind of magic operated by treating chosen objects as the images of other objects or people. Such images were not merely symbolic: each participated in the substantive reality of what it represented, so that changes wrought in an image could be reproduced in its counterpart.[60] Thus, when an individual stuck pins or thorns in the representation of an enemy, the image served as much more than a symbol: it was an actual extension of a person; harm inflicted upon the image would also be undergone by the enemy.[61] Charms operated in a similar way to image magic. Specific formulas and ceremonies could produce physical change in an object or person: a spell or ritual was taken to represent a given effect, so that its performance brought about the effect. Just as an effigy was mutilated to harm the individual represented, so the recitation of a spell brought about the effect that it was understood to symbolize.[62]

Through the use of image magic, people could reach and transform anything or anybody. Goodwife Glover, a Catholic Irishwoman who lived in Boston and who used image magic to attack her enemies, was brought to trial in 1688 for afflicting the children of her neighbor John Goodwin. According to Cotton Mather's account, "Order was given to search the old womans house, from whence there were brought into the court, several small Images, or Puppets, or Babies, made of Raggs, and stuff't with Goat's hair,

60 Richard Shweder believes this magical concept of shared identity to be based on a fundamental human disability, the failure to distinguish between resemblance and correlation. According to Shweder, "a universal inclination to seek symbolic and meaningful connections among objects and events" leads humans to mistake superficial likeness for profound structural, functional, or qualitative correspondence (Richard Shweder, "Likeness and Likelihood in Everyday Thought: Magical Thinking in Judgements about Personality," *Current Anthropology*, 18 [1977]: 637).

61 John Skorupski describes this process as follows: "Some form of change is produced in an object, *s*, which is taken as standing for, or 're-presenting', the goal object, *g*. So, *s* 'is' *g*. Therefore, the same change is produced in *g*" (John Skorupski, *Symbol and Theory* [New York, 1976], p. 135).

62 See John Skorupski, *Symbol and Theory*, especially pp. 93–4. According to Skorupski, an "operative" ceremony brings about a consequence that takes effect when the ceremony is performed. "Operative acts are produced, then, by being said to be produced (the 'saying' need not be verbal, of course)" (p. 103). For the use of image magic in England, see George L. Kittredge, *Witchcraft in Old and New England*, chap. 3.

and other such Ingredients." Glover "acknowledged, that her way to torment the Objects of her malice, was by wetting of her Finger with her Spittle, and stroaking of those little Images."[63] Mather knew another, unnamed woman "whose Brother was tortured with a cruel, pricking, Incurable Pain in the Crown of his Head: which continued until there was found with her a Poppet in Wax, resembling him, with a pin stuck into the Head of it; which being taken out, he Recovered Immediately."[64]

At the Salem witch trials in 1692, a remarkable number of testimonies mentioned the use of poppets to inflict harm. A few examples:

> I doe it by Roling up a handcherchef and Soe Imagining to be a representation of a person.[65]

> the way of her afflicting was by sticking pins into things and Clothes and think of hurting them.[66]

> she had then two popets made and stuck pins in them to bewitch the said Children by which one of them dyed, the other [became] very sick.[67]

> he r|a|n a great pin into a poppets heart which killed the said Hawkins.[68]

Whether or not these particular claims were true, the people of Essex County were clearly familiar with the principle and practice of image magic. As in the case of Goodwife Glover, there was physical as well as anecdotal evidence for the existence and use of poppets by the accused. Two of Bridget Bishop's neighbors had found several poppets in her cellar while knocking down a wall for her; the poppets had pins stuck in them.[69] Another of the accused, Elizabeth Johnson, actually produced three poppets in court.[70]

63 Cotton Mather, *Memorable Providences* (Boston, 1689), pp. 7–8.
64 Cotton Mather, "Paper on Witchcraft," p. 265.
65 *Salem Witchcraft Papers,* II: 529.
66 Ibid., I: 135.
67 Ibid., II: 342–3.
68 Ibid., III: 762.
69 Ibid., I: 97.
70 Ibid., II: 504–5. For other references to image magic in the Salem testimonies, see ibid., I: 139, 211; II: 410, 514, 521, 523, 545, 627–8; III: 741, 768. I agree with Chadwick Hansen that at least some of the individuals accused of witchcraft in early New England had been employing magic to harm their enemies (Chadwick Hansen, *Witchcraft at Salem* [New York, 1969], chap. 5). John Demos and Carol Karlsen both have doubts about this, although Demos goes on to describe

Not all magical images were fabricated. Cotton Mather was informed that after he visited Goodwife Glover in prison, "she took a stone, a long and slender stone, and with her Finger and Spittle fell to tormenting it." He added: "though whom or what she meant, I had the mercy never to understand."[71] Robert Pike, a magistrate of Salisbury, Massachusetts, had heard of "spiteful and suspicious persons, that ha[d] sent for a handful of thatch from the house or the barn of him that they ... owed a spite to, and the house ha[d] been burnt as they had burnt the thatch that they fetched."[72] When Rebecca Stearns of Cambridge, Massachusetts, suffered a series of violent fits in the late 1650s, she and her mother suspected that the fits had been inflicted by their neighbor Winifred Holman and her daughter Mary. On one occasion when Rebecca was unwell, her mother went outside and saw Mary Holman "siting on hur knees at a holle of water: she tooke up water in a dish and held it up a prety haith[height] and dreaned[drained] it into another thing." Rebecca's mother returned to her and found her crying. When asked why she was crying, Rebecca "sayd she could not tell but she sayd she could not forbeare," whereupon her mother concluded that Mary Holman's strange antic with the water had caused Rebecca's crying fit. This is not to suggest that Mary Holman was actually employing image magic against Rebecca Stearns: her activity at the "holle of water" may have been completely innocent. But Rebecca's mother clearly understood how image magic worked and believed that she had seen it in action.[73]

Whereas image magic was used only to afflict, charms could serve both good and evil purposes. Healers sometimes used charms as part of their treatment. Cotton Mather knew a woman "who upon uttering some Words over very painful Hurts and Sores, did ... presently cure them."[74] Mather had heard that in some towns it was "a usual thing for People to cure Hurts with Spells."[75] The boundary between magical and non-magical medicine was often

the magical activities of accused witches. See John Demos, "Underlying Themes in the Witchcraft of Seventeenth-Century New England," *American Historical Review*, 76 (1971): 1312 n5, 1317 n18; *Entertaining Satan*, pp. 80–4; and Carol Karlsen, *The Devil in the Shape of a Woman: Witchcraft in Colonial New England* (New York, 1987), p. 132 n50.

71 Cotton Mather, *Memorable Providences*, p. 12.

72 Robert Pike, letter to Jonathan Corwin, 9 August 1692, in Charles Upham, *Salem Witchcraft*, 2 vols. (1867; Williamstown, Mass., 1971), II: 542.

73 Middlesex Court Files: Original Depositions and Other Materials from the Proceedings of the Quarterly Courts of Middlesex County, Massachusetts (Massachusetts Archives, Columbia Point, Boston, Mass.), folder 25, #3 in series of four documents on Holman case.

74 Cotton Mather, "Paper on Witchcraft," pp. 265–6.

75 Cotton Mather, *Wonders of the Invisible World* (1693; Amherst, Wisc., 1862), p. 96.

blurred in the early modern period. Traditional folk medicine combined three elements: commonsensical remedies, the application of medicinal plants and minerals, and the use of ritual charms. According to Protestant theologians, the inclusion or not of a charm indicated whether magic was involved, but many layfolk tended to confuse physicians in general with magical practitioners; such men and women did not make a clear distinction between medical and occult responses to illness.[76] Not all New England healers were magicians, but at least some did use magical charms. In his *Essay for the Recording of Illustrious Providences,* Increase Mather gave two examples of charms prescribed by healers in Boston.

> A man in Boston gave to one a Sealed Paper, as an effectual remedy against the tooth-ach[e], wherein were drawn several confused characters, and these words written, In Nomine Patris, Filii, et Spiritus Sancti, Preserve thy Servant, such an one.

> Not long since a Man left with another in this Town, as a rare secret a cure for the Ague, which was this: five letters, viz, x, a, etc, were to be written successively on pieces of Bread and given to the Patient, on one piece he must write the word Kalendant, and so on another the next day, and in five days (if he did believe) he should not fail of cure.[77]

The phrase "In Nomine Patris, Filii, et Spiritus Sancti" was derived from Catholic ritual, as was the formula recited by Rebecca Johnson's daughter when she used the sieve and scissors to find out whether her brother Moses Haggat was alive: "By Saint Peter and Saint Paul, if Haggat be dead, let this sieve turn around."[78] The recitation of Catholic prayers as an ingredient in magical ritual was a survival from belief in the supernatural powers of the medieval church.

Other New Englanders were believed to use charms or spells for less benevolent purposes. In the late 1680s, Wilmott Reed of Marblehead quarreled with Mistress Simms of Salem Town, who had accused Reed's maid, Martha Laurence, of stealing her linen. When Simms threatened to take legal action, Reed cursed her, wishing that "she might never mingere [urinate] or carcare [defecate], if she did not goe." Soon afterward, Simms "was taken with the distemper of the dry Belly-ake, and so continued many months during her stay in the Towne, and was not cured whilst she tarryed

76 See Keith Thomas, *Religion and the Decline of Magic,* pp. 226–7.

77 Increase Mather, *Essay for the Recording of Illustrious Providences* (Boston, 1684), p. 261.

78 *Salem Witchcraft Papers,* II: 507.

in the Countrey."[79] When Mercy Short visited the Boston gaol during the witch crisis of 1692, Sarah Good, one of the accused, asked her for some tobacco. Mercy refused, "throwing a Handful of Shavings at her and saying, That's Tobacco good enough for you." Sarah Good, enraged by this insult, "bestowed some ill words upon her," whereupon Mercy "was taken with . . . Fits" that lasted for several weeks.[80] A few years prior to this, Mercy Disborough of Fairfield, Connecticut, told Thomas Benit "that she would make him as bare as a birds taile." Thereafter, he lost several of his livestock. Thomas Benit believed that there was a direct link between Disborough's curse and his subsequent misfortune: by speaking of the evil she willed upon him, Disborough had caused the evil to occur.[81]

New Englanders were not defenseless against occult attack. They could use magic to undo as well as to cause harm. Countermagic, a technique that reversed image magic, demanded no special training and was often used by people who did not regard themselves as cunning folk. When someone used image magic to injure a person or damage an object, a two-way channel of communication was believed to open between practitioner and victim. The mischief could be undone, and the malefactor identified, by inflicting harm upon the damaged object or something closely associated with the injured person; this harm would then be translated back to the individual responsible. The purpose of countermagic was as much to identify and punish the malefactor as it was to heal the victim: it exacted revenge.[82] Since the occult channel between afflicter and afflicted was already open, countermagic did not require any particular skill.

One of the commonest countermagical techniques involved burning the affected object in a fire: the person responsible would be drawn to the fire, or be found to have burns if examined afterwards. As minister John Hale pointed out, this method assumed a "sympathy in nature" between the damaged object and the malefactor's body.[83] In or prior to 1665, Margaret Garrett of Hartford, Con-

79 Ibid., III: 717.

80 Cotton Mather, "A Brand Pluck't Out of the Burning," in George L. Burr, ed., *Narratives of the Witchcraft Cases* (1914; New York, 1952), p. 260.

81 Willys Papers, W–33, 6 June 1692, testimony of Thomas Benit. See also the case of Jane Walford in Nathaniel Bouton, ed., *Documents and Records Relating to the Province of New Hampshire*, 5 vols. (Concord, N.H., 1867–80), I: 217–18, 18 April 1656, testimony of Susannah Trimmings.

82 E. E. Evans-Pritchard discusses the use of "vengeance-magic" in *Witchcraft, Oracles, and Magic among the Azande* (Oxford, 1937), esp. pp. 388–9.

83 John Hale, *A Modest Enquiry*, p. 79.

necticut, found one side of a cheese she had made full of maggots. She suspected foul play and flung the cheese into the fire, whereupon Elizabeth Seager, who was in the barn, "Cryed out exceedingly." Seager came into the house and "cryed out she was full of Paine, and sat wringeing of her body and crying out, what do I aile? what do I aile?" Garrett concluded that Seager had used occult means to damage the cheese.[84]

New Englanders used countermagic to cure both livestock and human beings suffering from inexplicable ailments. When an animal fell ill for no apparent reason, the owner might suspect that his livestock had been "bewitched." If so, he might decide to injure the animal in the hope of undoing the "bewitchment" and identifying the individual responsible. In 1658, Goody Hand testified in court that Elizabeth Garlick of Easthampton, Connecticut, had bewitched a sow: Hand told the court that her neighbors "Did burne the sowes tale [tail] and presently Goody Garlicke Did come in."[85] When Henry Grey's heifer fell ill in 1692, he decided to experiment with countermagic. First, he cut off a piece of the heifer's ear. When this did no good, "he sent for his Cart whip and gave the Cow a stroak with it." Within an hour, the animal was well. Next morning, neighbor Mercy Disborough "Lay on the bed and strethr [stretched] out her arme and said . . . I am allmost kild." This confirmed Grey's prior suspicion that Disborough had caused the heifer's illness.[86]

Physical mistreatment of the sort meted out to bewitched animals was unacceptable when dealing with human victims. Instead, the hair or urine of the afflicted would be heated over a fire. In 1685, one of the children of Samuel Shattock, a Quaker who lived in Salem Village, fell ill. The Shattocks called in a doctor, who concluded that the boy was "under an ill hand." A few days later, neighbors cut off some of the boy's hair and boiled it in a skillet. If the experiment worked, the person who had caused the child's illness would be burned or drawn to the fire. After the hair had boiled for some time, Mary Parker "Came in and asked if [Shattock] would buye Soom Chickens." The neighbors were sure that Parker had no chickens to sell at that time and so concluded that she had been drawn by the boiling hair.[87] When Katherine Branch, a ser-

84 Willys Papers, W–4, 17 June 1665, testimony of Margaret Garrett. See also the testimony regarding a bewitched pudding in the case of Hugh Parsons: John Pynchon Notebook (New York Public Library), printed in Samuel Drake, *Annals of Witchcraft in New England* (1869; New York, 1972), pp. 219–20, 248–9.

85 *Records of the Town of Easthampton,* I: 135. For similar examples, see *Salem Witchcraft Papers,* II: 445; John Hale, *A Modest Enquiry,* p. 17; and Middlesex Court Files, folder 25, #2 in series of four documents on Holman case.

86 Willys Papers, W–33, 6 June 1692, testimony of Henry Grey and Ann Godfrey.

87 *Salem Witchcraft Papers,* II: 635–6.

vant girl in Stamford, Connecticut, became bewitched in 1692, "som[e] persons atempted to Cutt off a lock of the said Kates hayr," presumably planning to burn or boil it.[88]

Another popular form of countermagic entailed heating the victim's urine in a bottle, sometimes with nails and pins. This may have derived from the use of pins to stab images and was clearly intended to injure the malefactor. As Cotton Mather put it, "the Urine must be bottled with Nails and Pinns, and such Instruments in it as carry a Shew of Torture with them, if it attain its End."[89] Over twenty seventeenth-century witch-bottles have been found in England. All have urine-traces; some contain pins, nails, and representations of the human heart, cut out of cloth or felt and then pierced. Most of these English specimens are stoneware vessels with bearded human masks, known to contemporaries as *greybeards* or *bellarmines*.[90] The malevolent faces on these vessels served to symbolize the malefactor against whom the bottle was directed: this was image magic at its most grimly anthropomorphic.[91]

No witch-bottles have been discovered in New England, but, as the following incident shows, colonists were familiar with the technique. In 1682, the household of Quaker George Walton in Portsmouth, New Hampshire, was disturbed by the "throwing about" of stones, bricks, hammers, spits, and other domestic utensils. This disruption was blamed on neighbor Hannah Jones, with whom Walton was involved in a land dispute. Richard Chamberlain, Secretary of the Province of New Hampshire, was living with the Waltons at the time and recorded their unsuccessful response.[92] They

88 Willys Papers, W–21, 28 June 1692, report of Jonathan Selleck.

89 Cotton Mather, *Memorable Providences*, p. 59.

90 This may have been a derogatory reference to Robert Bellarmine, the Jesuit scholar who engaged in a heated controversy with James I over the Oath of Allegiance.

91 See Ralph Merrifield, "Witch Bottles and Magical Jugs," *British Journal of Folklore*, 66 (1955), 195–207; Ralph Merrifield and Norman Smedley, "Two Witch-Bottles from Suffolk," *Proceedings of the Suffolk Institute of Archaeology*, 28 (1958–60), 97–100; and Norman Smedley and Elizabeth Owles, "More Suffolk Witch-Bottles," ibid., 30 (1965), 88–93.

92 Richard Chamberlain had arrived in New Hampshire with English proprietor Robert Mason in December 1680. The New Hampshire colonists had consistently ignored the territorial claims of Mason's family, but now Mason was determined to secure full recognition of his proprietorship. Mason had nominated Chamberlain as Secretary of New Hampshire so that he could assist him in his mission. When the colonists proved recalcitrant, Mason returned to England to press his case, leaving Chamberlain behind to bear the brunt of local hostility. George Walton's dispute with Hannah Jones was over land forfeit to the Mason claim: Walton had bought some of the land from Mason. Thus, the apparently supernatural incidents in Walton's house may have been an attack on both Walton himself and his guest (George L. Burr, ed., *Narratives of the Witchcraft Cases*, pp. 55–7).

"set on the Fire a Pot with Urine and crooked Pins in it, with design to have it boil." The Waltons had been "advised" that boiling the urine would end their ordeal and "give Punishment to ... the wicked Procurer or Contriver of this Stone Affliction." Unfortunately for the Waltons, the malefactor was one step ahead of them. Just as the urine began to change temperature, a stone appeared, broke the top of the pot and knocked it off its stand, spilling the urine. The Waltons refilled the pot and put it back over the fire, but another stone broke the handle off and again knocked the pot over so that the urine escaped. Once the pot was refilled and repositioned a second time, a third stone appeared and broke the pot into several pieces, "and so the Operation became frustrate and fruitless."[93]

Seven years later, Cotton Mather published an account of another "Urinary Experiment," which took place in Northampton, Massachusetts. One of the townsmen there had been "taken with many Ails and pains that increased on him to great Extremity." The sick man had recently quarreled with a neighbor whose wife was "under Suspicion for Witchcraft." His friends suspected that she was responsible for the illness and so decided to try countermagic as a remedy. They "went to the Traditional Experiment of Botteling Urine; but they could get no Urine from him, a strange Hole through the Urinary Passage shedding the water before they could receive it into the vessel." The thwarted friends were convinced that this "strange Hole" was a subterfuge by whoever had caused the illness. Meanwhile, the victim "languish[ed], decay[ed], and die[d]." After his death, a jury of inquest confirmed that there was "an Hole ... quite thro[ugh] his Yard," which had "hindered their Saving of any Urine, and gave a Terrible Torture to him." According to Mather, "all concluded with good Reason, the Occasion of his Death to be something preternatural."[94]

Not all countermagical experiments were unsuccessful. When fifteen-month-old Moses Godfrey of Hampton, New Hampshire, fell ill in 1680, Goodwife Godfrey and her daughter Sarah decided to experiment with the child's urine. Sarah "took some embers out of the fire and threw them upon the child's water; and by and by Rachel Fuller [a suspected neighbor] came in and looked very strangely."[95] In 1681, Michael Smith came "very sick" to Hannah

93 Richard Chamberlain, "Lithobolia," in George L. Burr, ed., *Narratives of the Witchcraft Cases,* p. 74. For other examples of witch-bottles, see *Salem Witchcraft Papers,* I: 308; III: 772–3.

94 Cotton Mather, *Memorable Providences,* pp. 60–1.

95 Nathaniel Bouton, ed., *Documents and Records Relating to the Province of New Hampshire,* I: 416, 14 July 1680, testimony of Goodwife Godfrey.

Weacome's house in Boston; Smith claimed that healer Mary Hale "had bewitched him." Weacome "advised the people that watched with him, to take the water of said Michaell and close it in A Bottell." This having been done, Weacome then locked the bottled urine in a cupboard. As long as the bottle remained there, Goody Hale "did not seace [cease] walking to and fro, about the House of the said Weacome." After about an hour, some of those inside the house "Desired the Bottell to be unstoped." Immediately this was done, Goody Hale left.[96]

At first sight, it might seem odd that magic was widespread in Puritan New England, the one place where it should have been utterly discarded. Magic was surely a vital part of the corrupt world Puritans sought to leave behind them in England. Indeed, the close correspondence between folk magic and Catholic ritual made the former doubly abhorrent to the Puritan sensibility. Yet magical traditions persisted even in the New-English Israel. There are three reasons for this apparent anomaly. First, not all New Englanders were Puritans. Second, some members of the godly community were driven to magic by fears and uncertainties arising from predestinarian theology. And third, godly colonists who used magical techniques, for whatever reason, were generally disinclined to problematize their behavior: these layfolk were much less rigorous in their beliefs and practices than their ministers would have liked. Their attitude toward the supernatural world was essentially pragmatic and inclusive.

Migrants to the northern colonies were driven by a broad range of motives, only some of which were religious. William Bradford, governor of Plymouth Colony, attested that "many wicked persons and profane people" came over to New England. In their eagerness to attract recruits, both the promoters back in England and the settlers themselves had been willing to admit "untoward" applicants.[97] Thomas Dudley, deputy-governor of Massachusetts, also recognized that some of the colonists came over "for worldly ends" and that they included a significant contingent of "profane and debauched persons."[98] Certainly, many people had migrated for religious reasons: longing for a more godly life in a thoroughly Puritan community, eager to evangelize among the Indians, perhaps escaping from religious persecution in England. But others

96 Suffolk County Court Files, vol. 24, #1972, testimony of Hannah Weacome.

97 William Bradford, *Of Plymouth Plantation, 1620–1647*, ed. Francis Murphy (New York, 1981) pp. 356–7.

98 Thomas Dudley, letter to Countess of Lincoln, in Alexander Young, ed., *Chronicles of the First Planters of the Colony of Massachusetts Bay* (1846; Williamstown, Mass., 1978), pp. 324–5.

were motivated by the availability of land and economic opportunity in the colonies, the desire to be with family and friends, attractive publicity about New England, or perhaps a spirit of adventure. The New England population was, in Bradford's words, "a mixed multitude."[99] Not surprisingly, this heterogeneous group included people who used magic without any hesitation or sense of wrongdoing.

Some of those who turned to magic were clearly not Puritans. Goodwife Glover, who tormented her enemies by "stroaking... little Images," was a Gaelic-speaking Catholic.[100] Katherine Harrison, the fortune-teller who claimed to have read a book by William Lilly, was described in court as "a sabbath breaker." Her master in Hartford, Connecticut, John Cullick, had "turned the saide Catherin out of his service" because of her "evile conversation in word and deede."[101] Thomas Whitteridge's wife, who consulted a fortune-teller in 1672 and was literally scared to death by his predictions, was apparently "a woman of no commendable life."[102] Yet the constituency for magic within New England also included people whose lives were otherwise highly "commendable." In 1692, when several girls in Salem Village began to suffer bizarre fits, locals suspected that the children had been bewitched. One villager, Mary Sibley, experimented with countermagic in an attempt to cure her niece, Mary Walcott. Sibley was a full member of the village church and reputedly a devout woman.[103] This was not an isolated incident. According to Cotton Mather, there were "manifold Sorceries practised by those that ma[d]e a profession of Christianity."[104] Despite clerical condemnation of such practices, magic proved to be stubbornly persistent even within the covenanted community. Magic appealed to such people in part because it enabled them to alleviate spiritual anxieties created by Puritanism itself. Those anxieties arose from the difficulties of achieving assurance of salvation.

The entire thrust of Puritan devotional life was toward those fleeting moments during which believers sensed unequivocally the presence within them of God's grace. The first of these moments came during the process of conversion. Once the believer had stripped away all delusions of self-worth and was consumed by hunger for Christ, he or she would experience the transforming

99 William Bradford, *Of Plymouth Plantation*, p. 357. For a full discussion of this subject, see David Cressy, *Coming Over: Migration and Communication between England and New England in the Seventeenth Century* (New York, 1987), chap. 3.
100 Cotton Mather, *Memorable Providences*, p. 8.
101 Willys Papers, W–11, 23 September 1668, testimony of Elizabeth Smith.
102 William Adams, "Memoirs," pp. 17–18.
103 Deodat Lawson, "A Brief and True Narrative," in Cotton Mather, *Wonders of the Invisible World*, p. 215. This case is discussed in detail below (chap. 2).
104 Cotton Mather, *A Discourse on Witchcraft*, p. 25.

ecstasy of divine mercy and love. This sensation, hopefully to be repeated many times during the remainder of one's life, was profoundly emotional and often explicitly sensual. Submission to Christ was, paradoxically, self-empowering. By recognizing their own impotence and surrendering utterly to God, believers made of themselves vessels for divine puissance: they were transformed from pathetic sinners into mighty saints.[105]

For those who became convinced that they had indeed received grace, dependence upon God was both glorious and liberating. But not all believers experienced the ecstasy of divine love. Church membership in New England was open only to those who could testify convincingly to personal experience of saving grace. Many people held back from membership because they were not fully certain that they had felt the breath of Christ within them.[106] Jonathan Mitchell, the minister at Cambridge, admitted that the "severity" of this procedure had deterred "some truly gracious souls" from seeking admission.[107] During the second half of the seventeenth century, a growing proportion of the godly refused to attend the Lord's Supper, in response to the ministers' insistence that only those confident of grace should do so.[108] According to Cotton Mather, the "most common" reason given by Bostonians for not attending the sacrament was that they "fear[ed]" they were "unfit for the Supper of the Lord."[109] Jane Turell, wife of the minister at Medford, was reluctant to approach the Lord's Table, lest "coming unworthily she should eat and drink Judgment unto herself." Mistress Turell was much distraught by her situation: indeed, she "was often in an Agony," longing "that she might draw near to God with a true Heart, and in the full Assurance of Faith."[110] Some people were driven to utter despair by their sense of spiritual emptiness. In 1637, a young woman, "having been in much trouble of

105 Charles Lloyd Cohen describes conversion as a "potent fusion of humility and strength, the grace of love transfigured into iron wilfulness" (Charles Lloyd Cohen, *God's Caress: The Psychology of Puritan Religious Experience* (New York, 1986), p. 274. See also Dewey Wallace, *Puritans and Predestination* (Chapel Hill, 1982), pp. 195–6: "The piety of predestinarian grace as an experience was particularly focused on providing assurance and certainty, as anxieties dissolved in the experience of being seized, in spite of one's unworthiness, as one of the chosen of that awesome and yet gracious numen upon which one was totally dependent."

106 David D. Hall, *Worlds of Wonder, Days of Judgment*, pp. 130–1.

107 Cotton Mather, *Magnalia Christi Americana*, II: 67.

108 David D. Hall, *Worlds of Wonder, Days of Judgment*, pp. 156–9. See also Edmund Morgan, "New England Puritanism: Another Approach," *William and Mary Quarterly*, 18 (1961): 241–2.

109 Cotton Mather, *Companion for Communicants* (Boston, 1690), p. 76.

110 Benjamin Colman, *Reliquiae Turellae, et Lachrymae Paternae* (Boston, 1735), pp. 110–11.

mind about her spiritual estate, at length grew into utter desperation, and could not endure to hear of any comfort, so as one day she took her little infant and threw it into a well, and then came into the house and said, now she was sure she should be damned, for she had drowned her child."[111] Such an extreme response was doubtless unusual, but many New Englanders were disturbed by uncertainty about their spiritual estate. For them, dependence upon God was anything but liberating or reassuring.

Even those who did undergo conversion often remained extremely doubtful of their salvation. Assurance was itself dangerous, since indications of grace were notoriously elusive and unreliable. Ministers warned their congregations that those who deluded themselves that they had grace were guilty of "hypocrisy": a heinous sin, however innocent or well-meaning. Not surprisingly, some people wondered if their own experiences of the divine presence had been delusive. John Stedman of Cambridge believed for a time that he had undergone spiritual regeneration, but then came to have "many fears and doubts about [his] estate."[112] John Stansby, also of Cambridge, became convinced that he was "as devilish a hypocrite as ever lived."[113] Mary Norton of Wenham thought at first that she had embraced Christ and "was full of Joy," but "afterward came to question whether this was indeed the time."[114] Some Puritans actually cultivated anxiety as a sign of grace. "The greatest part of a Christian's grace," wrote Thomas Shepard, "lies in mourning for the want of it."[115] Spiritual comfort, then, was attainable only through psychological torment.[116]

None of this is to suggest that humanity's role in spiritual regeneration was entirely passive. Even though it was God who be-

111 John Winthrop, *Journal,* I: 230. See also *ibid.,* II: 29, 93; John Hull, "Diary," *Transactions of the American Antiquarian Society,* 3 (1857): 195–6; Noahdiah Russell, "Diary," *New England Historical and Genealogical Register,* 7 (1853): 56; Charles Pope, ed., *Records of the First Church at Dorchester* (Boston, 1891), p. 33; and Robert Middlekauff, *The Mathers: Three Generations of Puritan Intellectuals, 1596–1728* (New York, 1971), p. 377 n4.

112 Thomas Shepard, "The Confessions of Divers Propounded to be Received," ed. George Selement and Bruce Woolley, *Publications of the Colonial Society of Massachusetts,* 58 (1981): 74.

113 Thomas Shepard, "Confessions," p. 88. See also pp. 36, 52, 100, 113.

114 John Fiske, "Notebook," ed. Robert Pope, *Publications of the Colonial Society of Massachusetts,* 47 (1974): 52.

115 Thomas Shepard, "Journal," in Michael McGiffert, ed., *God's Plot: The Paradoxes of Puritan Piety, Being the Autobiography and Journal of Thomas Shepard* (Amherst, Mass., 1972), p. 198.

116 Michael McGiffert describes this as "the central paradox of Puritan piety": "to be anxious is to be assured; to be assured is to be, or become, anxious" (Michael McGiffert, ed., *God's Plot,* pp. 20, 25). See also Edmund Morgan, *Visible Saints* (New York, 1963), p. 70: "This was the constant message of Puritan preachers: in order to be sure one must be unsure."

stowed grace, believers could prepare themselves for the coming of the Spirit. Puritan divines such as Thomas Shepard taught that individuals could cultivate a desire for grace that would make their hearts fit receptacles for God's greatest gift. Preparation consisted of repentance and self-humiliation: the contrite would recognize their sins, convince themselves of their utter worthlessness, and thus prepare themselves to surrender to God's mercy. English Puritan thinkers of the late sixteenth and early seventeenth centuries had produced a vast literature dealing with preparation. This literature exercised a profound influence over the development of New England theology and devotional life. Yet identifying the precise role played by preparatory exercises in an individual's regeneration proved to be extremely controversial. Indeed, a growing emphasis on preparation in the sermonic literature of the 1630s led to accusations by the so-called Antinomians that the New England ministry was leading its flock back to a doctrine of salvation by works.[117]

Preparationism survived these attacks and, despite continuing controversy, came to occupy a significant place in the religious culture of seventeenth-century New England. Yet even though preparation did allow men and women a participatory role in the salvation process, it offered no guarantees. Just as nobody could be certain that they were elect, so nobody could tell if they had prepared effectively. Thus, preparation was not necessarily reassuring. In fact, intense predisposition to saving grace tended to aggravate the anxieties caused by uncertainty of salvation.[118] There was another sense in which preparation intensified rather than alleviated the tensions engendered by Puritan theology. Although God bestowed the will and ability to prepare, just as he gave grace itself, preparation did imply a partial transfer of responsibility to the self.[119] This would have been reassuring if the men and women involved had faith in their own capability, yet the whole purpose of preparation was to undermine self-worth. Thus, the more successfully people prepared, the more they would doubt their ability

117 See David D. Hall, ed., *The Antinomian Controversy, 1636–1638: A Documentary History* (Middletown, Conn., 1968).

118 According to Norman Pettit, "the lost soul could be left in utter confusion between preparation and conversion. . . . Uncertainty of outcome could lead, and often did, to an inner tension and agony of soul" (Norman Pettit, *The Heart Prepared: Grace and Conversion in Puritan Spiritual Life* [New Haven, Conn., 1966], pp. 18–19).

119 The reconciliation of free will and divine sovereignty was made possible by a distinction between primary (divine) and secondary (human) causation. This enabled ministers to justify human effort within the context of free grace.

to prepare.[120] Giles Firmin, a former deacon of the First Church in Boston who returned to England and became minister of Shalford, Essex, criticized New England preparationists for focusing attention on human inadequacy rather than Christ's mercy. "Some eminent Divines," he lamented, "have . . . layed blocks in the way, which have caused much trouble of spirit to loaden and afflicted Souls, who have been flying to Christ for Refuge." Firmin remembered hearing about a "Maid-servant who was very godly, and reading . . . Mr Shepard's book . . . was so cast down, and fell into such troubles, that all the Christians that came to her could not quiet her spirit."[121]

Preparatory exercises did not end with initial conversion: they encompassed an entire lifetime of devotional discipline that would guide the soul to a state of readiness for salvation. Ideally, believers would fluctuate constantly between spiritual anxiety and relief, between the terrifying realization of personal inadequacy and the stunning revelation of God's forgiveness, between the agony of abandonment and the ecstasy of Christ's embrace.[122] Many Puritans were able to accept the instability inherent in their spiritual lives. They derived comfort from the knowledge that they were not alone in their uncertainty, from the sharing of experiences and feelings with family members and friends, from collective worship and sermons in which ministers spoke of God's mercy, and from ritual

120 Perry Miller saw the enlargement of man's role in determining salvation as psychologically positive. According to Miller, Puritan theologians "reduce[d] the actual intrusion of grace to a very minute point." As a result, believers "enjoyed clear sailing to the haven of assurance." (Perry Miller, *The New England Mind: The Seventeenth Century* [New York, 1939], p. 395; "The Marrow of Puritan Divinity," in *Errand into the Wilderness* [Cambridge, Mass., 1956], p. 71). The first of these claims is an exaggeration. The second, as Andrew Delbanco has pointed out, derives "a great deal more from our automatic resistance to the idea of arbitrary governance, and from our commitment (however chastened by historical awareness) to the ideal of individual autonomy, than from a consideration of how the doctrine felt to seventeenth-century New Englanders" (Andrew Delbanco, *The Puritan Ordeal* [Cambridge, Mass., 1989], p. 3). Far more convincing is Delbanco's argument that "the encroaching doctrines of covenant and preparation – even as they placed more and more responsibility on God's human partner in the transaction of grace – produced in America a generation not of rationalist presumption but of morbid anxiety" (p. 62). The culture of preparation "reduced at least some New Englanders to the condition of paralyzed dread" (p. 143). Preparationists "had misdirected attention from the solace of Christ and had become obsessed with the inadequacy of the self" (p. 211).

121 Giles Firmin, *The Real Christian* (London, 1670): To the Christian Reader, p. iii; Introduction, p. ii.

122 See Charles Hambrick-Stowe, *The Practice of Piety*, especially pp. 21–22; and Michael McGiffert, ed., *God's Plot*, pp. 25–6.

fasting and prayer through which they purged themselves of sin.[123] Support of this kind enabled many people to engage in a lifelong cycle of doubt and assurance, of spiritual death and resurrection. In doing so, they reenacted the passion of Christ and thus came closer to personal union with their Savior. They accepted this recurrent experience as both normative and desirable. Others, however, sought at least occasional relief from a sense of impotence and uncertainty. Magic offered one such outlet.

There was a close symmetry between New England's theological and magical orientations: divination provided a release for precisely those tensions engendered by religious doctrine. The anxieties induced by predestinarian theology turned upon an individual's future; this may help to explain why most magical divination in New England served to predict the future. In England, many people had access to at least a few preachers who did not necessarily hold identical theological positions. The spiritual environment in England was far from closed, and those unable to endure the rigors of one ministry might seek at least occasional relief in other quarters. New Englanders, by contrast, did not have ready access to alternative theological viewpoints. The range of positions held by preachers was relatively narrow: New England pastors were, with few exceptions, unrelentingly predestinarian. It is, then, hardly surprising that magical divination in the northern colonies was more oriented toward fortune-telling than in England. Some of those New Englanders who turned to divination were devout people who needed a sense of future certainty, however limited or short-term. Knowing one's "future Husbands Calling," for example, was certainly insignificant when compared with the issue of salvation, but such knowledge did offer some certitude about the future, a kind of certitude that Puritanism was unlikely to offer.[124] Some New Englanders went further and used divining techniques in an attempt to penetrate the mystery of election itself. According to Cotton Mather, such people let their bibles fall open and then determined "the state of their souls" from the first word they focused on.[125] Clearly, these colonists turned to magic not in defiance but in default of Puritanism.

That willingness to use magic in the service of religion testifies to an open-ended pragmatism that constitutes the third and perhaps most significant reason for recourse to magic in early New England. By no means all those "that ma[d]e a profession of Chris-

123 David D. Hall evokes these aspects of Puritanism in *Worlds of Wonder, Days of Judgment,* chaps. 3 and 4.

124 John Hale, *A Modest Enquiry,* p. 133.

125 Cotton Mather, A *Discourse on Witchcraft,* p. 27.

tianity" discriminated between the supernatural strategies sanctioned by Puritan doctrine and those it condemned. Instead of eschewing all magical traditions and techniques, some layfolk included magic and astrology as well as organized religion in an eclectic worldview. This is not to suggest that all, or even most, godly layfolk used magic: each congregation contained a core of individuals whose faith was quintessentially Puritan in its exclusivity. But others were less rigorous, and thus willing to employ magical techniques if and when they seemed useful. Ignorance of official opposition to magic may explain in part godly recourse to magical techniques: even in towns and villages as thoroughly ministered as those of New England, by no means was everybody well informed. As we will see, some of those who used magic were surprised and horrified when ministers confronted them and explained that their actions were illicit. Increase Mather was convinced that some "practise[d] such things in their simplicity."[126] But although some layfolk did not realize that magic was offensive to Puritan theology, others may have heard but chose to ignore official strictures on the subject; at the very least, those strictures conveniently slipped their minds from time to time. Theological rigor may have meant less to some people than did the practical and emotional advantages to be gained by using magic. Such colonists did not necessarily make a self-conscious decision to disregard official teaching: they merely set it aside when convenient. Their commitment to orthodoxy was selective and intermittent, but nonetheless sincere.[127] In order to fulfill all their needs, they turned sometimes to religion, sometimes to magic.

Yet this was not simply a question of "need," nor of the contrasting "functions" performed by magic and religion. New Englanders espoused diverse and sometimes contradictory forms of belief because such had been the norm in English culture for over a thousand years.[128] Puritan theology and the guardians of Puritan faith, potent though each was, could not overcome completely the spirit of promiscuity that suffused English supernaturalism. Thus,

126 Increase Mather, *An Essay for the Recording of Illustrious Providences,* p. 260.

127 For a similar formulation, see David D. Hall, *Worlds of Wonder, Days of Judgment,* pp. 15–16.

128 As Keith Thomas points out, men and women turned to magic "for highly practical purposes and in a distinctly utilitarian frame of mind" (Keith Thomas, "An Anthropology of Religion and Magic, II," *Journal of Interdisciplinary History,* 6 [1975]: p. 102). But underlying those "utilitarian" motives were inherited beliefs about the working of the universe. I would agree with Hildred Geertz that supernatural beliefs have plausibility only if they fit into "a conventional cognitive map in terms of which thinking and willing, being anxious and wishing, are carried out" (Hildred Geertz, "An Anthropology of Religion and Magic, I," *Journal of Interdisciplinary History,* 6 [1975]: p. 84).

some New Englanders incorporated religious formulas into magical rituals, whereas others used magic in order to achieve spiritual goals. Like many English men and women before them, these colonists took disparate beliefs and mixed them together in order to concoct for themselves a workable, if intellectually untidy, mental world.

Some of those New Englanders who used magic were, from a Puritan point of view, "profane and debauched persons." But others were respectable, godly people who either did not grasp or quietly ignored the tensions between magic and Congregationalist theology. These colonists alternated between religious and magical strategies, according to circumstance and their current frame of mind. For such men and women, the relationship between religious faith and magical practice tended to be extremely hazy. Other New Englanders, however, were much less flexible and much more self-conscious about the implications of their faith. These rigorously exclusivist brethren, led by the clergy, condemned magic in no uncertain terms. As a result, recourse to magic caused tension and conflict within the communities of early New England. It is to the discord that arose from the persistence of magical tradition in the northern colonies that we now turn.

2

THE SERPENT THAT LIES IN THE GRASS UNSEEN

CLERICAL AND LAY OPPOSITION TO MAGIC

> They say, that in some Towns it has been a usual thing for People to cure Hurts with Spells, or to use detestable Conjurations, with Sieves, Keys, and Pease, and Nails, and Horseshoes, and I know not what other Implements, to learn the things for which they have a forbidden, and an impious Curiosity. 'Tis in the Devils Name, that such things are done; and in Gods Name I do this day charge them, as vile Impieties.
>
> Cotton Mather, *Wonders of the Invisible World*

On 2 May 1687, Joseph Beacon was lying in bed. In retrospect, Beacon could not be sure whether he was asleep or awake, but he suspected the latter. As he lay there, he saw an apparition of his brother, who lived in London, "distanced from him a thousand Leagues." The apparition appeared at about five o'clock in the morning. Beacon saw that his brother's "Countenance was very Pale, G[h]astly, Deadly, and he had a bloody wound on one side of his Fore-head." Understandably "Affrighted," he cried out, "What's the matter, Brother? How came you here!" The apparition replied, "Brother, I have been most barbarously and injuriously Butchered, by a Debauched Drunken Fellow, to whom I never did any wrong in my Life."

Joseph Beacon was "extreamly astonished" by the vision of his murdered brother. His family observed "an extraordinary Alteration upon him," and so Beacon gave them a detailed account of what he had seen and heard. After a week had passed, the shock began to wear off. But several weeks later, toward the end of June, Beacon received the following news "by the common ways of Communication":

> the April before, his Brother going in haste by Night to call a Coach for a Lady, met a Fellow then in Drink, with his Doxy [sweet-heart] in his hand: Some way or other the Fellow thought himself Affronted with the hasty passage of this Beacon, and immediately ran into the Fire-side of a Neighbouring Tavern, from whence he fetch[e]d out a Fire-fork, wherewith

> he grievously wounded Beacon in the Skull; even in that very part where the Apparition show[e]d his Wound. Of this Wound he Languished until he Dyed on the Second of May, about five of the Clock in the Morning at London.

The ghastly apparition had told the truth. The limitations of the physical world had been overcome: Joseph Beacon and his brother had seen and spoken with each other, although separated by a thousand leagues; Beacon knew immediately what he would not learn through other channels for over a month.[1]

Cotton Mather received this account directly from Joseph Beacon, accepted its veracity, and published it as "A Narrative Of An Apparition Which A Gentleman In Boston Had Of His Brother, Just Then Murthered In London." Any other New England clergyman would have done the same. For all their determination to break with the "superstitions" of the past, Puritans were just as convinced as other English men and women that the universe was an enchanted place, filled with amazing portents and prodigies. Puritans, both clerical and lay, inhabited a world of "wonders": of comets, hailstorms, lightning, fires, deformed births, dreams, visions, prophecies, and omens. All events that seemed to interrupt the natural order were believed to carry supernatural significance, although the specific meaning of a given wonder was usually mysterious. The lore of wonders that pervaded seventeenth-century English culture and which the colonists brought with them to New England derived from folklore, classical meteorology, apocalyptic prophecy, and natural philosophy. Transmitted both orally and through printed matter, this hodge-podge of traditions endowed extraordinary events with an occult significance that was all the more potent for being unspecific. The open-ended nature of wonder lore enabled people of different faiths to appropriate wonders for their own use. Puritans viewed all extraordinary events as providential in their expression of God's power and purpose. They believed that wonders revealed not only God's ascendancy over the world, but also his attitude toward humanity at the moment when a wonder occurred. The specific meaning of each wonder was impenetrable, as was divine providence itself; but it could be understood in broad terms as a sign of God's approval or anger (usually the latter). For that reason, Puritans were eager to record and digest all supernatural incidents, and to ponder their significance.[2]

1 Cotton Mather, *Wonders of the Invisible World* (1693; Amherst, Wisc., 1862), pp. 107–9.

2 This paragraph is much indebted to David D. Hall's discussion of wonder lore and its origins in chapter 2 of *Worlds of Wonder, Days of Judgment: Popular Religious Belief in Early New England* (New York, 1989).

In private journals, church records, and published texts, Puritans reported and shared wonder tales. The most ambitious collection of such tales to be produced by a seventeenth-century New Englander was Increase Mather's *Essay for the Recording of Illustrious Providences*. This work, first printed in Boston in 1684, was received enthusiastically on both sides of the Atlantic: it was reprinted four times during the 1680s, twice in Boston and twice in London. In his *Essay*, Mather related "Memorable Events" that ranged from "Remarkable Tempests" and "Sea Deliverances" to "Answers of Prayer" and "Judgments of God upon Sinners" such as Quakers and drunkards. Mather undertook the project after finding a manuscript collection of wonder stories in the papers of John Davenport.[3] In May 1681, he showed the manuscript to a group of ministers convened in Boston; they agreed to help him in completing the project, committing themselves to "diligently enquire into, and Record such Illustrious Providences as have hap[pe]ned, or from time to time shall happen, in the places whereunto they do belong." Mather acknowledged himself "Engaged to many for the Materials" gathered in his book. This was, then, a collective enterprise, presented to the people of New England "that men would praise the Lord for his goodness, and for his wonderful works to the Children of Men."[4]

Colonial fascination with "Illustrious Providences" dates from the very beginning of New England settlement. John Winthrop, for example, preserved careful and detailed accounts of extraordinary incidents: "especial providences of God as were manifested for the good of these plantations."[5] According to Winthrop, on 18 January 1644, at about midnight, three men approaching Boston harbour by sea saw two lights rise out of the water, "in form like a man." These lights traveled through the air toward the town for about a quarter of an hour. A week later, at eight o'clock in the evening, the two lights reappeared. This time, a third light, which looked "like the moon," rose and joined with them. They "closed in one, and then parted, and closed and parted divers times" before dis-

3 The Reverend John Davenport died in 1670, soon after moving from New Haven to Massachusetts at the invitation of the First Church in Boston.

4 Increase Mather, *An Essay for the Recording of Illustrious Providences* (Boston, 1684), title page, Preface, pp. v, x, xii, p. 311. Robert Middlekauff discusses Mather's *Essay* in *The Mathers: Three Generations of Puritan Intellectuals, 1596–1728* (New York, 1971), chap. 8, esp. pp. 143–8. For other examples of works chronicling portents and prodigies, see William Bradford, *Of Plymouth Plantation, 1620–1647*, ed. Francis Murphy (New York, 1981); Edward Johnson, *Johnson's Wonder-Working Providence*, ed. J. Franklin Jameson (New York, 1910); and Nathaniel Morton, *New-England's Memorial* (Cambridge, 1669).

5 John Winthrop, *Journal*, ed. James Hosmer, 2 vols. (New York, 1908), I: 163.

appearing. That same evening, wrote Winthrop, several "godly persons" heard a voice on the stretch of water between Boston and Dorchester, "calling out in a most dreadful manner, boy, boy, come away, come away." A fortnight later, people on the other side of town heard the same voice.[6]

Puritan interest in "especial providences" continued throughout the century.[7] In July 1665, the inhabitants of several towns on Long Island were surprised to hear the sound of guns and drums coming in from the sea. Their surprise must have turned to amazement when, at ten o'clock one clear morning, they beheld "companies of armed men in the air, clothed in light-coloured garments, and the commanders in red." The eminently respectable Puritan diarist John Hull received news of this remarkable spectacle and recorded it for posterity.[8] Hull also described a portentous dream experienced by a Long Island man that same year. The man "dreamed he fought with devils, and they took his hat from him." Soon afterwards, he was "found dead . . . killed, as supposed, by lightning, and his hat some few rods from him, cut as it were by art."[9] Hull did not try to interpret these wonders; nor did Winthrop. To do so would have been both presumptuous and futile, since divine providence was inherently mysterious. But neither did they express any doubt as to the objective reality of these bizarre phenomena: Puritan diarists related such incidents as indisputable fact.

The sharing of wonder tales that made possible Increase Mather's *Essay for the Recording of Illustrious Providences* was not limited to that particular enterprise: Puritans regularly exchanged information about supernatural occurrences. The Reverend Noahdiah Russell, a tutor at Harvard College, was part of one such network. Russell recorded in his diary an incident that took place at Lynn, Massachusetts, in March 1682. One afternoon, a hailstorm shattered many windows in Lynn. The night came on so dark that an elderly townsman named Mr. Handford went outside to see if there was a new moon. To his amazement, Handford beheld "a strange black cloud" in which there appeared "a man in arms complete, standing with his legs straddling and having a pike in his hands which he held across his breast." Handford's wife and "many others" also

6 Ibid., II: 155–6. See also ibid, II: 346.

7 David D. Hall points out that wonder lore was "falling out of favor within learned culture" by the late seventeenth century. But "tradition remained strong" and even educated colonists "continued to invoke the wonder" (David D. Hall, *Worlds of Wonder, Days of Judgment,* p. 110).

8 John Hull, "Diary," *Transactions of the American Antiquarian Society,* 3 (1857): 218. Hull was a merchant, silversmith, mintmaster, and also the treasurer of Massachusetts.

9 John Hull, "Diary," p. 220.

saw the apparition. After a while, the "man in arms" vanished and in his place came "a spacious ship seeming under sail though she kept the same station." Those who saw this second apparition said that the ship was "the handsomest of ever they saw with a lofty stern, the head to the south, the hull black, the sails bright; a long and resplendant streamer came from the top of the mast." Eventually, the "spacious ship" also disappeared and the sky began to clear. A week later, Jeremiah Shepard, the minister at Lynn, described this incident in a letter to Margaret Mitchell of Cambridge. It was from Mitchell that Noahdiah Russell heard about the apparitions.[10]

Inclusive and eclectic as Puritans were in their appropriation of wonder lore, they by no means welcomed or approved all occult phenomena. Visions and prophecies were acceptable only if they reinforced Congregationalist theology: the orthodox denounced revelations experienced by Quaker prophets and dissenters like Anne Hutchinson as "the strong delusions of Satan."[11] Not all supernatural occurrences, Puritans believed, were the result of divine intervention: the Devil could also bring about such effects. Clergymen condemned "false" prophecy not just because they believed it to be diabolical, but also because personal revelation shifted power away from the institutional church as embodied in the ministry and toward autonomous individuals. Clerical opposition to heterodox revelation was as much professional as moral and doctrinal.

The issue of power and its origin also underlay clerical objections to magic. Ministers perceived magical practitioners as a challenge both to their own authority and to God's control of access to occult realms. Whereas "illustrious providences" occurred at God's command, fortune-telling and other kinds of magic involved the human manipulation of supernatural forces.[12] Clergymen argued that the knowledge and power that magic offered was a blasphemy against God's omnipotence and the mystery of his design. Just as ministers believed in spectral ships and spectral armies, so they did not doubt that magic worked. Yet human beings, they insisted, could not bring about magical effects. Ministers believed that people who employed magic had no power of their own and that magical experiments

10 Noahdiah Russell, "Diary," *New England Historical and Genealogical Register,* 7 (1853): 53–4.
11 Increase Mather, *An Essay for the Recording of Illustrious Providences,* p. 345.
12 See David D. Hall, *Worlds of Wonder, Days of Judgment,* p. 100: "Prophecy and magic were alike in helping people to become empowered, prophecy because it overturned the authority of mediating clergy and magic because it gave access to the realm of occult force."

succeeded as a result of diabolical intervention. Clerics feared that the Devil used magic to lure people into his service. At first, those who experimented with magical techniques would not realize that they were relying on the Devil's services, but sooner or later, he would claim their souls as a reward. In the clerical mind, anybody who operated in collusion with the Devil, whether consciously or not, was a witch; magical practitioners relied upon a diabolical agency, and so were guilty of diabolical witchcraft.

Not surprisingly, ministers were horrified to discover that colonists practiced magic and consulted magical experts. "It is a sad thing," wrote Increase Mather, "that ever any person should dare to do thus in New England.... Dreadful guilt is upon the Souls of them, that have gone to Enquire of such vile Creatures, and so of the Devil by them.... Much more is it Evil to be a Practitioner in this Iniquity."[13] According to the clergy, magic of any kind (fortune-telling, image magic, charms, or countermagic) was an abomination in the sight of God. In public lectures and private confrontations, ministers sought to educate their flock in the spiritual dangers posed by magical experimentation and so to purge their communities of magic.[14]

"In many parts of the World," lamented John Hale, the minister at Beverly, Massachusetts, diviners "have been countenanced in their diabolic skill and profession; because they serve the interest of those that have a vain curiosity, to pry into things God has forbidden, and concealed from discovery by lawful means." Clerics like Hale argued that the knowledge provided by divination was neither natural nor derived from God; therefore, it must come from the Devil. All those who "divin[ed] about things future," "discover[ed] things secret, as stollen Goods," and "inform[ed] of persons and things absent at a great distance" did so through "the

13 Increase Mather, *A Discourse Concerning the Uncertainty of the Times of Men* (Boston, 1697), pp. 24–5.

14 Stuart Clark points out that Protestant writings on magic and witchcraft were generally pastoral, not legal or philosophical, in nature (Stuart Clark, "Protestant Demonology: Sin, Superstition, and Society," in Bengt Ankarloo and Gustav Henningsen, eds., *Early Modern European Witchcraft: Centres and Peripheries* [Oxford, 1990], p. 56).

In the discussion that follows, I point out minor differences between the ministers in their attitudes toward magical practice, but, for the most part, the clergymen who spoke out on this subject offered the same interpretation of magic and voiced similar concerns. I do not wish to suggest, however, that the ministry constituted an ideological monolith on all issues. At Salem in 1692, for example, clergymen disagreed with each other on the crucial issue of spectral interpretation (for which see Chapter 6).

assistance of a familiar spirit."[15] In 1669, when Katherine Harrison of Wethersfield, Connecticut, appeared in court on charges of witchcraft, the magistrates asked local ministers whether fortune-telling was proof of complicity with Satan. The ministers responded that

> those things, whether past, present or to come, which are indeed secret, that is, cannot be knowne by humane skill in Arts, or strength of Reason arguing from the course of nature, nor are made knowne by divine revelation either mediate or intermediate, nor by information from man, must needes be knowne (if at all) by information from the Devill.[16]

In *Angelographia,* a treatise exploring the role played by spirits in human affairs, Increase Mather assured his readers that God condemned those who went to "ungodly Fortune-Tellers, to reveal such things, as cannot be known, but by the help of Evil Angels."[17] Deodat Lawson, preaching at Salem Village in 1692, condemned use of "the Sive and Seyssors, the Bible and Key; [and] the White of an Egge in a Glass." According to Lawson, the knowledge these techniques yielded came "from the Devil, not from God."[18] "Tis horrible," raged Cotton Mather, "that in this land of Uprightness, there should be any such Pranks of Wickedness."[19]

Healing magic, the ministers argued, was just as reprehensible as divination. Medicinal charms, they reasoned, could not derive their power from God, since people who used charms credited them with mechanical efficacy: God responded to supplication, not command. If magical healing was neither natural nor God-given, it must be diabolical in origin. Cotton Mather accordingly warned his congregation that medicinal charms were "Watch-words to the Devils."[20] "It has been a usual thing," Mather complained, "for People to cure Hurts with Spells.... 'Tis in the Devils Name, that such things are done; and in Gods Name I do this day charge them, as vile Impieties."[21] Clergymen were shocked by the inclusion of re-

15 John Hale, *A Modest Enquiry Into the Nature of Witchcraft* (1702; Bainbridge, N.Y., 1973), p. 165.
16 Willys Papers: Records of Trials for Witchcraft in Connecticut (Annmary Brown Memorial, Brown University Library, Providence, R.I.), W–18, 20 October 1669, Opinion of Ministers in the case of Katherine Harrison.
17 Increase Mather, *Angelographia* (Boston, 1696), p. 25.
18 Deodat Lawson, *Christ's Fidelity the Only Shield against Satan's Malignity* (Boston, 1692), p. 65.
19 Cotton Mather, *A Discourse on Witchcraft* (Boston, 1689), p. 27.
20 Ibid., p. 26.
21 Cotton Mather, *Wonders of the Invisible World,* p. 96. According to Mather, curses operated in much the same way: "When foul-mouth[e]d men shall wish harm unto their Neighbours, they give a Commission unto the Devils to perform what they desire" (Cotton Mather, *A Discourse on Witchcraft,* p. 24).

ligious words and phrases in charms of this kind. Samuel Willard lamented that the Devil had "taught men to use the name of God, or of Christ, or of some notable Sentence that is recorded in God's Word, (which is also his name) either for the keeping of Devils out of places, or for the Curing of these or those Maladies that men labour of." This was "nothing else but plain conjuration, and an horrible abusing of the Name of God to such purposes as serve egregiously to the Establishing of the Devils Kingdom in the hearts of men."[22] Increase Mather also condemned the "use of any of the sacred Names or Titles belonging to the Glorious God, or to his Son Jesus Christ, as Charms." Mather reminded his readers that "God in his word doth with the highest severity condemn all such practices, declaring not only that all Enchanters and Charmers are not to be tolerated amongst his People; but that all who do such things are an abomination to him."[23]

According to Cotton Mather, some Puritans took these clerical injunctions too literally. When Margaret Rule of Boston became possessed in 1693, the devils tormenting Rule prevented her from hearing any words that evoked God or godliness. Yet she could hear the letters of such words if they were spelled out and so could be made to understand those engaged in discourse with her; this proved an effective way of outmaneuvering the possessing devils. But, complained Mather, "there were some so ridiculous as to count it a sort of Spell or a Charm for any thus to accommodate themselves to the capacity of the Sufferer." As a result, "little of this kind was done." Whether or not such scruples were "ridiculous," it must have been heartening to Mather and his colleagues that at least some Bostonians were so rigorous in their disavowal of magical charms.[24]

Ministers were also concerned about the use of countermagic as a defense against witchcraft. They demanded that illness or misfortune be understood in providential terms, as a judgment from God, and that all temptations to blame specific individuals or engage in magical remedies be resisted. Suffering, they insisted, was the consequence of sin and an invitation to moral reformation. Whether God inflicted suffering himself or allowed Satan to do so, perhaps by means of a witch, was of little consequence: ultimate responsibility lay with the sufferer.[25] In 1692, Deodat Lawson re-

22 Samuel Willard, *The Danger of Taking God's Name in Vain* (Boston, 1691), p. 10.
23 Increase Mather, *An Essay for the Recording of Illustrious Providences,* p. 260.
24 Cotton Mather, "Another Brand Pluck't Out of the Burning," in George L. Burr, ed., *Narratives of the Witchcraft Cases* (1914; New York, 1952), pp. 315–16.
25 This effort to shift attention away from the agent of misfortune toward divine

minded the congregation at Salem Village that the only effective antidote against affliction, of whatever kind, was repentant prayer: this opened up the sinner's heart to Christ, who then acted as mediator on man's behalf, so that God would "assuredly and shortly suppress the malice of Satan."[26]

> Prayer is the most proper and potent antidote against the old Serpent's venomous operations. When legions of devils do come down among us, multitudes of prayers should go up to God. Satan, the worst of all our enemies, is called in Scripture a dragon, to note his malice; a serpent, to note his subtlety; a lion, to note his strength. But none of all these can stand before prayer.[27]

The title of this sermon, which was published in Boston soon after its delivery in church, encapsulated neatly Lawson's argument: *Christ's Fidelity the Only Shield against Satan's Malignity.*

Yet, Lawson continued, some New Englanders used other means to remove affliction. These "unwarrantable projects" included "Burning the Afflicted persons hair; paring of nails, stopping up and boyling the Urine; [and] Their scratching the accused, or otherwise fetching Blood of them."[28] Lawson condemned countermagic as "using the Devil's shield, against the Devil's sword."[29] Just as malevolent witches inflicted harm only by the Devil's help, so those who fought witchcraft with countermagic succeeded only through the intervention of infernal spirits. It was the Devil who had brought about the original affliction and now the Devil obligingly removed it. In doing so, he encouraged the observance of rituals no less dependent upon his agency than maleficent witchcraft. Increase Mather argued that all countermagic involved an implicit diabolical covenant:

providence and the victim's failings was a common trait of Protestant writings on witchcraft (Stuart Clark, "Protestant Demonology," esp. p. 60).

26 Deodat Lawson, *Christ's Fidelity,* p. 39.

27 Ibid., p. 73.

28 The drawing of blood, especially from the face, was a time-honored way of undoing a witch's spell. Samuel Shattuck testified at Salem in 1692 that a passing stranger had offered to "fetch blood of" Bridget Bishop, who was suspected of having bewitched Shattuck's son (Paul Boyer and Stephen Nissenbaum, *The Salem Witchcraft Papers: Verbatim Transcripts of the Legal Documents of the Salem Witchcraft Outbreak,* 3 vols. [New York, 1977], I: 99). See also Keith Thomas, *Religion and the Decline of Magic* (1971; Middlesex, England, 1973), p. 649; and George L. Kittredge, *Witchcraft in Old and New England* (1929; New York, 1956), pp. 47, 169, 236, 290.

29 Deodat Lawson, *Christ's Fidelity,* pp. 62, 64. John Hale described countermagic as "going to the Devil to find the Devil" (John Hale, *A Modest Enquiry,* p. 21).

> if the Devils do either operate or cease to do mischief upon the use of such things it must needs be in that they are signs which give notice to the Evil Spirits what they are to do; Now for men to submit to any of the Devils Sacraments is implicitly to make a covenant with him.[30]

Countermagic, in the ministers' view, was morally equivalent to the original act of witchcraft. Those who used countermagic to heal mysterious illnesses or to identify the malefactors responsible became servants of the Devil: as Increase Mather put it, "the person thus recovered cannot say, The Lord was my healer, but [should say], The Devil was my healer."[31] Cotton Mather, who spoke out against countermagic in 1689, urged his congregation to abandon "superstitious Preservations" in favor of three alternative "amulets": prayer, faith, and a holy life.[32]

The clergy had two fundamental objections to magic. First, they believed that magic relied upon a diabolical agency. Those who used magical techniques might believe that they themselves had somehow harnessed occult forces so as to bring about the desired effect, but in fact they had been duped by the Devil. Magical practitioners had no independent power; they could achieve nothing without external assistance. Magic, wrote John Hale, was "wrought by the Devil's power, and not by any natural power of the Sorcerer."[33] Second, in trying to understand and manipulate the world around them, those who used magic disregarded providential theology, which entrusted all knowledge and power to God's control. From the ministers' perspective, those who experimented with magic or consulted magical practitioners were guilty of "hubris": they refused to accept their allotted place in the world and sought to usurp God's rightful authority.

New Englanders who used magical techniques differed from the clergy in their understanding of magic in two respects. First, they did not believe that magic was inherently evil. After all, those skilled in magical practice were as likely to harness it in the service of the community as they were to misuse it against neighbors and acquaintances. Some layfolk saw no harm in benevolent magic and branded as witches only those who used magic for evil purposes.[34]

30 Increase Mather, *An Essay for the Recording of Illustrious Providences*, pp. 248–9. See also Cotton Mather, *A Discourse on Witchcraft*, p. 25.

31 Increase Mather, *An Essay for the Recording of Illustrious Providences*, p. 266.

32 Cotton Mather, *A Discourse on Witchcraft*, pp. 19–20.

33 John Hale, *A Modest Enquiry*, p. 79.

34 There are occasional references in the sources to "white" witches and "healing" witches, but the appellation "witch" on its own seems always to have carried a negative connotation.

From this perspective, witchcraft was simply a misuse of occult power, the flipside of a valued social service. Second, whereas ministers condemned all forms of magic as diabolical, some of their parishioners saw no reason to implicate the Devil in either good or evil magic. They perceived magic in pragmatic terms, as a harnessing of occult power for practical ends. They did not think about where this power came from; they just used it. "Such have an implicit faith," lamented John Hale, "that the means used, shall produce the effect desired, but consider not how; and so are beguiled by the Serpent that lies in the grass unseen."[35]

The very fact that magic could be used for both good and evil purposes placed cunning folk in an ambiguous and vulnerable position. Some of those who ended up in court on charges of witchcraft had long served their communities as healers or fortunetellers; in fact, witnesses often referred to these services as proof that the suspect had occult power.[36] Elizabeth Morse of Newbury, Massachusetts, a healer and midwife, was suspected of using her skills to harm as well as to cure her neighbors. One townsman declared that he was uncertain whether she was "a Witch, or a cunning Woman." William Morse, Elizabeth's husband, was aware "that his wife was accounted a witch, but he did wonder that she should be both a healing and a destroying witch." Others were less reluctant to believe that Morse was skilled in both "healing" and "destroying." Indeed, the former implied the latter, whether or not the practitioner actually used her "destroying" ability.[37] In 1692, Ephraim Foster told the court at Salem that he had heard accused witch Samuel Wardwell of Andover "tell dority Eames hur forten [fortune]." Eames apparently declared "after[ward] that she believed Wardwell was a witch or els he Cold never tell what he did."[38] The precise meaning of Eames's remark is unclear, although Foster clearly interpreted it as negative. Eames's description of Wardwell as "a witch" suggests that she believed all cunning folk to be at least potentially malevolent. Assuming that to be the case, it is instructive that Eames nevertheless had Wardwell tell her fortune. Her doing

35 John Hale, *A Modest Enquiry*, p. 131. Writing about early modern England, Clive Holmes notes that "insistence upon the diabolical origins of benificent witchcraft never took root except within a small cadre of godly laymen" (Clive Holmes, "Popular Culture? Witches, Magistrates, and Divines in Early Modern England," in Stevan Kaplan., ed., *Understanding Popular Culture: Europe from the Middle Ages to the Nineteenth Century* [New York, 1984], pp. 102–3).

36 This was also the case in England and Europe, for examples of which see Stuart Clark, "Protestant Demonology," p. 78 n103.

37 "Trials for Witchcraft in New England" (Houghton Library, Harvard University), printed in Samuel Drake, *Annals of Witchcraft in New England* (1869; New York, 1972), pp. 281, 287.

38 *Salem Witchcraft Papers,* III: 787.

so testifies to the ambivalent position cunning folk occupied in the minds of their neighbors: however dangerous, they were also invaluable as healers and fortune-tellers.

Any kind of divining skill could rebound on the practitioner and result in an accusation of witchcraft. In 1679, when Caleb Powell offered to discover, through occult craft, who was bewitching the Morse household in Newbury, Massachusetts, William and Elizabeth Morse repaid his offer of assistance by accusing Powell himself of bewitching them.[39] When Elizabeth Godman was tried for witchcraft in 1653, several witnesses mentioned her mysterious possession of information on assorted matters to which, it was claimed, she was not privy by any natural channel: she "could tell sundrie things that was done at the church meeting before meeting was done" and knew that "Mrs Atwater had figs in her pockets when she saw none of them." Such abilities were "suspicious" and good cause for "fear."[40] Two years later, in 1655, Goodwife Batchelor of Ipswich, Massachusetts, was accused of witchcraft. James How, Thomas Medcalfe, and Francis Bates each deposed that "Goodwife Batchelor had several times said that some of Goodman Medcalf's and Goodman Howe's cattle would die, some would escape, and others would live." A rather unsurprising prediction; but when "it came to pass as she said, although they all seemed well when she told it," James How accused Goodwife Batchelor of having bewitched the cattle.[41]

Healers were especially vulnerable to accusations of witchcraft if they applied their skills to a patient whose condition then worsened. Margaret Jones of Charlestown, Massachusetts, tried for witchcraft in 1648, was known as a medical practitioner. Jones was suspected of "a malignant touch" because many of her patients were "taken with deafness, or vomiting, or other violent pains or sickness." According to John Winthrop, she told those who refused her medicines that "they would never be healed, and accordingly their diseases and hurts continued, with relapse against the ordinary course, and beyond the apprehension of all physicians and surgeons."[42] In 1680, in Hampton, New Hampshire, John and Mary Godfrey's fifteen-month-old son died under suspicious circumstances; neighbor Rachel Fuller was thought to have been responsible. During a visit to the Godfreys' home while the child was sick, Fuller had

39 *Records and Files of the Quarterly Courts of Essex County*, 9 vols. (Salem, Mass., 1911–78), VII: 355.
40 Charles J. Hoadly, ed., *Records of the Colony or Jurisdiction of New Haven*, 2 vols. (New Haven, Conn., 1857–8), II: 31, 33.
41 *Records and Files of the Quarterly Courts of Essex County*, III: 403–4.
42 John Winthrop, *Journal*, II: 344.

enacted a bizarre ritual. First, she "turned her[self] about, and smote the back of her hands together sundry times, and spat in the fire." Next, she took some herbs, "rubbed them in her hand and strewed them about the hearth by the fire." Fuller then sat down and said to Goody Godfrey, "Woman, the Child will be well." Soon after Fuller left, Mehitable Godfrey came to her mother and told her that their visitor was at the back of the house, "acting strangely." Goody Godfrey and Sarah, another daughter, looked outside:

> [They] saw Rachel Fuller standing with her face towards the house, beating herself with her arms, as men do in winter to heat their hands, and this she did three times; and stooping down and gathering something off the ground in the interim between the beating of herself, and then she went home.

Rachel Fuller had been quite explicit that her ritual was intended to effect a cure, but the child died. Fuller's strange behavior prompted the Godfreys to accuse her of murder by witchcraft.[43]

Even healers who used neither charms nor occult rituals were vulnerable to accusations of witchcraft, so hazy was the boundary between magical and non-magical treatment. When Goodwife Simons of Easthampton, Connecticut, "had her fits" sometime before 1658, Goodwife Bishop went to the local healer Elizabeth Garlick for "Dockweede," a medicinal herb. There is no evidence that Garlick prescribed charms for Simons or any other of her patients. Yet when Garlick was tried for witchcraft in 1658, Bishop testified to Garlick's healing activities as incriminating evidence. Bishop evidently believed that medical skill implied magical skill and that Garlick was prone to use her expertise against as well as for her neighbors.[44]

43 Nathaniel Bouton, ed., *Documents and Records Relating to the Province of New Hampshire,* 5 vols. (Concord, N.H., 1867–80), I: 416, 14 July 1680, testimony of Goodwife Godfrey.

44 *Records of the Town of Easthampton,* 5 vols. (Sag Harbor, N.Y., 1887–92), I: 134–5. For a detailed discussion of the Garlick case, see John Demos, *Entertaining Satan: Witchcraft and the Culture of Early New England* (New York, 1982), chap. 7. A number of other accused witches were also healers, including Anna Edmunds of Lynn (*Records and Files of the Quarterly Courts of Essex County,* II: 226–8, V: 55, VI: 180); Ann Burt, also of Lynn (*Records and Files of the Quarterly Courts of Essex County,* IV: 207–9); Katherine Harrison of Wethersfield, Connecticut (Willys Papers, W–16); Mercy Disborough of Fairfield, Connecticut (Willys Papers, W–33); Winifred Holman of Cambridge, Massachusetts (Middlesex Court Files: Original Depositions and Other Materials from the Proceedings of the Quarterly Courts of Middlesex County, Massachusetts [Massachusetts Archives, Columbia Point, Boston, Mass.], folder 25); Jane Hawkins of Boston (John Winthrop, *Journal,* I: 266–8); Mary Hale of Boston (Suffolk County Court Files: Original Depositions and Other Materials from the Pro-

Female healers were much more likely to be accused of witchcraft than were their male counterparts, partly because they were unprotected by the professional status accorded to male "doctors."[45] Only one male healer, Dr. Roger Toothaker of Billerica, was accused of witchcraft in seventeenth-century New England. All other accused medical practitioners were women. It should be borne in mind that there were in fact very few male doctors in the northern colonies. Indeed, it might be tempting to see the gender distribution in such cases as reflecting nothing more than the proportion of female to male practitioners, were it not for the fact that women were generally more vulnerable than men to accusations of witchcraft: seventy-nine percent of accused witches in early New England were female.[46] Witch accusations were often directed against women whose situation (whether through economic independence, medical skill, or occult knowledge) challenged gender norms that placed women in positions subordinate to men.[47] The power wielded by cunning folk was potentially threatening whether in the hands of a man or a woman, in that it could be used for both good and evil; but it was especially threatening if the magical practitioner was a woman, since occult expertise assured her a position of authority in the local community quite contrary to her normative status as a woman. Thus, it is hardly surprising that most accused

ceedings of the Quarterly Courts of Suffolk County, Massachusetts [Massachusetts Archives, Columbia Point, Boston, Mass.], vol. 24, #1972); and the unnamed woman who was suspected of having afflicted Margaret Rule in 1693 (Cotton Mather, "Another Brand Pluck't Out of the Burning," p. 311).

45 Carol Karlsen, *The Devil in the Shape of a Woman: Witchcraft in Colonial New England* (New York, 1987), pp. 142–3. Karlsen goes further in suggesting that one function of New England witchcraft was "to discredit women's medical knowledge in favor of their male competitors." This rests on the assumption that male and female practitioners were "in direct competition," which may or may not have been the case in early New England. Certainly, there is no evidence to suggest a conscious female defiance of male medical practice such as Joyce Gibson asserts for early modern England in *Hanged for Witchcraft: Elizabeth Lowys and Her Successors* (Canberra, Australia, 1988). I do not address here the specific issue of midwifery, for which see John Demos, *Entertaining Satan*, p. 80, and Carol Karlsen, *The Devil in the Shape of a Woman*, p. 142.

46 Carol Karlsen, *The Devil in the Shape of a Woman*, pp. 48–9.

47 Carol Karlsen argues convincingly that situation rather than behavior made women vulnerable to accusations of witchcraft. According to John Demos and Richard Weisman, witches were characterized as such in part because they were ill-tempered and quarrelsome (John Demos, *Entertaining Satan*, pp. 86–94; Richard Weisman, *Witchcraft, Magic, and Religion in Seventeenth-Century Massachusetts* [Amherst, Mass., 1984], pp. 85–91). Yet Karlsen points out that these women were no more disagreeable or contentious than their neighbors. Their behavior became unusually threatening as a result of their anomalous situations: aggression signified not just a failure to live up to ideals of harmony, but also a "refusal to accept their 'place' in New England's social order" (Carol Karlsen, *The Devil in the Shape of a Woman*, pp. 118–19).

cunning folk were women: the legal prosecution of magical practitioners as witches was as much an expression of fears relating to female power and independence as it was an attempt to punish what appeared to be an abuse of magical skill.

New Englanders who used magic or consulted magical practitioners realized that occult power was dangerous if misused. Consequently, cunning folk, male and female, were often distrusted. But people who turned to magic did not see it as intrinsically evil: they defined magic as good or evil according to the purpose it served. Ministers, however, refused to make that distinction: they believed that all those who used magic were allies, whether witting or unwitting, of the Devil. It was particularly worrisome to the clergy that some of those who resorted to magic were respectable, godly people who apparently did not realize that experimenting with magic was contrary to Puritan doctrine. These people most likely feared the Devil, but did not perceive magic as necessarily diabolical. Increase Mather believed that some "practise[d] such things in their simplicity, not knowing that therein they gratifie[d] the Devil."[48]

> Many who practise these nefarious Vanities little think what they do. They would not for the World (they say) make a Covenant with the Devil, yet by improving the Devils signals, with an opinion of receiving benefit thereby, they do the thing which they pretend to abhor.[49]

Thus, people who professed to fear and hate the Devil had unknowingly pledged themselves to his service through the performance of magical rituals. They had been, in John Hale's words, "beguiled by the Serpent that lies in the grass unseen."

In campaigning against magic, the ministers' principal target was not willful defiance of Puritan doctrine, but what they saw as misinterpretation and ignorance: "simplicity" rather than conscious sin. John Hale, like Increase Mather, believed that some of those who used magic were unaware of their offense. Hale declared himself willing to excuse "a tanto [in some degree], though not a toto [completely], those that ignorantly use[d] charms, spells, writings or forms of words, etc being taught them by others."[50] Some of Hale's parishioners were better informed than others. One "ancient Woman" came to him for "advice" because she was worried about a particular incident in her past. She told Hale that "when

48 Increase Mather, *An Essay for the Recording of Illustrious Providences*, p. 260.
49 Ibid., pp. 248–9.
50 John Hale, *A Modest Enquiry*, p. 131.

she was a Maid, she had a curiosity to know who should be her Husband, and was informed of a Doctor that would shew Maids their future Husbands in a glass." The said "Doctor" showed her the image of a man that proved to resemble exactly her future husband. The woman asked Hale "whether she had done well or evil in going to the Dr." Hale replied that "she did evil in going thereby to the Devil." He explained as follows:

> The Dr. could not bring into the glass the shadow of a man absent and unknown, by any natural cause, or means by him used. Therefore it was from the Devil, who raised this Spectre in likeness of a man then unknown.

Hale suspected, moreover, that "the Dr. doing this frequently for his Money, must know he did it by a familiar Spirit, and therefore was a Conjurer in some league explicite, or implicite, with Satan."[51]

Hale was anxious to dissuade his parishioners from magical experiments, but his efforts in that direction were not always successful. In 1670, thirty-five-year-old Dorcas Hoar expressed to Hale "great repentance for the sins of her former life," which included having borrowed "a book of Palmistry." Hale explained that "it was an evill book and evill art," whereupon Hoar "seemed . . . to renounce, or reject all such practices." Yet several years later, Hale's daughter Rebecca and townsman Thomas Tuck both reported that Dorcas Hoar was still in possession of a fortune-telling book. John Samson, who had originally lent Hoar the "book of Palmistry," told Hale that he had long since sold the volume, which he said was quarto size. Both Rebecca Hale and Thomas Tuck claimed that the book they had seen was the size of a grammar, which led Hale to conclude that Hoar had acquired another volume and was still at least interested in fortune-telling, if not actually practicing it. In 1692, when Dorcas Hoar was accused of witchcraft, Hale visited her in prison and questioned her about these reports. Hoar denied that she had seen any book other than John Samson's and assured Hale that she had told no fortunes since her promise of reformation. Hale did not believe her and so presented his findings to the witch court as incriminating evidence.[52] Assuming that Rebecca Hale and Thomas Tuck were telling the truth, Dorcas Hoar's protestations of innocence were almost certainly disingenuous: in 1670, she may perhaps have been sincere in her determination to renounce palmistry, but since then she had reverted, despite Hale's

51 Ibid., pp. 134–5.
52 *Salem Witchcraft Papers,* II: 397–9.

having explained to her that such behavior was offensive to God. Hoar resumed her interest in divination not because she was ignorant of official teaching on the subject, but because she chose to ignore that teaching.

In general, Hale believed, people who used magic had "an implicit faith that the means used [would] produce the effect desired, but consider[ed] not how." Yet Hale did meet one man who had thought about the origins of magical power and who believed that God had given him "the gift of healing." According to Hale, the man used medicinal charms he believed to be "Scripture words," taught to him by an old woman (he could not read himself). This healer's belief that his powers came from God and his use of "Scripture words" as charms exemplified the lack of any conscious antagonism to religion on the part of magical practitioners. Hale did not "believe that this man was a Wizard (though in danger of it) because he did it ignorantly in misbelief." Hale explained to the healer that "part of his words were Scripture, and part not," and that their efficacy "came by the devil." The man "seemed convinced of his error, and promised reformation."[53] There are no other examples in the surviving records of New Englanders claiming that magical power came from God.[54] Layfolk who incorporated religious words and phrases into magical charms may have believed that magic was God-given; or they may have included religious formulas simply because these were traditional, without giving any thought to the possible implications. Increase Mather at least recognized the former possibility when he emphasized that people who had been cured through countermagic should not say, "The Lord was my healer."[55] It may also be significant that Deodat Lawson thought it necessary to remind his congregation that divination came "from the Devil, not from God."[56]

53 John Hale, *A Modest Enquiry*, pp. 131–2. There have been many Christian communities in which healing is considered to be a legitimate religious phenomenon, but the Puritans had excluded the charismatic as well as the sacramental from their version of Christianity.

54 Several healers did draw a connection between religious faith and medical efficacy. When Jane Hawkins "practised physic, she would ask the party, if she did believe." Ann Burt of Lynn was reported to have told Sarah Townsend that "if she could believe in her God she would cure her body and soul." When Rebecca Stearns fell ill in the 1650s, Winifred Holman offered "to cuer her with the blising of God." But there is no evidence that any of these healers used magical charms as part of their treatment, or that they saw magical efficacy as sanctioned by God (John Winthrop, *Journal*, I: 266–8; *Records and Files of the Quarterly Courts of Essex County*, IV: 207; Middlesex Court Files, folder 25, #1).

55 Increase Mather, *An Essay for the Recording of Illustrious Providences*, p. 266.

56 Deodat Lawson, *Christ's Fidelity*, p. 65.

If Hale was willing to believe in the innocence and benevolent intentions of at least some cunning folk, Cotton Mather had his doubts:

> I suspect that there are none of that sort; but rather think, There is none that doeth good; no, not one. If they do good, it is only that they may do hurt.

Mather urged his congregation not to trust magical practitioners, even those who apparently did "only Good-Turns for their Neighbours."[57] If cunning folk could "effectually use Divels to cure Hurts," it was reasonable to conclude that they could "cause them also."[58] Mather conceded that some of those less experienced in magical practice did not realize the dangers involved. He feared that the Devil used seemingly harmless magical experiments to lure people into his service. "It has been acknowledged," he wrote, "by some who have sunk the deepest into this horrible Pit, that they began at these little Witchcrafts."[59] Mather suspected that "the frequent and consistent practice of certain Magical Ceremonies may have Invested many Persons with the Diabolic Ministry of Witches, who have not been well aware of what they have been adoing."[60] The ministers' task was thus twofold: to dissuade layfolk from consulting magical practitioners and to make them understand the dire spiritual consequences of experimenting with magic themselves.[61]

Clergymen sought to combat magic not only in private confrontations with individual offenders, but also in public lectures and disciplinary proceedings. In 1689, Cotton Mather gave a sermon on witchcraft in which he assured his congregation that all "Magical Ceremonies" were a form of witchcraft:

> This is the Witchcraft of them, that with a Sieve, or a key will go to discover how their lost Goods are disposed of. This is the Witchcraft of them that with Glasses and Basons will go to discover how they shall be Related before they dy. They are a sort of Witches who thus employ themselves.[62]

57 Cotton Mather, *A Discourse on Witchcraft,* pp. 5–6.

58 Cotton Mather, "Paper on Witchcraft," *Proceedings of the Massachusetts Historical Society,* 47 (1914): 266.

59 Cotton Mather, *Wonders of the Invisible World,* p. 96.

60 Cotton Mather, "Paper on Witchcraft," p. 258.

61 In general, Protestant evangelists and demonologists paid far more attention to the dangers of beneficent magic than to malevolent witchcraft: the corrupting influence of the former was particularly worrying because it was so insidious (Stuart Clark, "Protestant Demonology," pp. 62–9).

62 Cotton Mather, *A Discourse on Witchcraft,* p. 27.

Three years later, in the midst of the Salem witch panic, Deodat Lawson denounced the use of countermagic against witchcraft in a guest sermon delivered from the pulpit of Salem Village Church.[63] That same year, Francis Dane, the minister at Andover, heard that some of his parishioners were using "the Sive, and Cisers [scissors]" and so "the Sabboth after . . . spake publiqly concerning it."[64] Clergymen sometimes went beyond words in their efforts to drive home the dangers of magical experimentation. In July 1687, Increase Mather had two divination glasses broken at a church meeting.[65] In 1694, two young women belonging to Boston's Second Church, Rebecca Adams and Alice Pound, were found guilty of "consulting an ungodly fortune-teller in the Neighbourhood, with desires to be informed of some secret and future things." Adams and Pound had to give a public acknowledgment of their misconduct, "and so the church was reconciled with them."[66] Dramatic ritual events such as these were an effective way of underscoring the ministers' objections to magic. Yet some godly New Englanders remained ignorant of those objections, or perhaps ignored them when convenient.

The substance of the ministers' objections to magic remained the same throughout the seventeenth century, but the intensity of their concern did not. Although New Englanders made use of magical techniques throughout the century, it was apparently not until the 1680s that clergymen mounted a campaign against magic. Most surviving denunciations of magical practice date from the last two decades of the century. During those years, ministers attacked magic in sermons and learned treatises. Increase Mather, Cotton Mather, Deodat Lawson, and Samuel Willard each berated their congregations for using magic and explained to them in detail why such practices were offensive to God. Once delivered in church, these sermons were published to ensure a wider circulation of their message. Treatises such as Increase Mather's *Essay for the Recording of Illustrious Providences* and John Hale's *Modest Enquiry into the Nature of Witchcraft* (published in 1702) also discussed the Devil's involvement in magical experiments and denounced popular recourse to such "vile Impieties." But why this sudden interest in magic?

The chronological focus of extant clerical attacks may reflect in

63 Deodat Lawson, *Christ's Fidelity,* delivered in March 1692, subsequently published (Boston, 1693).
64 *Salem Witchcraft Papers,* III: 881.
65 Samuel Sewall, *Diary,* ed. M. Halsey Thomas, 2 vols. (New York, 1973), I: 144.
66 Boston Second Church Records (Massachusetts Historical Society), Book 2.

part the growing number of printers and printing presses in the Boston area during the latter part of the century.[67] As a result of this expansion in printing capacity, the number of published sermons rose dramatically, although the vast majority still slipped into oblivion unless preserved in manuscript notation. In a statement on the witch trials of 1692, the Reverend Francis Dane mentioned that he had recently lectured in Andover against the use of magical divination. Were it not for this passing reference, we would not know that he had done so, since Dane's sermons have not survived. Other sermons denouncing magic, from earlier and later decades, have probably perished.[68] The individual confrontations described by John Hale in his treatise are undated and may have taken place earlier in the century; Hale had served as pastor at Beverly since 1665.

Many of the surviving diatribes against magic were penned by Increase and Cotton Mather, both Bostonians, who jointly dominated the colonial press during the final decades of the seventeenth century. The predominance of their work in any discussion of clerical opposition to magic reflects the extraordinary productivity of father and son as authors, not necessarily a lack of concern on the part of ministers who lived outside Boston. Indeed, the fact that Francis Dane and John Hale were active against magic out in the rural backwaters of Andover and Beverly suggests a broad-based clerical movement, and also confirms the widespread currency of magical practice.

Even taking into consideration the impact of an expanding printing industry, the concentration of clerical attacks on magic during the last two decades of the century seems striking. There were, in fact, good reasons for New England ministers to become more sensitive to magical practice during those years. As the decades passed, clergymen perceived a decline in the quality of spiritual life and in their own status within New England society. As an increasing number of people became involved in commerce, ministers identified "a worldly Spirit" taking hold of the northern colonies.[69] A relatively stable, communitarian, and homogeneous

67 See John Tebbel, *A History of Book Publishing in the United States:* I, *The Creation of an Industry, 1630–1865* (New York, 1972), pp. 13–50.

68 *Salem Witchcraft Papers,* III: 881. I have not been able to find any manuscript notes for sermonic attacks on magic; but as the Dane reference shows, it would be rash to conclude that such attacks did not take place. I have found a 1656 manuscript sermon by Jonathan Mitchell, the pastor at Cambridge, inveighing against judicial astrology (for which see Chapter 4).

69 "The Necessity of Reformation . . . Agreed Upon by the Elders and Messengers of the Churches Assembled in the Synod at Boston in New-England," 10 Sep-

society was giving way to a more complex world in which merchants and their priorities seemed to challenge the spiritual values that ministers embodied.[70] As early as 1662, Michael Wigglesworth claimed that "holiness" and "heavenly frames" had been replaced by "Carnality" and "an Earthly mind." Wigglesworth accused New Englanders of "luke-warm Indifferency" and "key-cold Deadheartedness."[71] In 1676, Increase Mather reminded New Englanders that "Religion and not the World was that which our Fathers came hither for."[72]

Three years later, in 1679, the reforming synod that met in Boston lamented what the clergy saw as "a great and visible decay of the power of Godliness amongst many Professors in these Churches." The ministers argued that recent misfortunes (the devastating war with the Indians in 1675–6, a smallpox epidemic, two major fires in Boston, and deteriorating relations with the Stuart government in London) betokened "holy displeasure." According to the synod's report, the causes of God's anger were clear: widespread neglect of devotional exercises in the home, "sloth and sleepiness" in church, sabbath-breaking, intemperance, "Sinful Heats and Hatreds," slander, lies, and the breaking of promises. The ministers also denounced "Covetousness" and an "Inordinate affection to the world," citing in particular "Traders, who sell their goods at excessive Rates" as well as "Day-Labourers and Mechanicks [who] are unreasonable in their demands."[73] Throughout the 1670s and 1680s, an overwhelming majority of sermons addressed the issue of spiritual decline, drew attention to signs of "holy displeasure," and urged New Englanders to repent, lest God withdraw altogether his protection from them.[74]

tember 1679, in Williston Walker, ed., *The Creeds and Platforms of Congregationalism* (1893; Boston, 1960), p. 431.

70 See Bernard Bailyn, *The New England Merchants in the Seventeenth-Century* (1955; New York, 1964), especially chap. 5; and Richard Dunn, *Puritans and Yankees: The Winthrop Dynasty of New England, 1630–1717* (Princeton, 1962), pp. 59–190.

71 Michael Wigglesworth, "God's Controversy with New England," *Proceedings of the Massachusetts Historical Society,* 12 (1871–3): 88. See also John Higginson, *The Cause of God and His People in New England* (Cambridge, 1663).

72 Increase Mather, *An Earnest Exhortation to the Inhabitants of New-England* (Boston, 1676), p. 16.

73 "The Necessity of Reformation," in Williston Walker, ed., *Creeds and Platforms,* pp. 424, 427–32.

74 See Harry Stout, *The New England Soul: Preaching and Religious Culture in Colonial New England* (New York, 1986), esp. pp. 62–3, 75–6. In arguing that the ministers perceived a decline in spiritual fervor, I do not mean to suggest that their perception was necessarily accurate. For contributions to the debate on "declension," see Jon Butler, *Awash in a Sea of Faith: Christianizing the American People* (Cambridge, Mass., 1990), pp. 60–3; David D. Hall, *Worlds of Wonder, Days of Judgment,* chap. 3; Theodore Dwight Bozeman, *To Live Ancient Lives: The Primitivist Dimension in Puritanism* (Chapel Hill, 1988), Appendix 2; Patricia Bonomi,

At the same time that the clergy was becoming increasingly concerned about "great and visible decay" within their churches, the sectarian challenge to orthodox Congregationalism was becoming much more serious. This was due in part to the growing number of Anglicans, Quakers, and Baptists present in New England.[75] But perhaps even more worrisome to the established clergy were political changes that threatened Congregationalist hegemony. Hitherto, the colonial governments of New England, excepting Rhode Island, had sanctioned only Congregationalism. Colonial regimes enjoyed almost complete political autonomy and so were able to pursue this policy despite the English crown's detestation of Congregationalists. But in 1684, the government in London revoked the charter that had given Massachusetts the right of self-government. Two years later, six other charters were revoked, and all the colonies stretching northward from New Jersey were incorporated into a new imperial system called the Dominion. Edmund Andros, royal governor of the Dominion, was an Anglican: he insisted on liberty of conscience and worship for members of the Anglican faith. This was anathema to Congregationalists. The Dominion collapsed in 1689, but the new charter that William and Mary ratified in 1691 was hardly a return to the earlier "status quo." The 1691 charter guaranteed freedom of worship to all Protestant confessions and enlarged the political community to include formerly disenfranchised groups such as Quakers and Anglicans, a direct blow to Congregationalist supremacy in New England.[76]

Under these circumstances, it is hardly surprising that ministers became extremely sensitive to all forms of competition, including magic. Quakers, Baptists, Anglicans, magical practitioners: in the

Under the Cope of Heaven: Religion, Society and Politics in Colonial America (New York, 1986), p. 7; Harry Stout, *The New England Soul,* chaps. 3 and 4; Kenneth Silverman, *The Life and Times of Cotton Mather* (New York, 1984); Darrett Rutman, *Winthrop's Boston: A Portrait of a Puritan Town, 1630–1649* (Chapel Hill, 1965); the exchange between Rutman and Edmund Morgan in *William and Mary Quarterly,* 19 (1962): 408–21, 642–4; and Perry Miller, *The New England Mind: From Colony to Province* (Cambridge, Mass., 1953), Book 1.

75 After the Restoration, a substantial number of Anglican merchants migrated to New England (Bernard Bailyn, *The New England Merchants in the Seventeenth Century,* pp. 122, 124, 138). When Anglican Edmund Andros arrived in Boston to assume control of colonial government in 1686, he brought with him friends and associates of like faith. Quaker conversions multiplied after the arrival of evangelist George Keith in 1688. There were, moreover, four Baptist churches in Massachusetts by the end of the century: one in Boston (founded in 1665) and three in old Plymouth Colony (part of Massachusetts since 1691). There were six other New England Baptist churches, all situated in Rhode Island (William McLoughlin, *New England Dissent, 1630–1833: The Baptists and the Separation of Church and State,* 2 vols. [Cambridge, Mass., 1971], I: 9–10).

76 For a more detailed discussion of the Dominion and its impact, see Chapter 6.

clerical mind, these were all part of a diabolical plot to subvert the New-English Israel. The campaign against magic should be understood as part of a larger rearguard action by the ministry, which also included denunciation from the pulpit of "Indifferency" within church congregations and the publication of treatises attacking sectarianism.[77] During the last quarter of the century, as the clergy became increasingly worried about developments both inside and outside the covenanted community, so they became more inclined to attack magic as yet another challenge to their authority.

The tensions between magic and Puritan theology did not exist solely in the minds of clergymen; they also gave rise to conflicts between layfolk. Not all godly New Englanders engaged in or approved of magical experimentation. Some layfolk shared their ministers' attitude toward magic and reacted unequivocally when they saw neighbors using magical techniques. Since magic was utterly practical in its objectives, clerical and lay opposition to magic necessarily impinged upon a number of practical issues. Foremost among those issues was response to illness and misfortune.[78]

It was when individuals became ill or suffered some kind of loss that confrontations between users or advocates of magic and those who opposed magic were most likely to occur. In times of illness or suffering, some layfolk would blame witchcraft and turn to countermagic in an attempt to retaliate against whoever was responsible for their condition. Yet providentialist theology taught that suffering should be understood as a judgment from God, and that the only effective response was repentance and moral reformation. This held true, according to providentialists, regardless of whether a natural explanation could be found for the sufferer's condition. If, on the one hand, God had inflicted a natural illness, spiritual renewal would be just as crucial as medical treatment in bringing about the patient's recovery. If, on the other, God had allowed a human witch to act as the instrument of his wrath, the ultimate cause of affliction was still the sufferer's own spiritual inadequacy. If the human agent deserved punishment, this should be left to God himself, or a godly court of law; individual retribution was not acceptable.

Resort to countermagic differed from a providentialist response

77 See, for example, James Allen, Joshua Moodey, and Samuel Willard, *The Principles of the Protestant Religion Maintained* (Boston, 1690); and Cotton Mather, *Little Flocks Guarded against Grievous Wolves* (Boston, 1691).

78 Indeed, according to Stuart Clark, the primary concern of Protestant writings on magic, witchcraft, and demonology was misfortune and its interpretation (Stuart Clark, "Protestant Demonology," p. 59).

to suffering in two significant respects: first, those who used countermagic had decided to blame suffering on somebody else instead of seeing their condition as divine punishment for their own moral turpitude; second, if another human was responsible for their condition, they wanted to identify and punish the malefactor instead of leaving both to God or a godly court. Such people acted as spiritual vigilantes: they arrogated to themselves a judicial power and authority that, according to Puritan doctrine, belonged only to God and his official representatives. As New Englanders faced misfortune, they had to choose between different responses. Should the afflicted open their hearts to God and trust in the ultimate justice of divine providence? Or should they seek out the origin of their misfortune? And should they engage in some kind of magical remedy? Such decisions could be personally traumatic and socially divisive.

Before afflicted individuals could even contemplate using countermagic, they had to be willing to blame their condition on a malevolent neighbor or acquaintance. John Hale lamented that some people blamed all their misfortunes on witchcraft, "and thereby in suffering times [were] apt to be jealous of their Neighbours that c[a]me frequently to their Houses in their day of adversity, as causes of these afflictions by some charming or inchantment."[79] Others, wrote Cotton Mather, refused either to blame or to seek revenge, choosing instead "to Recommend all to God, and rather to endure Affliction, than to have it Removed to his Dishonour, and the Wounding of their own Consciences."[80]

Ministers kept a close watch over their parishioners in times of suffering, hoping to save them from the spiritual error of shirking responsibility for their condition. Some of their flock behaved in a quite exemplary manner. Cotton Mather related the afflictions of an unnamed woman who fell ill after eating some food given to her by a neighbor who was suspected to be a witch. The woman's response was to pray, although she was so sick that she could barely utter more than one syllable at a time. "Lord," she gasped, "Thou hast been my Hope, and in Thee I will put my Trust; Thou hast been my Salvation here, and wilt be so for ever and ever." Immediately, the woman's fit left her and she afterward recovered completely.[81] In 1693, when Margaret Rule of Boston became possessed, some of her neighbors suspected that a woman who had recently "threatened" Rule was responsible for the affliction. Never-

79 John Hale, *A Modest Enquiry*, p. 67.
80 Cotton Mather, *Memorable Providences* (Boston, 1689), To the Reader, p. iv.
81 Ibid., p. 74.

theless, reported Mather, "the pious People in the Vicinity" were determined "to try ... whether incessant Supplication to God alone might not procure a quicker and safer Ease to the Afflicted, than hasty Prosecution of any supposed Criminal; and accordingly that unexceptionable course was all that was ever followed."[82]

Less satisfactory, from Mather's perspective, was the case of Philip Smith. When Smith fell ill in 1684, he too prayed for relief: "Such Assurances had he of the Divine Love unto him, that in Raptures he would cry out, Lord, stay thy hand, it is enough, it is more than thy frail servant can bear!" But Smith also voiced his suspicion that neighbor Mary Webster was responsible for his illness. Webster had been tried for witchcraft in 1683: the court had acquitted her, but not everybody believed that she was innocent.[83] On hearing Smith's suspicions against Webster, a group of young men went to her house, dragged her outside, hung her up until almost dead, cut her down, rolled her in the snow and then buried her in it, leaving her for dead. Clearly, these young men were not willing to leave Webster's punishment to God.[84]

Some people were torn between different responses to misfortune. When Elizabeth Godman appeared in court on charges of witchcraft in 1655, Goodwife Thorpe testified that one of her cows had recently fallen ill. Thorpe suspected that Godman had bewitched the animal, but, after a considerable internal struggle, she resolved to set aside these suspicions and to focus on prayer. This is the report of her statement to the court:

> she thought there was something more than ordinary in it, and could not but think that she was bewitched; [but] God helped her to examine herselfe, and to be humbled for her unbeleife, and to seeke him twice or thrice to deliver the beast ... she sought God earnestly to resist the evill spirit, and if the beast was ill by that meanes he would deliver it, and presently the Lord answered and the beast was well and continewes so.[85]

A year later, when Mary Parsons of Northampton, Massachusetts, was tried for witchcraft, William Hannum told the court that he had argued with the accused on three occasions. Each quarrel had been followed by the mysterious death of livestock belonging to him: first a cow, then a sow, and finally an ox. Hannum suspected that Parsons was responsible, "though I desire," he told the court,

82 Cotton Mather, "Another Brand Pluck't Out of the Burning," p. 311.
83 Cotton Mather, *Memorable Providences*, p. 55.
84 Samuel Drake, *Annals of Witchcraft in New England*, p. 179.
85 Franklin Dexter, ed., *New Haven Town Records*, 2 vols. (New Haven, Conn., 1917), I: 250, 7 August 1655, testimony of Goodwife Thorpe.

"to look at the overarchinge hand of God in all." Either Hannum felt guilty that he was unable to see his misfortune solely in terms of divine providence, or else he realized that he should at least appear to be so.[86]

Even clergymen were not exempt from temptations of this kind. In 1693, one of Cotton Mather's children died from an obstruction in the bowels soon after birth. The suspicious circumstances surrounding this death might have prompted a less staunch providentialist to blame his misfortune on witchcraft. A few weeks before Abigail Mather gave birth, she saw a specter in their porch, "which Fright caused her Bowels to turn within her." The specters that had recently begun to torment their neighbor, Margaret Rule, bragged to Rule that they had given Mather's wife the "Fright" in the hope of "doing Mischief unto her Infant at least, if not unto the Mother." As soon as the baby was born, a local woman who was suspected of being a witch wrote a letter to Cotton's father, Increase Mather, railing against Cotton and assuring Increase that "Hee little knew, what might quickly befall some of his Posterity." But Cotton Mather was made of sterner stuff than to give way under pressures of this kind. He wrote in his diary,

> I made little use of, and laid little Stress on this Conjecture, desiring to submitt unto the Will of my Heavenly Father, without which, Not a Sparrow falls unto the Ground.

Mather believed that misfortune should be understood in providential terms: whatever the immediate cause of the baby's death, this was ultimately a judgment from God.[87]

Some of those who did blame suffering on witchcraft decided to use countermagic against the malefactor. As we have already seen, clergymen denounced such initiatives in no uncertain terms. The Salem witch crisis provides a clear example of direct confrontation between ministry and laity on this issue. In early 1692, when several girls in Salem Village began to suffer strange fits, their relatives reacted to the situation in very different ways. The Reverend Samuel Parris, whose daughter Elizabeth Parris and niece Abigail Williams were among the afflicted, adopted a course of prayer and

86 Middlesex Court Files, folder 16, #665. See also the testimony given against Parsons by William Hannum's wife, in which Goodwife Hannum expressed a similar ambivalence (also #665). Some families divided in response to such crises. When Zachariah Davis blamed Elizabeth Morse for "his loss of calves," his father told William and Elizabeth Morse that he was "rather troubled his son should so judge" and that "he judged it a hand of God" (Joshua Coffin, *A Sketch of The History of Newbury* [Boston, 1845], p. 127).

87 Cotton Mather, *Diary*, ed. Worthington C. Ford, 2 vols. (1911; New York, 1957), I: 164.

fasting. Parris also called in the local doctor, William Griggs, hoping that the immediate cause of the children's condition might be natural and that medical treatment would assist in their recovery, but Griggs concluded that Elizabeth and Abigail were "under an Evil Hand" and so withdrew. Parris was now advised by his fellow ministers to "sit still and wait upon the Providence of God."[88] But Mary Sibley, a member of Parris's congregation and the aunt of another afflicted girl, Mary Walcott, took matters into her own hands and turned to countermagic in an attempt to cure her niece. Sibley asked the minister's Caribbean slaves, Tituba and her husband, to prepare a urine-cake. They later confessed that, without the knowledge of their master or mistress, they had taken some of the girls' urine, mixed it with meal to make a cake, baked it, and then fed the cake to a dog. Sibley may have entrusted the experiment to Tituba because the minister's slave had a reputation for magical expertise: under interrogation by the witch court, Tituba admitted that "her Mistress in her own Country . . . had taught her some means to be used for the discovery of a Witch."[89] In any case, the experiment seemed to work, since the girls were now able to see "particular persons hurting of them."[90]

Parris soon heard about the urine-cake and found out that it had been made at Mary Sibley's request. Parris "discoursed" Sibley in his study, reducing her to "tears and sorrowful confession." Two days later, he denounced her from the pulpit for adopting this "diabolical" strategy:

> I do truly hope and believe, that this our sister doth truly fear the Lord, and am well satisfied from her, that what she did, she did it ignorantly, from what she had heard of this nature from other ignorant, or worse, persons. Yet we are in duty bound to protest against such actions, as being indeed a going to the Devil for help against the devil.[91]

Samuel Parris was sufficiently convinced of the Devil's presence in Salem Village that a villager's willingness to experiment with countermagic would not have been in itself surprising to him. Much more unnerving was that a member of his own congregation had used countermagic, refusing to place her entire trust in God. For

88 John Hale, *A Modest Enquiry*, pp. 23, 25.
89 Ibid., p. 25.
90 Deodat Lawson, "A Brief and True Narrative," in Cotton Mather, *Wonders of the Invisible World*, p. 213. This recipe seems to have been English rather than Caribbean in origin. For references to urine-cakes in England, see George L. Kittredge, *Witchcraft in Old and New England*, p. 435 n237.
91 Samuel Parris, "Records of Salem-Village Church," in Danvers First Church Records (Microfilm copy: Essex Institute, Salem, Mass.), 27 March 1692.

Parris, who liked to conceive of the world as engaged in a bipolar struggle between good and evil, this was an unwelcome blurring of the boundary between the godly and the diabolical.

Clergymen were not alone in objecting to the use of countermagic against witchcraft. The need to choose between magical and religious remedies also caused dissension between layfolk. Because such disagreements rarely found their way into legal records or clerical writings, they remain largely invisible to the historian. But descriptions have survived of two incidents that evoke the tensions likely to arise within a community or neighborhood as a result of bewitchment. When Goodwife Chandler of Newbury, Massachusetts, fell into a long sickness prior to her death in 1666, she claimed that Elizabeth Morse had bewitched her, and that every time Morse came to see her, she felt worse than before. One day, a neighbor suggested that a horseshoe be nailed to the threshold, claiming that this would prevent any witch from coming into the house. The next morning, Goodwife Chandler took her staff, struggled to the door and nailed on a horseshoe. As long as it remained there, Elizabeth Morse refused to enter the house: she would kneel down by the door and talk, but she would not go in, even though she visited several times in a day. When Chandler's daughter asked Goodwife Morse why she would not enter, Morse replied, "it was not her Mind to come in." Meanwhile, another of Goodwife Chandler's neighbors, William Moody, had heard that there was a horseshoe nailed on her door. He became extremely angry, condemned the measure as "a Piece of Witchery," and knocked the horseshoe down. Elizabeth Morse no longer feared to enter the house. A week later, Goodwife Chandler got yet another neighbor, Daniel Rolfe, to fasten the horseshoe a second time, but Moody now took off the horseshoe, put it in his pocket, and carried it away. This left Goodwife Morse free to come and go as she pleased, causing much grief to the ailing Goodwife Chandler.[92] As the controversy over Chandler's horseshoe demonstrates, recourse to magic could engender spontaneous conflict between lay men and women, independent of any clerical intervention.[93]

Conflicts between layfolk over response to suffering did not necessarily take the form of a neat, clear-cut struggle between godly

92 "Trials for Witchcraft in New England" (Houghton Library, Harvard University), printed in Samuel Drake, *Annals of Witchcraft in New England,* pp. 275–6: 17 May 1680, testimony of Esther Wilson.

93 Richard Weisman describes William Moody's actions as an "informal exercise of ecclesiastical sanctions" (Richard Weisman, *Witchcraft, Magic, and Religion,* p. 60). Weisman means to suggest, I assume, that Moody somehow embodied or represented ministerial opposition to the use of magic. But this, I think, is to miss the point, namely, that this was a spontaneous conflict between layfolk.

people who turned to prayer and ungodly people who embraced countermagic. The case of the Goodwin afflictions in Boston illustrates this point. When the children of John Goodwin became bewitched in 1688, several neighbors suggested that he use countermagic against whoever was responsible. According to Goodwin, "many did say, (yea, and some good people too) [that] were it their case, they would try some Tricks, that should give ease to their Children."[94] By "good people," Goodwin meant godly people, people like Mary Sibley, the church member in Salem Village who used countermagic against her niece's tormentors. But the Goodwins refused to use anything other than religious means to obtain relief. Accordingly, they asked neighboring ministers to keep a day of prayer at their house, which they did along with some other devout people.[95] Yet John Goodwin's own account of the ordeal describes this as "a time of sore Temptation." Countermagic "might ensnare . . . Souls," but it apparently worked: "For the present," Goodwin wrote, "it might offer some relief to our Bodies."[96] Moreover, the people urging him to use countermagic were "good people," godly people. The Goodwins eventually decided to rely on prayer and fasting, placing the fate of their children in the hands of God, but for a time they were sorely tempted to use countermagic.

People who used magical techniques might not see the dangers in doing so, but, wrote John Hale, the Devil was assuredly using such devices to seduce New Englanders, "that by Sorceries, Inchantments, Divinations and such like, he may lead them captive at his pleasure."[97] Ministers were particularly concerned that some of those who used or recommended magic were otherwise respectable, godly people. Even members of the covenanted community adopted magical as well as religious strategies in order to combat the challenges of their day-to-day existence. This inclusive mentality appalled not only the clergy, but also their more exclusivist parishioners. Corporate considerations as much as concern for individual moral welfare underlay this horrified response. When Mary Sibley had Tituba and her husband bake a urine-cake, when "good people" urged John Goodwin and his wife to use countermagic against their occult enemy, when worried individuals used divination to ascertain their spiritual estate, they unwittingly posed a fundamental threat to New England's spiritual mission: the es-

94 Cotton Mather, *Memorable Providences,* p. 49.
95 Ibid., pp. 5–6.
96 Ibid., p. 49.
97 John Hale, *A Modest Enquiry,* pp. 16, 165.

tablishment of a pure and exemplary community, free of the corrupt practices that had polluted even the Church of England.

Resort to magical experiments was much more than personal in its implications, since it invited the wrath of God upon both the guilty individuals and the community in which they lived. In the aftermath of the Salem witch hunt, Increase Mather wrote that the use of magical aids such as "Sieves, and Keys, and Glasses" explained in part why God had "let loose evil Angels upon New England."[98] As the clergy became less confident of New England's spiritual future and their own hitherto privileged position within the community, they sought to increase public awareness of the dangers involved in magical experimentation. They believed that magic, like "key-cold Dead-heartedness" within their churches and sectarianism without, was an instrument of the Devil in his campaign against the godly. The ministers feared that magic would destroy New England by delivering its people into Satan's clutches: God's Israel in the Wilderness would become the Devil's Dominion.

98 Increase Mather, *Angelographia,* pp. 25–6.

3

ENTERTAINING SATAN

SIN, SUFFERING, AND COUNTERMAGIC

And the man said, "The woman whom thou gavest to be with me, she gave me of the tree, and I did eat."

And the Lord God said unto the woman, "What is this that thou hast done?" And the woman said, "The serpent beguiled me and I did eat."

Gen.3.12,13.

Samuel Parris, pastor at Salem Village, Massachusetts, was convinced that when Mary Sibley, a member of his church, turned to countermagic in an attempt to cure her niece, she did so "ignorantly."[1] Sibley was apparently an unwitting transgressor, who did not realize that experimenting with magic was illicit. Other godly layfolk also used magical techniques "in their simplicity," to use Increase Mather's words. Lay recourse to magic shocked New England ministers, yet the clergy themselves may have been partly responsible for this state of affairs. Ambiguity in Puritan teaching on one central issue, the allocation of responsibility for human sin and misfortune, may have prompted layfolk to turn to countermagic as a defense against affliction. Inadvertently, from their own pulpits, the New England clergy promoted a rival supernatural agency.

Liability for sin and suffering was a matter of crucial importance to Puritans, yet there was no consensus within the godly community on this issue. Samuel Parris saw the afflictions in Salem Village as divine punishment for the villagers' backslidings; he felt that this was as much his as their responsibility and so adopted a course of repentant prayer and fasting. Sibley, on the other hand, preferred to see her niece's condition as the result of another person's malevolence; she determined to retaliate, using countermagic as a weapon against the malefactor. Whereas Parris blamed himself for

1 Samuel Parris, "Records of Salem-Village Church," in Danvers First Church Records (Microfilm copy: Essex Institute, Salem, Mass.), 27 March 1692.

the situation, Sibley located responsibility elsewhere. Such discrepancies were not unusual. Individual responses to the issue of liability varied from one person to another; this holds true for clergymen as well as for layfolk. Lack of consensus on this issue derived from ambiguity within Puritan theology itself. At the center of that ambiguity stood the Devil.

When New England ministers addressed their congregations in sermons and treatises, one of their objectives was to educate layfolk in the constant threat posed by the Devil.[2] Most sermons contained at least some passing reference to Satan, although ministers seldom took him as their central theme: the Devil's significance was pervasive rather than topical. In treatises that dealt specifically with issues relating to the Devil, the ministers were able to explore their subject in greater detail; the substance of these essays corresponded closely to that of their sermons. As the references to Satan in these sermons and treatises are pieced together, a detailed picture emerges of the Devil, his place within an elaborate mythology, and his role in the generation of human sin.[3]

The ministers taught that Satan was an actual being. He was leader of the fallen angels, "a numberlesse number of those Invisible Immortall created spirits the Angells made by God in a good

2 In doing so, the clergy drew on a demonological tradition common to Protestants and Catholics alike in seventeenth-century Europe. Early modern European demonology is discussed by Jeffrey Burton Russell, *Mephistopheles: The Devil in the Modern World* (Ithaca, N.Y., 1986), chaps. 2 and 3; and Stuart Clark, "Protestant Demonology: Sin, Superstition, and Society," in Bengt Ankarloo and Gustav Henningsen, eds., *Early Modern European Witchcraft: Centres and Peripheries* (Oxford, 1990), pp. 45–81.

3 The following summary of New England Puritan diabology is based on a reading of clerical treatises and approximately five hundred sermons, half printed and half in manuscript. Most of the sermons were preached in Massachusetts. Relatively few survive from the first half of the century, but those that are available suggest a diabology consistent with later years. This sermonic literature does not indicate any marked increase or decrease in clerical concern with the Devil over the course of the seventeenth century. During the 1690s, ministers produced a number of publications dealing with the witch crisis of 1692; not surprisingly, these included discussion of the Devil's implication in the witch conspiracy. But sermons of the 1690s did not become any more preoccupied with matters diabolical than before. The one exception to this was the body of sermons produced by Cotton Mather, who did refer to the Devil much more frequently during those years. For further discussion of Puritan diabology, see Edward Trefz, "A Study of Satan, with Particular Emphasis upon His Role in the Preaching of Certain New England Puritans" (Th.D. dissertation, Union Theological Seminary, 1952); "Satan as the Prince of Evil: The Preaching of New England Puritans," *Boston Public Library Quarterly*, 7 (1955): 3–22; and "Satan in Puritan Preaching," *Boston Public Library Quarterly*, 8 (1956): 71–84, 148–59. See also Elizabeth Reis, "Satan's Familiars: Sinners, Witches, and Conflicting Covenants in Early New England" (Ph.D. dissertation, University of California, Berkeley, 1991).

estate," who had rebelled against God and, as a consequence, were driven out of Heaven. Wounded pride had impelled Satan and his followers to rebellion: when God instructed the angels to minister to the needs of humankind, a newly created and inferior being, some of the angels refused on the grounds that this would be humiliating. As a result of their "witting and wilfull Sin and pride," the rebel angels fell, irrecoverably, from divine favor.[4] The fallen angels now determined to avenge themselves by destroying the kingdom of God. The first step toward this end was to be the moral destruction of God's new and favored creation. Thus did the human soul become the battlefield for a dramatic struggle between the forces of Heaven and Hell.[5] Just as angelic pride had been the cause of Satan's rebellion, so Satan used human pride to seduce men and women away from God.[6] "Gods great Enemy, and the ringleader of Rebellion against him" was determined to win over every man and woman.[7] As humanity divided into "the Children of God and the Children of the Devil," each individual's moral fate had cosmic significance as a potential trophy in the Devil's war against God.[8]

The diabolical alliance had three components: the rebel angels as a group, their leader, and the men and women whose souls they had already conquered. Ministers used the word *Devil* to indicate each of these components. Devil was a flexible term: it could signify not only a specific being, but also evil in a collective or even abstract form. To designate the fallen angels by a singular name was not inappropriate, since it underlined their "onenes and union in sundry respects." They were all angels; they had all fallen; they were "all full of wicked malice and enemyes to all righteousness"; they all united "against the glory of god and Xt [Christ] and the salvation of men"; and "they so combine[d] their forces and practises as if

4 Jonathan Mitchell, "Continuation of Sermons Concerning Man's Misery" (Massachusetts Historical Society), 15 August 1655. See also Cotton Mather, *Speedy Repentance Urged* (Boston, 1690), p. 10.

5 This sequence of events is also narrated in Deodat Lawson, *Christ's Fidelity the Only Shield against Satan's Malignity* (Boston, 1692), pp. 1–2.

6 See, for example, Increase Mather, *The Folly of Sinning* (Boston, 1699), p. 50; John Williams, *Warnings to the Unclean* (Boston, 1699), p. 53; Cotton Mather, *The Gospel of Justification by the Righteousness of God* (Boston, 1700), p. 21.

7 Samuel Willard, *The Child's Portion* (Boston, 1684), pp. 29–30. See also William Adams, *The Necessity of the Pouring Out of the Spirit from on High* (Boston, 1679), p. 39.

8 Samuel Willard, *The Child's Portion*, p. 45. For examples of the dualism that underlay this cosmology, see John Norton, *Three Choice and Profitable Sermons* (Cambridge, Mass., 1664), pp. 27, 36; Joshua Moodey, *Souldiery Spiritualized* (Cambridge, Mass., 1674), p. 20; William Adams, *The Necessity of the Pouring Out of the Spirit from on High*, p. 38; Increase Mather, *Some Important Truths* (Boston, 1684), p. 42; Joseph Belcher, *The Worst Enemy Conquered* (Boston, 1698), p. 25.

they were all but one Devill."[9] The word Devil also suited human recruits to the alliance against God. These were "vile and wicked persons, the worst of such, who for their villany and impiety [did] most resemble Devils and wicked Spirits."[10] According to Increase Mather, sin "turn[ed] men into... Devils incarnate."[11] The most explicit expression of human allegiance to Satan was witchcraft: the witch actually signed a covenant with the Devil and promised to do his bidding. But any act of ungodliness or refusal to give oneself entirely to communion with Christ was effectively "a making War against him."[12] "Denying to come unto the Lord Jesus Christ" was "the most horrid Act of Enmity and Rebellion against the Glorious God." All such resistance was "like the Sin of Witchcraft."[13]

The rebel angels used a threefold strategy to recruit men and women to their ranks. First, they diverted human attention from spiritual concerns to the pleasures of the flesh. Ministers often associated "the flesh, world and Devil" in an unholy trinity.[14] Flesh, they argued, was "the principal agent in all disobedience."[15] Second, the Devil encouraged dissension within the godly community: "divisions, especially in the Church of God, [were] in a great measure to be ascribed to the policy of Satan."[16] Third, the Devil was "enemy

9 Jonathan Mitchell, "Continuation of Sermons Concerning Man's Misery," 15 August 1655.

10 Samuel Parris, "Sermons 1689–1695" (Connecticut Historical Society), 27 March 1692, p. 148.

11 Increase Mather, *Angelographia* (Boston, 1696), p. 125.

12 Samuel Parris, "Sermons 1689–1695," 11 September 1692, p. 156.

13 Cotton Mather, *Unum Necessarium* (Boston, 1693), p. 95; Cotton Mather, *Optanda* (Boston, 1692), p. 23. See also John Williams, *Warnings to the Unclean* p. 42.

14 See, for example, Daniel Russell, "Sermon Notes, 1677" (Massachusetts Historical Society), p. 53; Samuel Wakeman, *A Young Man's Legacy* (Cambridge, Mass., 1673), p. 36; Joshua Moodey, *Souldiery Spiritualized* (Cambridge, Mass., 1674), p. 20; Edward Taylor, *Upon the Types of the Old Testament*, 2 vols. (Lincoln, Neb., 1989), II: 591; and Benjamin Wadsworth, *Good Souldiers a Great Blessing* (Boston, 1700), p. 28.

15 John Norton, "Notes on Sermons of Jonathan Mitchell, 1654–5" (Massachusetts Historical Society), 1 February 1654. Joseph Belcher described "Flesh and Spirit" as "diametrically opposite one unto another... the greatest contraries in the whole world, as contrary as light and darkness, as life and death, as good and evil, as Heaven and Hell." These opposing principles were necessarily "up in armes, indeavoring to vanquish and expell each other" (*The Worst Enemy Conquered* [Boston, 1698], pp. 17–8).

16 William Hubbard, *The Happiness of a People in the Wisdom of Their Rulers Directing and in the Obedience of Their Brethren Attending* (Boston, 1676), p. 17. According to Thomas Shepard, Satan was always ready to use "the divisions and scandals of God's people to promote his Hellish designs" (Thomas Shepard, *Eye-Salve* [Cambridge, Mass., 1673], p. 31). See also Samuel Arnold, *David Serving His Generation* (Cambridge, Mass., 1674), pp. 8, 15; Joshua Moodey, *Souldiery Spiritualized*, pp. 24, 26; Samuel Parris, "Sermons 1689–1695," p. 233; John Cotton, "Plymouth Church Records, 1667–99," *Publications of the Colonial Society of Massachusetts*, 22 (1920): 159.

of all truth" and sought to corrupt men and women through lies.[17] The most virulent form of lie was heresy. Satan did not limit himself to any one heretical tradition, but encouraged all forms of religious error, from Antinomianism at one extreme to Arminianism and Catholicism at the other.[18] He also encouraged his victims to become either completely unconcerned about the state of their souls, or utterly obsessed with their spiritual unworthiness. Satan often used the mystery of election to assault the faith of weaker Christians: despair of election or complacent assurance were equally sinful and both delighted Satan.[19]

The Devil pursued his victims with diligence and skill. He was "continually about men observing and watching of them and taking his best opportunities to tempt."[20] According to Puritan divines, there were "Devils enough to Beleaguer the whole Earth." There was "not a place under Heaven where Satan ha[d] not his Troops; not a person without some of these cursed Spirits haunting and watching him."[21] Satan was "a great naturalist, Skilled in [the] Constitution and inclinations of man."[22] His characteristic strategy when approaching humankind was to use stealth: the Devil was known for his "subtilty," "Wiles," "snares," "Ambushes," "hellish designs" and "execrable devises."[23] As Samuel Willard put it,

17 Richard Mather, *The Summe of Certain Sermons upon Gen. 15.6* (Cambridge, Mass., 1652), Preface, p. ii. See also Thomas Walley, *Balm in Gilead to Heal Sion's Wounds* (Cambridge, Mass., 1669), p. 14; Increase Mather, *A Call from Heaven* (Boston, 1679), p. 109; Cotton Mather, *The Way to Prosperity* (Boston, 1690), p. 29.

18 See Charles Chauncy, *God's Mercy* (Cambridge, Mass., 1655), pp. 31–2; Richard Mather, *A Farewell Exhortation to the Church and People of Dorchester* (Cambridge, Mass., 1657), p. 5; Thomas Shepard, *Eye-Salve*, pp. 14, 31; Samuel Parris, "Sermons 1689–1695," pp. 153, 232; Cotton Mather, *A Good Man Making a Good End* (Boston, 1698), p. 36.

19 The Devil terrified some people "with the most fearful representations of Sin, and the Law, and the Wrath of God," while others were "confident in their unregenerate state... perswaded by Satan to think there [was] no danger, God [would] not punish them for their Sins" (Samuel Willard, *The Truly Blessed Man* [Boston, 1700], pp. 15, 51, 530). See also Samuel Willard, *The Heart Garrisoned* (Cambridge, Mass., 1676), p. 5; Leonard Hoar, *The Sting of Death* (Boston, 1680), p. 9.

20 Jonathan Mitchell, "Continuation of Sermons Concerning Man's Misery," 10 October 1655.

21 Peter Thacher, *The Saint's Victory and Triumph over Sin and Death* (Boston, 1696), p. 19. See also Incease Mather, *The Folly of Sinning*, p. 6.

22 Jonathan Mitchell, "Continuation of Sermons Concerning Man's Misery," 10 October 1655.

23 Increase Mather, *An Earnest Exhortation* (Boston, 1676), p. 3; Increase Mather, *An Arrow against Profane and Promiscuous Dancing* (Boston, 1684), p. 25; William Stoughton, *New-England's True Interest Not to Lie* (Cambridge, Mass., 1670), p. 30; Samuel Willard, *The Heart Garrisoned*, p. 11; Thomas Shepard, *Eye-Salve*, p. 31; Samuel Parris, "Sermons 1689–1695," 1 October 1693, p. 231.

> The Devil hath learnt more wit at length than to ask men to throw themselves down from the pinnacle of the Temple prostrate at his feet, at a leap, the very sight and apprehension whereof would appear amazing and frightful; but he hath gotten fair and easie winding stairs, where a man shall neither see back from whence he came, nor forward whither he is going; and hath also many a Landing where he may stand still and breath; and thus by slow paces and easie degrees he draws men insensibly away from the Truth.[24]

Satan's patience did not derive from any lack of passion. His enmity toward mankind was "bloody and malicious."[25] The Devil's temptations were like "darts . . . headed with desperate Malice . . . Fiery in respect of the Fiery Wrath with which Satan shoots them . . . full of Indignation against God and his Saints . . . a Spark of Hell in every Temptation."[26] Satan tormented the godly with "Preternatural Vexations . . . [and] Killing Mischiefs."[27] He had no mercy even for those who committed themselves to his service: as Samuel Parris pointed out, "the Devil . . . will pay you no other wages, than of being your Eternal Tormenter."[28]

Satan hated all human beings, but he particularly loathed "the Covenant People of God, and those that would Devote themselves intirely to his Service," especially in England and New England.[29] According to Puritans, England was "first of Nations" to throw off "that Grosse darknes of Popery which had Covered and overspred the Christian world." As a result, the Devil was particularly enraged against godly English men and women.[30] New England Puritans prided themselves on being even more hateful to Satan than their brethren across the Atlantic. They believed that the native Americans were Devil-worshipers and that New England had belonged to Satan until the Puritan migration. Their transformation of the

24 Samuel Willard, *Heavenly Merchandize* (Boston, 1686), pp. 158–9. See also Urian Oakes, *The Unconquerable, All-Conquering and More-Than-Conquering Souldier* (Cambridge, Mass., 1674), pp. 10, 25; William Adams, *The Necessity of the Pouring Out of the Spirit from on High,* p. 39; Cotton Mather, *Warnings from the Dead* (Boston, 1693), p. 9.

25 Increase Mather, *Practical Truths Tending to Promote the Power of Godliness* (Boston, 1682), p. 197.

26 Peter Thacher, *The Saint's Victory and Triumph over Sin and Death* (Boston, 1696), pp. 19–20.

27 Cotton Mather, *Early Religion* (Boston, 1694), p. 63. See also Increase Mather, *Two Sermons Testifying against the Sin of Drunkenness* (Cambridge, Mass. 1673), p. 18.

28 Samuel Parris, "Sermons 1689–1695," 11 September 1692, p. 156.

29 Deodat Lawson, *Christ's Fidelity,* p. 26.

30 William Bradford and Nathaniel Morton, "History of the Plymouth Church, 1620–1680," *Publications of the Colonial Society of Massachusetts,* 22 (1920): 6.

diabolical wilderness into a monument to Christ infuriated the Devil, whose foremost priority it became to undermine the New England colonies.[31]

Determined though he was, especially against the New-English Israel, the Devil's efforts were all in vain. It was preordained that God would achieve complete victory over Satan: on the Day of Judgment, the apostate angels would be consigned to "the lake that burns with fire and brimstone," where they would suffer "the endless impressions of the fury of a provoked God."[32] But although Satan's defeat was inevitable, that did not deprive his struggle of significance, particularly from a human perspective. The race of Adam would not be freed from the afflictions of the Devil until the Day of Judgment itself.[33] Meanwhile, God allowed Satan to test human faith and to act as "the Executioner of the Wrath of God upon a sinful world." Whenever the forces of Hell assaulted the world, it was because "the Lord . . . permitted Satan so far to prevail as he did." God contained Satan's destructive urge "to winow" humankind and then sanctified it as a mandate "to cleanse Away the chaffe."[34]

The Devil, argued New England ministers, was a constant threat to the human soul. Men and women could respond effectively to God's proffered gift of grace only if they purged themselves of all those fleshly impulses that the Devil sought to cultivate in even the most saintly of believers. The godly must commit themselves to a continuous struggle against the Devil's temptations. If they resisted those temptations, they would share in God's victory over evil. If not, they would be carted away to Hell as the rubbish of human history. The triumph of good over evil was assured on a cosmic

31 See, for example, Cotton Mather, *Wonders of the Invisible World* (1693; Amherst, Wisc., 1862), p. 74.

32 Cotton Mather, *The Call of the Gospel* (Boston, 1686), p. 71; Samuel Willard, *Inpenitent Sinners Warned of Their Misery and Summoned to Judgement* (Boston, 1698), p. 19. See also Increase Mather, *A Sermon Preached on a Publick Fast* (Boston, 1682), p. 17; Samuel Willard, *Covenant-Keeping* (Boston, 1682), p. 49; Samuel Willard, *The Child's Portion,* pp. 203–4.

33 See Increase Mather, *The Day of Trouble Is Near* (Cambridge, Mass., 1674), p. 5: "Indeed, if the Devil were cast into the bottomless Pit, and shut up there, we might think that there would be less trouble in the World: But we know, that as yet though he be a Prisoner, yet he is a Prisoner at large, he hath a long Chain given him, and goeth with it ranging and raging up and down the World."

34 Cotton Mather, *Things for a Distress'd People to Think Upon* (Boston, 1696), p. 20; Increase Mather, *Practical Truths Tending to Promote the Power of Godliness,* p. 197; John Norton, "Notes on Sermons of Jonathan Mitchell, 1654–5," 18 January 1654. See also Increase Mather, *The Wicked Man's Portion* (Boston, 1675), p. 6; James Allin, *Serious Advice to Delivered Ones from Sickness* (Boston, 1679), p. 26; Urian Oakes, *The Sovereign Efficacy of Divine Providence* (Boston, 1682), p. 18.

level, but not on an individual human level. The ministers warned their congregations that the Devil was always at their side, studying their personal weaknesses, and exploiting every opportunity to lead them astray. Satan was a fearsome and indefatigable enemy.

Yet Puritan doctrine also emphasized the limitations of Satanic power. Clerics often reminded their congregations that the Devil was not actually responsible for human sin: he tempted particular men and women because they were already inclined toward sin and therefore fit candidates for his service; those who gave way to his temptations were impelled by their own corruption, not by Satan himself. Sinners could not abdicate responsibility for their thoughts and actions by blaming the Devil: they had received his overtures, they had done his bidding, and they would suffer as a consequence.

In February 1653, Jonathan Mitchell, the minister at Cambridge, enumerated for his congregation ten fruits of sin:

1 Every sinner in his naturall estate is forsaken of god, separated from god, hath Lost god.
2 He is become vile, hath Lost all his excellency.
3 God is His enemy.
4 He is already condemned to die.
5 He is a Slave of Satan.
6 All the things of the word are Curses to Him.
7 There remains for Him wrath to come in Death, Judgement and Hell.
8 Hee is utterly unable to come (or helpe himselfe) out of this estate. Bound hand and foot.
9 He is unwilling that god should Helpe Him . . .
10 Hee is utterly unworthy that god should make him willing or show him any mercy in this estate.

Only one item in that catalog of misery made direct reference to the Devil: the sinner was "a Slave of Satan." Mitchell did not mean to imply by this any divestment of personal liability: other items in the catalog focused on the sinner's own responsibility, his own unworthiness, his own unwillingness and inability to repent, his own vileness, his own damnation. Human beings sinned voluntarily, although tempted to do so by Satan, and thus bore responsibility for their own actions, even once the Devil's slave. Two years later, when Mitchell gave a short series of sermons on the Devil's power over humanity, he stressed that Satan's temptations could only activate an already existent propensity to sin. Satan could do nothing more than "blow the Coales of our Corruptions and Lusts and make them burn more fiercely." He could not "presse men to take up Armes for his Designes": sin was a "voluntary Act."[35]

New England ministers assured layfolk that the Devil could not succeed in tempting them to sin unless aided by their own corrupt impulses. Sin originated in a union of "forreign . . . and domestick adversaries": "warpings of corruptions within, and workings of temptations without," "the delusions of Satan, and the false reports of a carnal mind."[36] Original sin, which corrupted all descendants of Adam and Eve, had also arisen from a combination of human frailty and diabolical temptation. The Fall came about as a result of "volentary disobedience unto the Command [of God], through the instigation of Satan."[37] Nicholas Noyes, pastor of the church in Salem Town, Massachusetts, declared that the greatest danger to the human soul lay not in Satan's advances, but in man's own self:

> If there were no Devil to tempt, nor no evil Example among men, nor any temptation from a frowning or flattering World (which is all far otherwise) yet the inbred corruption of mens hearts, that are deceitful above all things, and desperately wicked, is enough to undoe all.[38]

Men and women who committed sin must recognize their own culpability not only in having given way to the Devil's temptations but also in having provoked God to unleash the Devil. God used Satan as an agent of his will: hence, diabolical temptations were "righteous judgements, as managed by Gods permissive Providence."[39] God sometimes allowed Satan to afflict particular men and women as a test of their faith, but usually he intended to punish them for their wickedness. Human sinners, then, were doubly guilty: first, in having deserved diabolical temptation; and second, in having succumbed to it.

Despite the ministers' insistence upon human responsibility for sin, some ambiguity inhered in their view, on the one hand, that Satan was empowered by humanity's own corruption and, on the

35 Jonathan Mitchell, "Continuation of Sermons Concerning Man's Misery," 1 February 1653 and 10 October 1655.

36 Joseph Belcher, *The Worst Enemy Conquered,* p. 6; John Whiting, *The Way of Israel's Welfare* (Boston, 1686), p. 8; Samuel Willard, *The Fountain Opened* (Boston, 1700), p. 149.

37 Edward Taylor, "Confession of Faith," in *Unpublished Writings of Edward Taylor,* 3 vols. (Boston, 1981), I: 28.

38 Nicholas Noyes, *New-England's Duty and Interest* (Boston, 1698), pp. 55–6. See also Urian Oakes, *The Unconquerable, All-Conquering, and More-Than-Conquering Souldier,* pp. 6, 10.

39 Samuel Willard, *The Truly Blessed Man,* p. 180.

other, that Satan was a formidable warrior in his own right. The clergy tried to make a careful distinction between Satan's power as tempter and man's role as guardian of his own soul: the Devil could do no more than tempt; only humans could respond to the temptation. Nevertheless, when taken at face value, the ministers' message left some logical loopholes: how could Satan himself pose a serious threat to the human soul if he had no power independent of God's will and human corruption? And if Satan was responsible for tempting men and women to sin, how was that different from being responsible for sin itself?

The ambiguity that underlay Puritan thinking on this subject was evident in the contrast between "occasional" and "regular" sermons. Regular sermons, which the clergy delivered to their settled congregations on the sabbath, emphasized issues relating to individual salvation. Occasional sermons, which marked public events such as political elections, artillery elections and fast-days, usually focused on the survival of the New England community at a corporate level. These occasional sermons tended to characterize any menace to the community as a diabolical plot and often magnified the threat posed by Satan and his instruments so as to underline the need for a renewed sense of common purpose. But regular sermons addressing individual salvation usually emphasized that Satan operated in the context of humanity's own corruption. As a result, New Englanders might hear one day that Satan and his agents posed a grave threat to their survival, and the next that the real threat was their own moral weakness. The theological contortions required to grasp the distinction could not have been within the compass of all those listening.[40]

Some ministers recognized and sought to counter a tendency on the part of layfolk to magnify the extent of Satan's responsibility for human sin. Samuel Willard reminded his listeners repeatedly that they must accept blame for their own lapses from godliness:

> The Devil indeed is called the Tempter, but remember, it is not his, but our fault if we are tempted.... Satan indeed waits for opportunity, and instigates the corruption in us, and so far he may be charged with it, but not so as to excuse our Concupiscence [worldly desires] from the blame and guilt.[41]

Satan, then, did no more than to "instigate" human corruption: he encouraged and even incited, but he did not compel. When

40 For a detailed analysis of these "regular" and "occasional" sermons, see Harry Stout, *The New England Soul: Preaching and Religious Culture in Colonial New England* (New York, 1986), pts 1 and 2.

41 Samuel Willard, *The Truly Blessed Man*, pp. 235, 499.

Elizabeth Knapp of Groton claimed to be possessed by the Devil in 1671, Willard criticized her neighbors for becoming obsessed with "the virulency of the enemy" and ignoring God's reasons for letting the Devil loose upon Elizabeth. Such a reaction "hinder[ed] the right efficacy of this Judgement upon the Soul."[42] In his 1701 sermon series, *The Christian's Exercise by Satan's Temptations,* Willard again urged his audience to recognize the extent of human culpability. When men and women were "by Temptation drawn into sin," they often tried "to extenuate [their] own fault, by seeking to throw it upon Satan." This, lamented Willard, was "a thing too frequent among such as profess themselves to be the Children of God." God would certainly punish the Devil "for all the malicious practises which he useth against his people," but human sinners were themselves blameworthy for having given way to temptation, which they "ought stedfastly to have resisted."[43]

According to Willard, responsibility for sin rested squarely on the shoulders of individual men and women, yet Samuel Parris sometimes gave quite the opposite impression. In 1690, Parris assured his congregation that "had there been no Saviour there had been no destruction of sin, the work of Satan, but we had perished therein." The Devil, declared Parris, "had Conquered Man before, and by the Death of Christ intended final obstruction of Deliverance."[44] Two years later, in the midst of the Salem witch crisis, Parris again alluded to Satan's formidable power: "if the Devil do but hold up his finger, give the least hint of his Mind, his Servants and Slaves will obey."[45] Remarks such as these might have suggested to some listeners that Satan rather than their own sinful impulses planted the seeds of sin. Parris himself, who fasted and prayed in the hope that God would forgive Salem Village for its sins and bring to an end the terrible afflictions there, saw diabolical assaults as operating in the context of human corruption. But dramatic statements about the Devil's conquest of humankind and the enslavement of men and women to Satanic whim may have pointed some of his parishioners in quite another direction. Similarly, when Cotton Mather described the crisis in Salem Village as the latest in a series of diabolical assaults designed to undermine the New England colonies, he opened the way for people to focus on the external agency of affliction rather than on its internal cause. Mather argued

42 Samuel Willard, *Useful Instructions for a Professing People in Times of Great Security and Degeneracy* (Cambridge, Mass., 1673), p. 31.
43 Samuel Willard, *The Christian's Exercise by Satan's Temptations* (Boston, 1701), p. 149.
44 Samuel Parris, "Sermons 1689–1695," pp. 78, 86.
45 Ibid., p. 154.

that God would not have allowed the witch crisis to occur had he not been angry with New Englanders; the colonists should repent of their sins and reform. Yet Mather's compelling descriptions of Satan's wrath, if taken out of context, could encourage layfolk to direct their attention outward. As Willard's sermons suggest, some colonists preferred to take that option.[46]

Extreme statements such as those made by Samuel Parris were exceptional, but many official pronouncements on the subject of sin were open to misinterpretation. Clerics often referred to the genesis of sin in formulaic terms, mentioning both Satanic temptation and individual corruption. In a letter to the church at Newbury, written in 1645, the Reverend John Fiske prayed that Goodman Badger would repent his "disorderly walking" and that God would not "leave him to Satan's temptation or a deluded heart."[47] The 1667 covenant for the church at Beverly committed members "to resist the temptations of Sathan, the world and [their] owne deceitfull harts."[48] In 1684, the church at Barnstable excommunicated Bethia Hinckley for "being so farr left of God unto the temptations of Satan and the corruptions of her own heart."[49] In describing diabolical temptation and human corruption as joint obstacles to godliness, ministers did not necessarily mean to suggest that Satan and the "deluded heart" bore equal responsibility for driving an individual to sin; telling people to repel the Devil did not in itself imply that Satan must share accountability when men and women transgressed. Yet such formulas could encourage ambiguity about where responsibility for sin should lie. Not all parishioners would have made a distinction between temptation to sin and responsibility for sin.

The underlying tension in clerical teaching between diabolical power and human responsibility was implicit and did not pose any overt threat to the credibility of Puritan thought. This tension was significant in practical terms, however. Clerical statements on the

46 Cotton Mather, *Wonders of the Invisible World*, pp. 74–5. This passage is discussed in greater detail in Chapter 6.

47 John Fiske, "Notebook," *Publications of the Colonial Society of Massachusetts*, 47 (1974): 38–9.

48 William P. Upham, ed., *Records of the First Church in Beverley, Massachusetts, 1667–1772* (Salem, Mass., 1905), p. 6.

49 "Records of the West Parish of Barnstable" (Massachusetts Historical Society). See also "Third Church Narrative," in Hamilton Andrews Hill, *History of the Old South Church, Boston, 1669–1884*, 2 vols. (Boston, 1890), I: 13, 26; Richard Pierce, ed., *Records of the First Church in Salem* (Salem, 1974), p. 135; John Wheelwright, letter to John Winthrop, 10 September 1643, in John Winthrop, *Journal*, ed. James Hosmer, 2 vols. (New York, 1908) II: 165–6; and Joseph Green's commonplace book (used by Green as a school textbook), *Massachusetts Historical Society Proceedings*, 34 (1943): 198, 233, 240, 241, 243, 246.

subject of liability embodied no single, consistent position. Instead, they presented a range of options, and so gave layfolk considerable leeway in deciding whom to blame for their sins and misfortunes.[50] As we will see, this helps to explain godly recourse to countermagic. Ministers attacked the use of countermagical techniques as a denial of personal culpability, yet the ambiguity inherent in their own teaching enabled layfolk to exculpate themselves, should they wish to do so. Puritan doctrine could be used to justify the location of evil outside the self.[51]

In 1657, Michael Wigglesworth recorded in his diary that he had attended "a conference where there was a question how to discern the temptation of Satan from those of our own concupiscence." Wigglesworth himself "reaped much resolution and comfort" from this discussion, of which unfortunately he gave no detailed account.[52] Neither ministers nor layfolk had a common attitude toward this crucial issue. Some assumed full responsibility for their sins; others were more inclined to blame the Devil. The majority tried to divide the burden of guilt between self and Satan. Most references to the Devil in diaries, personal testaments, and public records deal with the need to allocate responsibility for sin. It was when Puritans sought to account for their spiritual deficiencies that Satan figured most prominently in their thoughts.

In the privacy of their journals and diaries, ministers developed personal responses to the issue of liability that ranged from self-inculpation to something approaching self-absolution. If clerical diaries are organized along a continuum of blame for sin from self to Satan, then Michael Wigglesworth's can be placed at one extreme and Cotton Mather's at the other. It is striking how few references there are to the Devil in Wigglesworth's diary. Wigglesworth was determined to take full responsibility for his sins and rarely made

50 I agree with David D. Hall that layfolk "were in part the makers of their faith" (David D. Hall, "Towards a History of Popular Religion in Early New England," *William and Mary Quarterly*, 41 [1984]: 51). Hall shows that layfolk "were capable of rearranging the standard elements of the sermon to suit their needs" (David D. Hall, "On Common Ground: The Coherence of American Puritan Studies," *William and Mary Quarterly*, 44 [1987]: 226).

51 Andrew Delbanco argues for a fundamental change in the way that New Englanders perceived this issue over time. Delbanco suggests that by the end of the seventeenth century, New England ministers had shifted away from "the idea of sin as alienation from God" to a presentation of evil "as a monstrous thing outside the respectable self." But it is difficult to reconcile this view of the late seventeenth century with, for example, the sermons of Samuel Willard (Andrew Delbanco, *The Puritan Ordeal* [Cambridge, Mass., 1989], pp. 233–4).

52 Michael Wigglesworth, "Diary," ed. Edmund Morgan, *Publications of the Colonial Society of Massachusetts*, 35 (1946): 420.

any attempt to blame external forces. On one exceptional occasion, Wigglesworth did claim that "sathan cast objection into [his] mind."[53] On another, he referred to "the spirit of a Devil" in his heart, but here Wigglesworth was almost certainly using "Devil" in a metaphorical sense to describe his own sinful impulses: as he entertained sin, so he became diabolical.[54] Wigglesworth's reluctance to blame the Devil is all the more interesting in that he saw "detestable pride" as his foremost sin.[55] Wigglesworth made constant reference to his proud and rebellious spirit; he made it quite clear that he associated his own lapses with Satan's revolt against divine authority.

> I have rebell[e]d against and dishonour[e]d and disregarded my heavenly father, been a viper in his bosum where he has nourished me.
>
> This sin makes me likest unto the Devil. What made the Angels of light become damned spirits, but pride: this sin banish[ed] them out of heaven: am I then an heir of heaven, traveling thitherward, and do I give it entertainment?[56]

Wigglesworth bemoaned "the declensions and apostacys of [his] heart from god, unto a loos[e] frame of self-love and creature-exalting (and carnal lusts as much)."[57] After God had "pluck[ed] [him] out of sathans jaws and the belly of hell at last," and "preserv[e]d [him] in so many fearful dangers, from the fury of so many raging devils," Wigglesworth shuddered at the realization that he had entertained the sin of pride, giving "the Devils caus[e] to blaspheme, that one of [God's] children rebel[led] against him."[58] Wigglesworth regarded his behavior as devilish, but he did not perceive his sins as a direct product of Satan's designs. The Devil was an active force in Michael Wigglesworth's world, but sinful humans were less the victims of Satan than Satanic apostates who replicated the Devil's own abominations.

The autobiography and journal of Thomas Shepard, minister at Cambridge, Massachusetts, referred to the Devil more frequently than did Michael Wigglesworth's, but Shepard nonetheless accepted the burden of responsibility for sin. Just as Christ entered the hearts of those who "with fear heard what God spake and with

53 Ibid., p. 396.
54 Ibid., p. 352.
55 Ibid., p. 322.
56 Ibid., pp. 376, 423.
57 Ibid., p. 387.
58 Ibid., p. 421.

care received the word," so "by temptation... Satan entered in wicked men's hearts." Thus, the Devil did not cause sin, but took possession of those who were already sinful.[59] Shepard recognized that he himself was "the greatest enemy, worse than the Devil can be."[60] The Devil was certainly a potent adversary:

> I saw also that as Satan by external means of wicked men labors to suppress and silence preachers and means, so by inward efficacy he silenceth and suppresseth any good motion, any spirit of prayer.[61]

Yet the Devil's skill and power could never justify human capitulation. Men and women were no more exposed to the spirit of Satan than to God's benign influence: "a godly man resists the one and co-works with the other."[62] Shepard's life was plagued as much by Satan as by inner moral corruption, but Shepard blamed his sins on his own sinful nature, not on the Devil.

At the opposite end of the continuum from Michael Wigglesworth, Cotton Mather showed little reluctance to blame Satan for his own misfortunes and failings. In his sermons and published writings, Mather took care to emphasize that diabolical affliction fed upon human corruption: "Were it not for what is in us," he wrote, "for my part, I should not fear a thousand Legions of Devils."[63] Mather's diary also made occasional reference to his own responsibility for the evils that befell him.[64] Much more typical, however, are remarks that verge on the Manichean in their evocation of the Devil as an independent force, rather than as the subordinate instrument of God's just wrath.[65] In 1681, when exhaustion drove Mather to despair of his ability to carry out God's work, he held

59 Thomas Shepard, "Journal," in Michael McGiffert, ed., *God's Plot: The Paradoxes of Puritan Piety, Being the Autobiography and Journal of Thomas Shepard* (Amherst, Mass., 1972), p. 97.

60 Thomas Shepard, "Autobiography," in Michael McGiffert, ed., *God's Plot,* p. 45.

61 Thomas Shepard, "Journal," p. 195.

62 Ibid., p. 219.

63 Cotton Mather, *Wonders of the Invisible World,* p. 22.

64 For example: "In this Molestation, indeed I have had infinite Cause to acknowledge my own wicked Heart, as that Fountain of Sin, which gives my great Adversary the Advantage to molest me. And I must make a bitter Acknowledgement of my actual Miscarriages; by which I provoke the Holy One to permitt the Evil One to fall upon me, and I forfeit the gracious Assistance of the Lord" (Cotton Mather, *Diary,* ed. Worthington C. Ford, 2 vols. [1911; New York, 1957], I: 585).

65 Manichaeanism was a religious system, widely accepted from the third to the fifth century, that represented Satan as an independent being, co-eternal with God.

Satan responsible for introducing these "Discouraging Fears" into his mind.[66] In 1700, when he feared that his "serviceable" days were over, he blamed "the Devices of Satan" for having "brought [them] to an end."[67] In 1706, he wrote:

> I have been a Person buffeted with extraordinary Temptations, wherein Satan has designed with exquisite Contrivances, to spoil that work, which the sovereign Grace of God has intended me for.[68]

Mather emerges from these passages as a passive victim of the Devil's uncurbed energies, a far cry from the spirit of Wigglesworth's diary.[69]

Clerical teaching on liability for sin was amenable to a broad range of interpretations. As we have seen, fleeting references to the subject in sermons and other public pronouncements were usually formulaic, attributing sin to both Satanic temptation and human corruption. More detailed discussion provided layfolk with an ambiguous message that emphasized both the enormous threat Satan posed to human beings and his utter dependence upon human depravity. Layfolk took full advantage of the choices afforded to them by that ambiguity. Some adopted compact formulas that implied a divided responsibility: John Dane, a tailor who crossed the Atlantic around 1640, had hoped to "be more free here than there from temptations," but found in New England "a devell to tempt and a corrupt hart to deseve [deceive]."[70] Others developed more idiosyncratic solutions that ranged from one extreme to the other, as did the private meditations of their pastors.

Some of those who divided responsibility were probably mouthing clichés, perhaps with little thought to their actual meaning. In courtroom confessions, seventeenth-century criminals often blamed both Satan and self for the given crime. George Spencer, who admitted in 1641 to having had sexual relations with a sow, said that "he was driven by the power of the devill and the strength of his [corr]uptio[n] to doe the thing."[71] In 1649, James Clements claimed that he was impelled to lie about his negligence on the

66 Cotton Mather, *Diary*, I: 6.
67 Ibid., I: 347.
68 Ibid., I: 578.
69 See Robert Middlekauff, *The Mathers: Three Generations of Puritan Intellectuals, 1596–1728* (New York, 1971), p. 327.
70 John Dane, "A Declaration of Remarkabell Provedences in the Corse of My Lyfe" (Massachusetts Historical Society).
71 Charles J. Hoadly, ed., *Records of the Colony or Jurisdiction of New Haven*, 2 vols. (New Haven, Conn., 1857–8), I: 67, 2 March 1641.

watch "from the guilt of his conscienc[e] and working of Sathan."[72] Joanna Smith, presented to the Essex County court for fornication in 1682, blamed her sin on her "naturall wicked inclination" and "the temptations of the adversarye, and his wicked suggestions."[73] These confessions bear a suspiciously close resemblance to the format used in criminal indictments. In 1651, for example, Mary Parsons was indicted for murdering her own child, "not having the feare of God before [her] eyes nor in [her] harte, being seduced by the divill, and yeilding to his instigations and the wickedness of [her] owne harte."[74] The accused may have adopted official phraseology in order to placate the magistrates who were about to pass sentence upon them. The similarity in wording suggests that courtroom confessions mimicked a legal format and did not necessarily reflect sincere belief.

But the attribution of spiritual deficiencies to an alliance between the Devil and human corruption was not always formulaic or hackneyed. In other settings, layfolk developed diagnoses of their condition that bespoke profound engagement with the issue of liability and that recognized the role played by Satan without denying their own culpability. Captain Underhill, an excommunicate, was received back into the Boston Church in 1640 after delivering an impassioned statement in which he attributed his sinful condition to a complex interplay between his own moral corruption and the Devil's assaults:

> Many fearful temptations he met with beside, and in all these his heart shut up in hardness and inpenitency as the bondslave of Satan, till the Lord, after a long time and great afflictions, had broken his heart, and brought him to humble himself before him night and day with prayers and tears.[75]

In 1674, Samuel Danforth wrote in the Roxbury Church records that Margaret Cheany had just recovered from a lengthy "melancholick distemper." According to Danforth, Cheany bemoaned that she had been "long bound by Satan," but also recognized her own

72 Ibid., I: 489, 2 October 1649.

73 *Records and Files of the Quarterly Courts of Essex County,* 9 vols. (Salem, Mass., 1911–78), VIII: 298, 10 May 1682.

74 Nathaniel Shurtleff, ed., *Records of the Governor and Company of Massachusetts Bay in New England,* 5 vols. (Boston, 1853–4), IV: 48. This formula was used in indictments for crimes ranging from murder (John Noble and John F. Cronin, eds., *Records of the Court of Assistants of the Colony of Massachusetts Bay, 1630–1692,* 3 vols. [Boston, 1901–28], I: 32, 85), infanticide (I: 115, 228), blasphemy (I: 253–4; III, 211), rape (I: 22, 74), adultery (I: 56, 114–15), fornication (I: 125), and bestiality (I: 10, 87) to trading powder and shot with the Indians (I: 102).

75 Winthrop, *Journal,* II: 12–13, 3 September 1640.

responsibility for the distemper, "confessing and bewailing her sinful yielding to temptation."[76] In 1683, Thomas Dewy acknowledged cutting down a dam and recognized this to be "a thing offensive under many Considerations, which made [him] grieved in [his] Spirit, that the Adversary should get such advantage against [him], and to beg of God to pardon the evill there of."[77] Dewy, like Underhill and Cheany, believed that the Devil's ability to tempt men and women was dependent upon their own willingness to be tempted.

The position adopted by Underhill, Cheany, and Dewy recognized the potency of Satan's assaults and yet did not imply that Satan's might absolved them of responsibility for their condition. Other layfolk veered toward more extreme positions. When candidates for admission to church membership described in public their conversion experiences, they usually dwelt at length on their struggles with sin.[78] Most narrators accounted for sinful thoughts or actions in terms of their own corrupt impulses. This is hardly surprising, since conversion depended upon the believer's full recognition of personal culpability. Many conversion narratives referred to Satan only in the context of human responsibility for sin. John Stansby, for example, bemoaned that he had been "like the devil not only to hell [him]self but enticing and ha[i]ling others to sin." Stansby was convinced of his "hellish, devilish nature opposite to God and goodness." Indeed, he went so far as to accept personal blame for Christ's crucifixion:

> I saw as soon as ever I committed sin I was condemned, and that if pardoned it must cost the heart blood of Christ, and that I did as much as in me lie to drag Christ to the cross.[79]

But other narrators were disinclined to accept full responsibility for their sins and described themselves as having been, at least temporarily, victims of the Devil. John Collins spoke of himself as

76 Samuel Danforth, "Records of the First Church in Roxbury," *New England Historical and Genealogical Register,* 34 (1880): 362.

77 Edward Taylor, "Disciplinary Cases," in *Unpublished Writings of Edward Taylor,* p. 180.

78 For a discussion of surviving narratives and their reliability, see Charles Cohen, *God's Caress: The Psychology of Puritan Religious Experience* (New York, 1986), chap 5, esp. pp. 137–40. In addition to the three collections of narratives mentioned by Cohen (pp 137–8), a fourth has now been identified, transcribed, and published: Mary Rhinelander McCarl, ed., "Thomas Shepard's Record of Relations of Religious Experience, 1648–1649," *William and Mary Quarterly,* 48 (1991), 432–66.

79 Thomas Shepard, "The Confessions of Divers Propounded to Be Received," ed. George Selement and Bruce Woolley, *Publications of the Colonial Society of Massachusetts,* 58 (1981): 86.

having been "kept under the lash of Satan's terrors," while John Jones declared that he had been "a prisoner and kept by Satan."[80] Thomas Hincksman claimed that "the adversary prevailed so far as to force him to break off from the duty, Satan tempting him and telling him that twas not his right to seek after God."[81] These narrators may have been speaking metaphorically: the "lash of Satan's terrors," for example, did not necessarily refer to the actual figure of Satan. But even if so, their choice of language suggests an inclination to view evil as imposed upon rather than embraced by human sinners.

Other layfolk also claimed that the Devil overpowered them and forced them to sin. In 1637, Goodman Walker was questioned in a Salem Church meeting about his absence from the sacrament of the Lord's Supper. Elders asked Walker if he really desired communion with the church. Walker responded that "he would demur at it and his reason was because of his unfitness through God's visiting of him." One of the elders condemned this abdication of responsibility: "thus he charges God, not himself." Walker replied that he "charge[d]" not God but "the divil, because his fall came from his tempting of him."[82] Increase Mather noted in a diary entry for early 1676 that "old Negos" had been sent to speak with him. Negos was "a Lamentable object, crying out that the devill had power over him, and that there was no hope for him, that God had forsaken him, and answered him not."[83] Individuals who experienced difficulty in achieving or maintaining communion with Christ sometimes blamed their spiritual deficiencies on the Devil. Ann Foster, who confessed to witchcraft at Salem in 1692, claimed that Satan had prevented her from fulfilling her religious duties. Foster testified "that she formerly frequented the publique metting to worship god, but the divill had such power over her that she could not profit there and that was her undoeing."[84]

Surviving lay references to the Devil are mostly brief and often fragmentary; they frustrate as much as enlighten. But one individual left behind a more substantial discussion of Satan and his role in the drama of human sin. William Pynchon was a wealthy

80 Michael Wigglesworth, "Diary," p. 428; Thomas Shepard, "The Confessions of Divers Propounded to Be Received," p. 200.

81 John Fiske, "Notebook," p. 147.

82 Ibid., 240.

83 Increase Mather, "Diary," *Massachusetts Historical Society Proceedings*, 13 (1899–1990): 359.

84 Paul Boyer and Stephen Nissenbaum, eds., *The Salem Witchcraft Papers: Verbatim Transcripts of the Legal Documents of the Salem Witchcraft Outbreak*, 3 vols. (New York, 1977), II: 343.

merchant who arrived in Massachusetts with the Winthrop fleet and immediately became an important political figure in the Bay Colony. In 1635, Pynchon moved south to settle a new town in the Connecticut Valley: Agawam, later renamed Springfield. During the next fifteen years, Pynchon's relationship with the government in Massachusetts began to deteriorate as he supported demands for a more latitudinarian form of church government. In 1650, Pynchon became embroiled in theological controversy when he published *The Meritorious Price of Our Redemption,* a reappraisal of the atonement. New England ministers taught that human sin was imputed to Christ, who bore the wrath of God in order to redeem humanity. The central argument of Pynchon's book was that Christ's suffering was incidental to the atonement. According to Pynchon, the Son of God did not redeem men and women through "wounds, bruises, and stripes." Instead, he redeemed them through obedience to God's will, thus undoing the primal act of disobedience and all subsequent disobedient acts. Pynchon blamed Christ's suffering on the Devil: he argued "that Christ did not suffer any degree of God's wrath at all for us, but that all his sufferings were inflicted upon him from the rage and emnity of the old Serpent and his wicked instruments." The Devil's intention was to subvert the act of redemption: "he wounded him to make him grudge at his sufferings, and to make him unwilling to dy, that so he might spoile the perfection of his Mediatorial obedience." Pynchon granted that "God had a hand in all [Christ's] sufferings": after all, Satan could not act without "Gods allowance." However, God permitted Christ to be tortured in order to test his obedience, not because he had transferred his wrath from humanity to Christ.[85]

Despite Pynchon's concession that Satan acted only "by Gods determinate counsel and decree," his argument that "all the sufferings of Christ were . . . incited by the Devill" accorded Satan a crucial role in the penultimate act of the drama of redemption.[86] John Norton, the minister at Ipswich, who was commissioned by the General Court of Massachusetts to write a rebuttal of Pynchon's arguments, took up the matter of Satan's involvement in the Passion. According to Norton, Christ's suffering was a vital part of the atonement: he endured God's wrath on behalf of humankind. It was true that God used Satan to inflict that suffering, but Norton insisted that the Devil was a mere tool of the Almighty. Christ's agony on the cross was "much greater in respect of God, then it was in respect of Satan and his instruments"; "the righteous wrath

85 William Pynchon, *The Meritorious Price of Our Redemption* (London, 1650), Preface, p. ii; pp. 20, 21, 46.

86 Ibid., pp. 46, 64.

of God exceeded the unrighteous wrath of Satan." Norton castigated Pynchon for magnifying Satan's role: "God," he wrote, "is the first and universall efficient, not a meer counsellor, forespeaker, and permitter." According to Norton, "though Satan and men were the subordinate instruments, yet God himself was the Authour and principall efficient of them."[87] Pynchon had described Christ's suffering as "incited by the Devill (with Gods allowance)." His use of parentheses is telling.[88] Norton, on the other hand, saw the Devil as a mere instrument of God's wrath.[89]

William Pynchon was not the only layman in the Connecticut Valley to stress Satan's role in the drama of human depravity. Edward Holyoke, a friend of Pynchon and another of the original settlers at Agawam, wrote a treatise entitled *The Doctrine of Life,* published in London in 1658, in which he supported and developed many of Pynchon's arguments. In a remarkable passage that deserves quotation in full, Holyoke described the history of human corruption, focusing attention exclusively on the actions of Satan and Christ:

1 Satan brought man to offence, and so out of the favour of God, and to shame of face, and to the fear of Bondage; Christ the second Adam procured Reconciliation, Justification, and Adoption.
2 Satan brought mans soule to darknesse, sinfullnesse, or to death in sin; Christ the second Adam gives it knowledge, righteousnesse, and the life of holinesse.
3 Satan brought mans body to miseries, death and corruption; Christ the second Adam sustaineth it in this its pilgrimage, and perfectly restoreth it to life and incorruption in the Resurrection.
4 Satan caused the first Adam to be expelled from the Tree of Life, and the Paradise terrestiall, and brought all the world under curse, and so subject to vanity, and corruption; Christ the second Adam restoreth to the faithfull a comfortable, and sanctified use and service of the creatures, and will make a new world for his and their glory to dwell still with God, and to feed upon the Tree of life in the Paradise celestiall, and command Satan with his seed into eternall flames.

87 John Norton, *A Discussion of that Great Point in Divinity, the Sufferings of Christ* (London, 1653), pp. 15, 37, 38.
88 William Pynchon, *The Meritorious Price of Our Redemption,* p. 46.
89 For a detailed discussion of the background to this debate, see Philip Gura, *A Glimpse of Sion's Glory: Puritan Radicalism in New England, 1630–1660* (Middletown, Conn., 1984), chap. 11. I am grateful to Michael McGiffert for bringing Pynchon's work to my attention.

Holyoke's position was extreme and perhaps exceptional, although Samuel Willard's strictures against those eager "to extenuate [their] own fault, by seeking to throw it upon Satan" suggests otherwise. Declaring that Christ "destroy[ed] in mans nature, as a second Adam, the works of the Divill," Holyoke implied that humanity's role in the generation of sin was essentially passive. This came close to an outright denial of human responsibility for sin. Yet Holyoke had not actually rejected orthodox thinking on this issue: he had merely selected one possible interpretation of Puritan diabology and had then taken that perspective to its logical conclusion.[90]

Ambiguity in Puritan teaching about liability for sin gave individual believers considerable freedom of choice when confronting this issue in their own lives. For many people, the allocation of blame was a fairly straightforward process; but for others, such decisions were profoundly traumatic. Some of these tormented souls resolved the problem of culpability, albeit temporarily, by fusing Satan and self in claims of diabolical possession.

Diabolical possession was one of the most dramatic and disturbing manifestations of the supernatural world to which early modern Europeans and seventeenth-century New Englanders were exposed. Hundreds, maybe thousands, of men, women, and children became possessed during the late sixteenth and seventeenth centuries. For New England alone, we know of seventy-eight cases that occurred during the first century of settlement.[91] Medieval writers had produced numerous works describing possession cases and theorizing at length on the subject, but only after the late sixteenth century did diabolical possession become a widespread and frequent occurrence.[92] Europeans and New Englanders were fascinated and appalled by the spectacle of possession. They flocked to watch its victims contort and blaspheme; their pastors regaled them with sermons about the moral implications of diabolical affliction; and those among them who were literate could read theological and medical exegeses of the subject.

Possession was the inhabiting of a human body by a devil, who then controlled his victim's verbal and physical actions. Devils pos-

90 Edward Holyoke, *The Doctrine of Life, or of Man's Redemption* (London, 1658), pp. 16–17.

91 Carol Karlsen, *The Devil in the Shape of a Woman: Witchcraft in Colonial New England* (New York, 1987), p. 223. For a discussion of possession in early modern Europe, see Joseph Klaits, *Servants of Satan: The Age of the Witch Hunts* (Bloomington, Ind., 1985), chap. 5.

92 For examples of this medieval literature, see Jeffrey Burton Russell, *Satan: The Early Christian Tradition* (Ithaca, N.Y., 1981), pp. 230, 237–9; and Norman Cohn, *Europe's Inner Demons* (Hertfordshire, England, 1976), pp. 68–74.

sessed men and women either of their own accord or at the instigation of a witch. In many cases, the demoniac would accuse a witch of having incited a devil to attack. Some spiritual counselors encouraged such accusations, since disposing of a witch seemed much less daunting than did challenging a devil that had occupied of its own free will.[93] Possession was often preceded by an argument between the demoniac and a neighbor or acquaintance who was suspected of witchcraft.[94] Quarrels of this kind help to explain the timing of possession incidents, but they do not explain why people became demoniacs: after all, victims could have accused their enemies of witchcraft without becoming possessed. Much more significant as a cause of possession was inner spiritual conflict.[95]

Despite the spiritual and cultural diversity of the environments in which these incidents took place, a number of fundamental characteristics united the possessed of the sixteenth and seventeenth centuries. First, possession cases tended to occur in communities or households known for their spiritual intensity. A number of dramatic possession episodes took place in French convents during the seventeenth century. Most New England demoniacs came from godly families or lived in godly households. Ann Cole of Hartford, Connecticut, who became possessed in 1662, was "accounted a person of real Piety and Integrity."[96] The children of John Goodwin, who succumbed to possession in 1688, "had enjoyed a Religious Education, and . . . had an observable Affection unto Divine and Sacred things."[97] Among the first inhabitants of Salem Village to become possessed in 1692 were Elizabeth Parris, the minister's

93 See Joseph Klaits, *Servants of Satan*, pp. 111–12; and John Demos, *Entertaining Satan*, p. 116. Not all pastors agreed with this strategy: in New England, Cotton Mather discouraged Mercy Short and Margaret Rule from naming their tormentors, "lest any good Person should come to suffer any blast of Reputation, through the cunning Malice of the great Accuser" (Cotton Mather, "Another Brand Pluck't Out of the Burning," in George L. Burr, ed., *Narratives of the Witchcraft Cases* [1914; New York, 1952] p. 311).

94 See, for example, the confrontation between Martha Goodwin and Goodwife Glover (Cotton Mather, *Memorable Providences*, p. 3) and that between Mercy Short and Sarah Good (Cotton Mather, "A Brand Pluck't Out of the Burning," in George L. Burr, ed., *Narratives of the Witchcraft Cases*, pp. 259–60). The possessed at Salem in 1692 were certainly influenced by social conflicts within their community (Paul Boyer and Stephen Nissenbaum, *Salem Possessed: The Social Origins of Witchcraft* [Cambridge, Mass., 1974].

95 Carol Karlsen also argues that antagonistic relationships with suspect witches cannot explain possession, although she claims that such relationships were unusual in New England cases. The evidence does not support this latter assertion; Karlsen herself admits that there were "many exceptions" where such conflicts did occur (Carol Karlsen, *The Devil in the Shape of a Woman*, p. 225).

96 Increase Mather, *An Essay for the Recording of Illustrious Providences* (Boston, 1684), pp. 135–6.

97 Cotton Mather, *Memorable Providences*, p. 2.

daughter, and Abigail Williams, a niece who lived with the Parris family. The household of Thomas Putnam, Jr., a devout member of the Salem Village Church, was also afflicted: Putnam's wife, daughter, niece, and servant girl became possessed.[98]

Second, demoniacs on both sides of the Atlantic spoke and moved in ways that were culturally illicit: they became violent; they were lewd; they blasphemed. They embodied sin. Many of the nuns who became possessed in the French convent cases were evidently disturbed by forbidden sexual impulses that they either related or enacted during their fits. One young novice at Aix, Madeleine de Demandolx de la Palud, was convulsed by palpitations "representing the sexual act, with violent movements of the lower parts of her belly."[99] Possession enabled people like Madeleine de Demandolx, constrained by their own moral values and those of their environment, to express sinful desires without having to accept full responsibility for their behavior: the devils within them could act out forbidden fantasies on their behalf.[100] Across the Atlantic in Boston, Massachusetts, the Goodwin children were prevented by their possessing demons from doing housework, eating their meals, washing their hands, or lying still in bed. They were "cast into intolerable anguishes" by the prospect of "Religious Exercise," and also became insolent. The Goodwin children used possession to explore a variety of rebellious impulses their "Religious Education" otherwise precluded.[101]

Demoniacs seemed to derive intense satisfaction from such behavior. Yet at the same time, they condemned bitterly the demons who apparently compelled them. Possession episodes took the form of a struggle between the determination of a demon-within to embrace the illicit or sinful and the desire of the demoniac to repudiate such impulses. The third uniting characteristic of possession episodes during this period was that most demoniacs were obsessed

98 These were Ann Putnam, Sr., Ann Putnam, Jr., Mary Walcott, and Mercy Lewis. Mary Walcott lived with the Putnams.

99 Russell Hope Robbins, *The Encyclopedia of Witchcraft and Demonology* (New York, 1959), p. 24; Joseph Klaits, *Servants of Satan*, p. 118.

100 Joseph Klaits argues that one of the seventeenth century's distinguishing features was a massive campaign by religious reformers to suppress violence, sexual license, and other forms of physical spontaneity (Joseph Klaits, *Servants of Satan*, pp. 76–85). According to Klaits, there was a direct link between this reform movement and the proliferation of possession incidents in Europe: demoniacs could violate with impunity the new values of restraint and self-control; they were free to engage in behavior that otherwise they would have been expected to eschew (p. 117). See also Keith Thomas, *Religion and the Decline of Magic* (1971; Middlesex, England, 1973), pp. 572–4.

101 Cotton Mather, *Memorable Providences*, pp. 16–17, 33. See also Judith Devlin, *The Superstitious Mind: French Peasants and the Supernatural in the Nineteenth Century* (New Haven, Conn., 1989), p. 135.

with their moral condition. Possession usually followed the onset of crises caused by feelings of spiritual inadequacy. Madeleine de Demandolx, the novice at Aix, had gone through periods of bitter self-condemnation, was convinced of her moral turpitude, and repeatedly attempted suicide. A northern Englishman named Briggs, who was living in London as a student in 1574, became possessed soon after he convinced himself that he was an incorrigible sinner. Prior to the onset of possession, Briggs had also made several attempts to kill himself.[102] The first of the Goodwin children to become possessed, thirteen-year-old Martha Goodwin, "was in great distress of Mind, Crying out, That she was in the dark concerning her Souls estate, and that she had mispent her precious time."[103]

Most New Englanders who experienced possession admitted to having entertained sinful urges that clashed with their religious environment and gave rise to intense spiritual turmoil. Ambiguity in Puritan doctrine about liability for sin could intensify such crises. Those who were predisposed to locate blame either within themselves or elsewhere would adopt whichever aspects of Puritan teaching were most appropriate. But individuals who were torn between self-blame and self-absolution could find ample justification for both in clerical statements on the subject, and so sank deeper and deeper into spiritual dilemma. Possession provided a solution for those who were unable to resolve the extent of their own liability. Rather than accepting or rejecting responsibility for their condition, demoniacs did both: they displaced their sinful urges onto devils within them. This enabled them to blame their thoughts and actions on the devils that had taken possession of them, while admitting and bewailing the parlous spiritual state that had enticed devils in the first place.[104]

The most detailed account of diabolical possession to survive from early New England describes the torments of Elizabeth Knapp, a sixteen-year-old servant in the household of Samuel Willard, the minister at Groton. Elizabeth became possessed in the fall of 1671. Throughout the three months of her ordeal, she suffered periodic fits, outbursts of explosive energy which terrified those

102 Keith Thomas, *Religion and the Decline of Magic*, p. 574. See also Joseph Klaits, *Servants of Satan*, pp. 110–11.

103 Cotton Mather, *Memorable Providences*, p. 46.

104 Two recent studies by John Demos and Carol Karlsen interpret cases of possession in early New England (John Demos, *Entertaining Satan*, chap. 4; Carol Karlsen, *The Devil in the Shape of a Woman*, chap. 7). Demos approaches the subject from a psychoanalytic perspective and sees possession as the conversion of intrapsychic conflicts into somatic symptoms. Karlsen argues that possession was a ritual expression of otherwise stifled female dissatisfaction with "gender and class hierarchies." Both interpretations are discussed below.

around her.[105] Elizabeth became "violent in bodily motion, leapings, strainings, and strange agitations, scarce to bee held in bounds by the strength of three or four."[106] She ran around the house, "roaring and yelling extremely and fetching deadly sighs as if her heartstrings would have broken."[107] Elizabeth's fits began with a horrifying assault by her possessing devil:

> In the evening, a little before she went to bed, sitting by the fire, shee cryed out, oh my legs! And clapt her hand on them, immediately oh my breast! and removed her hands thither; and forthwith, oh I am strangled, and put her hands on her throat.[108]

In addition to suffering further attacks of this kind, Elizabeth also tried to hurt herself and became violent toward others, on one occasion "striking those that held her [and] spitting in their faces."[109] Elizabeth's oral symptoms were even more appalling: her possessing devil "belched forth most horrid and nefandous [nefarious] Blasphemies."[110] He told Elizabeth "that heaven was an ougly place, and that none went thither but a company of base roagues." He called Willard himself, Elizabeth's master and minister, "a blacke roague, who told them nothing but a p[ar]cell of lyes and deceived them."[111]

Willard's servant admitted that she was a fit receptacle for the Devil. Satan embodied rebellion and sin; Elizabeth was drawn to both. Between her fits, she spoke of "her discontent, that her condition displeased her, her labour was burdensome to her, shee was neither content to bee at home nor abroad."[112] Elizabeth's "discon-

105 For a detailed narrative of Elizabeth Knapp's possession, see John Demos, *Entertaining Satan*, pp. 99–111.

106 Samuel Willard, "A Briefe Account of a Strange and Unusuall Providence of God Befallen to Elizabeth Knapp of Groton," in *Groton in the Witchcraft Times* (Groton, Mass., 1883), p. 7.

107 Ibid., p. 11.

108 Ibid., p. 7.

109 Ibid., p. 17. The Goodwin children also made a number of attempts to harm themselves and others (Cotton Mather, *Memorable Providences*, p. 15).

110 Increase Mather, *An Essay for the Recording of Illustrious Providences*, p. 141.

111 Samuel Willard, "A Briefe Account," pp. 14, 17.

112 Ibid., p. 16. According to New England ministers, discontent made people especially vulnerable to the Devil's temptations. See, for example, Samuel Willard, *Useful Instructions for a Professing People*, p. 34, and Cotton Mather, *A Discourse on Witchcraft* (Boston, 1689), p. 23. Mary Johnson of Wethersfield, Connecticut, who confessed to witchcraft in 1648, testified that "her first Familiarity with the Devils came by Discontent" (Cotton Mather, *Memorable Providences*, p. 62). In 1653, Elizabeth Godman of New Haven prosecuted Goodwife Larremore for defamation: Larremore had said that she believed Godman to be a witch "because Mr Davenport aboute that time had occasion in his ministry

tent" was directed primarily against Samuel Willard, whose priviledged and apparently leisured position within the home and community depended upon her labour.[113] Since Willard was a minister of God, it was appropriate that Elizabeth should identify with Satan: just as he had rebelled against God, so she now rebelled against Willard. Elizabeth was also conscious of her spiritual failings and "complained against herselfe of many sins."[114] Yet she could not bring herself to accept full responsibility for her condition. Willard suspected that his servant had made a covenant with the Devil and that this was how he had come to possess her. During the first month of her ordeal, Elizabeth rejected her master's accusations, claiming that local witches had caused her affliction. But in late November, Willard persuaded Elizabeth to acknowledge that she had been tempted to sign a covenant. She actually confessed to having done so on two separate occasions in December; but each time she recanted, reverting to denial of personal culpability.

Elizabeth Knapp was torn between acknowledging and denying her state of sin, between becoming a witch and being a victim of witches. Claiming possession by the Devil enabled her to avoid clear-cut decisions about her own liability. During the possession fits, her sinful urges became those of the Devil within her: tempter and tempted became one. Elizabeth's direction of violent urges against both herself and those around her expressed the combination of self-blame and self-absolution that made possession so attractive to her. The explosive energy that characterized Elizabeth's fits bore eloquent testimony to the tremendous emotional release she experienced as both identity and responsibility were dissolved.[115]

Samuel Willard decided that his servant's case deserved public

to speake of witches, and showed that a froward discontented frame of spirit was a subject fitt for the Devill to worke upon in that way, and she looked upon Mrs Godman to be of such a frame of spirit" (Charles J. Hoadly, ed., *Records of the Colony or Jurisdiction of New Haven,* II: 29).

113 See Carol Karlsen, *The Devil in the Shape of a Woman,* pp. 246–7.

114 Samuel Willard, "A Briefe Account," p. 9.

115 For a different interpretation of the Knapp case, see John Demos, *Entertaining Satan,* chap. 4. According to Demos, Elizabeth's possession was a form of regression, enabling her to express "deep, intrapsychic lessons" acquired in infancy and early childhood; these "lessons" related to the denial of ego satisfaction and manifested themselves in rage, exhibitionism and the development of narcissistic transference relationships with figures of authority. Whereas Demos sees Elizabeth Knapp's possession as a reenactment of earlier experiences, I interpret her behavior as an attempt to resolve anxieties that looked to the future (that is, the possibility of salvation). I share David D. Hall's reservations about the application of twentieth-century psychoanalytic categories to cases involving seventeenth-century New Englanders. As Hall points out, this strategy rests on the assumption that "structures of the self" do not change over time (David D. Hall, "Witchcraft and the Limits of Interpretation," *New England Quarterly,* 58 [1985]: 270–1).

attention well beyond the community of Groton itself. Willard therefore wrote an account of Elizabeth's ordeal and sent it to his colleague Increase Mather, who included a brief summary of the case in his *Essay for the Recording of Illustrious Providences,* published in 1684. Five years later, Increase's son Cotton published an account of another possession episode. Cotton Mather's narrative appeared in a collection of short essays entitled *Memorable Providences.*[116] This time, the victim was an unnamed boy, who was tempted and then possessed by the Devil. The boy had spent his early childhood in Holland, where he had "used the Trade of inventing Lyes, and Stealing mon[e]y, Running away from his Father, spending of it at Dice, and with the vilest Company." His father, "a godly Minister," had tried to reform the boy by subjecting him to a rigorous discipline. At the age of ten or eleven, the boy ran away to Delft, where the Devil appeared to him, "counselling him not to hearken to the Word of God, nor unto any of his Father's Instructions, and propounding to him, to Enter into a Covenant with him." The boy was sorely tempted, but declined for the time being. His father, completely ignorant of this latest incident but despairing of his son's general behavior, joined with friends in a day of humiliation and then sent his son off to New England.[117]

Since the boy's arrival in New England, the Devil had "held a constant Discourse with him; and all about Ent[e]ring into a Covenant with him." The Devil tried "to allure him" with a series of promises,

> telling him many Stories of Dr. Faustus, and other Witches, how bravely they have lived, and how he should live deliciously, and have Ease, Comfort, and Money; and sometimes threatening to tear him in pieces if he would not.[118]

As before, the boy came close to signing, but "such dreadfull horrour did seiz[e] upon him ... from the Word of God, and such fears of his Eternal Perishing, that he could not do it."[119] The boy was now living at Tocutt, in the New Haven colony, with his epileptic brother, whom he used to tease by imitating his fits. By and by, he himself began to suffer real fits, which he took to be a punishment from God. The boy almost brought himself to seek help and confess his sins, "but when he was about to do it, the Devil still held his mouth, that he could not."[120] Eventually, he did confess his dealings

116 Cotton Mather, *Memorable Providences,* pp. 64–71.
117 Ibid., pp. 64–5.
118 Ibid., p. 65.
119 Ibid., p. 66.
120 Ibid., p. 67.

with Satan to the Reverend Abraham Pierson, minister at Tocutt. The Devil retaliated by taking possession of him and using him to deliver "horrible Blasphemies against the Name of Christ."[121] From time to time, the boy would break out of possession and begin to confess his former sins. On one occasion, he prayed "in such a manner so suitable to his Condition, so Aggravating his Sin, and pleading with God for mercy, and in such a strange, high, enlarged manner, as judicious godly persons then present, affirm[ed] they never heard the like in their lives."[122]

The boy in Mather's account was, like Elizabeth Knapp, the quintessential demoniac. The son of "a godly Minister," he knew that he was a sinner and so was tormented by "fears of his Eternal Perishing." The boy recognized his "Malice against the Word of God," but fluctuated between blaming himself and blaming Satan.[123] On the one hand, the Devil came to tempt him as a kindred spirit who, like Doctor Faustus, would gladly sell his soul in return for earthly pleasures. On the other, Satan was sufficiently uncertain of his chances that he felt it necessary to use threats. The boy's repeated attempts to confess indicate a sense of personal culpability, yet his very belief that he was tempted by the Devil placed him in a passive role. Eventually, he redefined the situation by becoming possessed. Possession constituted both abdication and recognition of responsibility. The boy was now an involuntary mouthpiece for the Devil; he had transformed himself into a victim and became the recipient of much public sympathy. Yet between fits he still recognized his own sinfulness, which he realized had prompted the Devil to approach him in the first place.

Diabolical possession laid bare the threat Satan could pose to an individual's spiritual autonomy. But at the same time, it also exposed the sufferer's fundamental culpability. Possession was often either preceded or accompanied by an attempt on the part of the devil to persuade his victim that she or he should become a witch. Although the possessed saw themselves as the victims of diabolical assault, they were also willing to confront the unwelcome fact that they themselves were fit candidates for the Devil's service. The children and young women who became possessed in 1692 claimed that the specters of local witches and the Devil himself had tried to recruit them. Several of the possessed testified that Mary Warren, a fellow demoniac, had become a witch; under pressure from the court, Warren confessed to having signed a diabolical covenant.

121 Ibid., p. 68.
122 Ibid., pp. 68–9.
123 Ibid., p. 65.

Other demoniacs admitted that they came close to capitulating.[124] As with Elizabeth Knapp and the boy at Tocutt, these cases evidenced a fundamental confusion of innocence and guilt in the minds of the possessed. It was this confusion that made possession attractive to them: as demoniacs, they became innocent without denying their guilt.

Individuals confronted the issue of culpability most directly and insistently as they prepared to convert. In a number of cases, possession coincided with and may well have been caused by anxieties about the regenerative process. This link helps to explain both the chronological distribution of possession cases and the disproportionate number of women who became demoniacs. All recorded cases of possession in early New England occurred during the second half of the seventeenth century, when a growing number of New Englanders failed to undergo conversion.[125] Ministers recognized that at least some of these people wanted to convert, but were not convinced that they had saving grace.[126] Inability to achieve assurance could lead to desperation, especially if individuals succeeded in convincing themselves of their utter worthlessness, but then despaired of Christ's mercy. Those unable to move beyond obsession with sin by seizing Christ might have been tempted to blame Satan for their inability to do so; yet this was not a promising option, since denial of personal culpability was itself a clear obstacle to conversion. Possession would enable such individuals to sidestep the issue of primary blame for failure to convert by fusing the two guilty parties: self and Satan. Religious commitment was much greater among women in late seventeenth-century New England.[127] Thus, women would have been more vulnerable than men to spiritual crises of this kind. Eighty-six percent of demoniacs in early New England were female.[128]

Several young women who became demoniacs were clearly worried about conversion. Martha Goodwin claimed "That she was in the dark concerning her Souls estate, and that she had mispent

124 *Salem Witchcraft Papers*, III: 793–804.

125 See David D. Hall, *Worlds of Wonder, Days of Judgment: Popular Religious Belief in Early New England* (New York, 1989), pp. 130–1, 156–9.

126 Others had no desire to do so; I do not mean to suggest that all unconverted New Englanders were would-be saints. See Jon Butler, *Awash in a Sea of Faith: Christianizing the American People* (Cambridge, Mass., 1990), p. 61.

127 Mary Maple Dunn, "Saints and Sisters: Congregationalist and Quaker Women in the Early Colonial Period," *American Quarterly*, 30 (1978): 590–592; Edmund Morgan, "New England Puritanism: Another Approach," *William and Mary Quarterly*, 18 (1961): 238–9. See also Laurel Ulrich, *Good Wives: Image and Reality in the Lives of Women in Northern New England, 1650–1750* (New York, 1980), pp. 215–26.

128 Carol Karlsen, *The Devil in the Shape of a Woman*, p. 223.

her precious time." Martha was only thirteen years old, but the Goodwin children were precocious: according to Cotton Mather, "those of them that were capable of it, seem'd to have such a Resentment [understanding or sense] of their eternal Concernments as is not altogether usual."[129] Elizabeth Knapp, a sixteen-year-old, bemoaned her "unprofitable life" and reported that the Devil "told hir [that] her time was past, and [that] there was no hope unlesse shee would serve him."[130] Ann Cole, who succumbed to possession in 1662, "had for some time been afflicted and in some feares about her spirituall estate."[131] Margaret Rule, who became a demoniac in 1693, was moving toward conversion during the six months prior to her possession: according to Cotton Mather's account, "she was observably improved in the hopeful symptoms of a new creature; she was become seriously concerned for the everlasting salvation of her soul, and careful to avoid the snares of evil company."[132] Rule's possession may well have been caused by anxieties relating to conversion.

One young woman came close to possession during a crisis that followed conversion; she was tormented by fears that her supposed regeneration was false, that "there was no saving grace wrought in her."[133] In 1684, James Fitch, minister at Norwich, Connecticut, sent Increase Mather an account of this unnamed young woman, recently assaulted by the Devil. The victim was "descended of very Godly parentage" and had "feared the Lord from her childhood," had undergone conversion, and so had been admitted to full communion with the church at Norwich. Recently, however, she had been

> most violently assaulted and vexed with Diabolicall sugestions, in a most blasphemous maner, especially in the time of religious dueties, so that her Phancy, cogitation, and memory were hurried and captivated by the Evill one.

Fitch decided that "she was [as] neer to a being possessed, as could be, and yet escape." He joined her father and other relatives in a private fast, but this did no good. All day long, the young woman claimed, "Satan mockt at the prayers, and helde before her minde

129 Cotton Mather, *Memorable Providences,* p. 2.
130 Samuel Willard, "A Briefe Account," pp. 12–13.
131 John Whiting to Increase Mather, 10 June 1682, *Collections of the Massachusetts Historical Society,* 4th ser., 8 (1868): 466.
132 Cotton Mather, "Another Brand Pluck't Out of the Burning," in George L. Burr, ed., *Narratives of the Witchcraft Cases,* p. 310.
133 James Fitch to Increase Mather, 1 July 1684, *Collections of the Massachusetts Historical Society,* 4th ser., 8 (1868): 475.

most blasphemous images, and Atheisticall misrepresentations of God and the things of God."[134]

The young woman "concluded [that] there had never been any thing of saving grace wrought in her, and despaired that it would be." In other words, she believed that her conversion had been a delusion.[135] The "poor dejected soule" in Fitch's charge does not appear to have revealed these fears until after the "assault" began, but she may well have doubted her conversion for some time. In common with those who became possessed, the woman at Norwich was torn between innocence and guilt: on the one hand, she was clearly convinced of her own spiritual inadequacy; on the other, she wanted to blame Satan for the "blasphemous images" that came into her mind. She came close to resolving this contradiction by seeing her "Phancy, cogitation, and memory" as "captivated by the Evill one." Yet in this case the fusion between Satan and self never became complete. Significantly, Fitch ended the woman's misery by convincing her, in a private consultation, that God was willing to forgive her sins; this enabled her to overcome her obsession with culpability. Fitch helped her to reenact the moment of conversion in which she had sensed Christ's mercy. Immediately, "she felt . . . a gospell peace and composure bearing rule in her heart" and had continued ever since "in a greater degree of firme composure than before she was thus buffeted."[136]

Other factors also inclined a disproportionate number of young women toward possession. Anthropologists argue that possession tends to occur within the least powerful constituent groups of a given society: powerless individuals, usually women, use possession to achieve public attention and (albeit temporary) social prestige.[137] This is certainly borne out by the distribution of cases in New England, where possession appealed to those with least social status: women and the young.[138] Possession not only offered young women

134 Ibid., p. 475.

135 Ibid., p. 475.

136 Ibid., pp. 475–6.

137 See Vincent Crapanzano and Vivian Garrison, eds., *Case Studies in Spiritual Possession* (New York, 1977), esp. pp. xi–xii, and I. M. Lewis, *Ecstatic Religion: An Anthropological Study of Spirit Possession and Shamanism* (Middlesex, England, 1971), esp. chaps. 3 and 4. For other anthropological and psychological studies of possession, see Carol Karlsen, *The Devil in the Shape of a Woman*, p. 337 n21, and A. R. Tippett, "Spirit Possession as it Relates to Culture and Religion: A Survey of Anthropological Literature," in John Montgomery, ed., *Demon Possession: A Medical, Historical, Anthropological, and Theological Symposium* (Minneapolis, 1976), esp. pp. 170–4. See also Joseph Klaits, *Servants of Satan*, 125–126.

138 According to Carol Karlsen's figures, most of the 59 female demoniacs whose ages are known were between 10 and 30 years old, with a concentration in the 16–25 range (Carol Karlsen, *The Devil in the Shape of a Woman*, pp. 223–4).

a temporary escape from social insignificance, but also enabled them to voice their anger and resentment toward New England society without having to acknowledge fully their dissatisfaction. As demoniacs, they shouted and screamed, cavorted and grimaced, insulted and disobeyed their parents or guardians, blasphemed against God and derided his ministers. Yet the possessed could blame their illicit behavior on the Devil within. Because their words and actions were apparently involuntary, they could challenge and violate cultural norms with impunity. These were godly young women, unwilling to engage in overt and self-conscious criticism of the social order. Possession allowed them to sidestep acknowledgment of their discontent by acting as the puppets of Satan.[139]

The assumption that women as daughters of Eve were especially vulnerable to the insinuations of the Devil further explains the preponderance of women among demoniacs. The Puritan view of woman as a moral entity was double-edged. On the one hand, divines lauded women as "helpmeets." They taught that the inculcation of self-disciplined virtue should take place primarily within the family and that household heads could not achieve this end without the assistance of their female partners. Women provided spiritual sustenance for their husbands and moral education for their children. As such, they constituted a "necessary good." On the other hand, despite their exaltation of godly womanhood and of the crucial roles played by individual women as mothers and wives, Puritans did not eschew the traditional notion that

Karlsen points out that demoniacs often had personal histories that further weakened their position within colonial society. Many of the possessed in 1692, for example, were orphans with little or no dowry and so dismal marital prospects. These young women had good reason to fear that their social status would not improve as they grew older and married (*The Devil in the Shape of a Woman*, pp. 226–30).

139 This paragraph is much indebted to Carol Karlsen's interpretation of possession in chap. 7 of *The Devil in the Shape of a Woman*. According to Karlsen, possession mediated between a woman's rage at her place in the world and her reluctance to engage in overt protest, which might result in her being branded as a witch. By identifying their dissatisfaction as diabolical intrusion, young women such as Elizabeth Knapp could acknowledge illicit impulses within themselves without conceding them any legitimate status. Possession symbolized both "female resistance" and "female capitulation" (p. 251). Both Karlsen and I see possession as a response to deeply felt but illicit and unwanted sensations: possession enabled the transgressive self to limit personal responsibility for the transgressive impulse. We also agree that the anxieties causing possession related to the demoniac's future prospects, whether in this world or the next. However, Karlsen argues that the "profound conflict" underlying possession related primarily to "immediate and ... personal" gender dissatisfaction rather than theological issues (pp. 235–6). I would argue that spiritual anxiety was equally significant as a cause of possession; and that theological issues can be "immediate and ... personal" in nature.

women were more prone to sin than men. After all, taught the ministers, it was Eve who gave way to Satan and who then seduced Adam. In discussing the case of Margaret Rule, Cotton Mather remarked that women were more likely to become possessed "for that reason, for which the old serpent made, where he did, his first address."[140] According to Mather, biology as well as history suggested that the Devil would approach women rather than men. Mather claimed that devils often gained access to men and women via "the Malignant Vapours and Humours of our Diseased Bodies." This helped to explain, in his opinion, why "one Sex may suffer more Troubles of some kinds from the Invisible World than the other," implying that female menstruation offered a regular and frequent avenue for diabolical intrusion.[141] Godly women who internalized these assumptions about the female propensity toward evil would have been more likely than men to perceive themselves as fit vessels for the Devil. Because they absorbed the gender stereotypes promulgated by religious doctrine, women became demoniacs in disproportionate numbers.

Possession, in providing a medium through which individuals could confront evil within the self, was an experience with which most New Englanders, male and female, could sympathize, at least to some degree. An occurrence of diabolical possession was as much a communal as it was an individual event: the ordeal of possession could always be guaranteed to create a public sensation. In 1671, the people of Groton gathered in "amazement and astonishment" to watch Elizabeth Knapp in her fits. So many townsfolk crammed into the house, complained Willard, that "there was no roome for privacye." These people were not just spectators: they questioned Elizabeth closely about her encounters with the Devil and on occasion helped to restrain her.[142] When the young woman at Norwich became distracted, the pastor and her father and other relatives gathered to observe a private fast. Later, the entire congregation at Norwich planned a day of fasting and prayer on her behalf.[143] The possessed boy at Tocutt also aroused intense public interest. On one occasion, over twenty people crowded into the room where he was praying to God for mercy.[144]

Townsfolk were doubtless drawn to such scenes by the drama of

140 Cotton Mather, "Another Brand Pluck't Out of the Burning," p. 313. For a full discussion of Puritan ambivalence toward women, see Carol Karlsen, *The Devil in the Shape of a Woman,* chap. 5.
141 Cotton Mather, "Another Brand Pluck't Out of the Burning," p. 313.
142 Samuel Willard, "A Briefe Account," pp. 11, 14.
143 James Fitch to Increase Mather, p. 475.
144 Cotton Mather, *Memorable Providences,* p. 69.

possession, by a prurient interest in the demoniac's sufferings, and by sheer curiosity. But there was a further and more profound reason for public interest. Local communities became gripped by the spectacle of the possessed because it spoke to a central spiritual issue: liability for sin. The struggles of the victim struck a resonant chord in the community at large: through another's possession, people could experience vicariously the emotional release provided by temporary fusion of self and Satan. For the afflicted individual and for the community as a whole, this was a profoundly cathartic process.[145] Most people managed to resolve issues of liability without resort to possession: some participated in group discussions such as that attended by Michael Wigglesworth; others addressed such issues on their own in private spiritual exercises. Many, it should not be forgetten, located blame without any hesitation or anxiety. Yet even for New Englanders who were not personally inclined to problematize issues of sin and guilt, cases of diabolical possession acted as a reminder that these issues were indeed fundamental and potentially disturbing.

The ambiguity in Puritan teaching that drove a small minority of colonists to the extreme of claiming possession may have led others to the practice of countermagic. This brings us to a significant (and ironic) link between Puritan theology and the assumptions underlying magic. Ambiguity and inconsistency in clerical statements about liability enabled people to look outside themselves for the cause of their troubles. This was crucial for those believers who resorted to countermagic as a defense against affliction. When layfolk reacted to misfortune by blaming and then counteracting a suspected witch, their ministers were horrified and reminded them that opening their hearts to God and repenting for their own spiritual failings was a much more effective route to recovery. Yet the ministers' own portrayal of the world as a dangerous place troubled by an active Devil might encourage even godly people to focus on external sources of evil and so to protect themselves by resorting to magic, particularly since some members of the religious community did not believe that magic was itself diabolical. Just as anxieties arising from predestinarian theology drove layfolk to exper-

145 See John Demos, *Entertaining Satan*, pp. 128–31, and Carol Karlsen, *The Devil in the Shape of a Woman*, p. 231. Demos argues that possession "made a uniquely gripping spectacle" because onlookers experienced "many levels of resonance." According to Karlsen, New England possession was first and foremost "a cultural performance, a symbolic religious ritual through which a series of shared meanings were communicated."

iment with magical divination, so confusion about moral responsibility may have encouraged colonists to use countermagic.

That many godly layfolk divided responsibility for evil between Satan and their own corrupt nature is particularly significant. Individuals who turned to countermagic did not necessarily absolve themselves of all blame for their condition. Some may have combined Puritan rituals of repentance with magical rituals of retaliation. Mary Sibley, the church member who commissioned a urinecake from Tituba and her husband, may well have engaged in devotional exercises as well as magical experiments, just as her pastor Samuel Parris combined a regimen of fasting and prayer with the ruthless prosecution of all suspect witches in and around Salem Village. In deciding to use countermagic, layfolk did not have to renounce religious strategies: the flexibility of Puritan doctrine concerning issues of liability enabled believers to avoid a stark choice.

Other facets of Puritan teaching further promoted the notion that evil originated beyond as much as within the self. The system of church discipline in early New England, which emphasized each member's responsibility to watch over the behavior of fellow saints, would have encouraged those already inclined to identify sin as lurking around them rather than emerging from within themselves. The clergy's characterization of hostile outsiders such as Indians and sectarians as servants of the Devil also fostered a conception of evil as alien and external.[146] On the other hand, ministers taught that God allowed Indians and sectarians to assault the northern colonies because the people of New England had sinned and deserved to suffer; although they recognized the need for mutual surveillance, clerics also insisted that the most effective form of discipline was self-discipline. Yet for all their determination to place self-examination at the very center of Puritan spirituality, the clergy provided layfolk with a moral structure that could and did sustain countermagic.

These characteristics of Puritan teaching help to explain why godly people turned to countermagic and why ministers had to argue with such vehemence that countermagic was unacceptable. People who used countermagic assumed that suffering was the result of affliction by outside forces and could be removed through magical ritual. Ministers insisted that the sources of sin and suffering were internal, as were the means for resisting them. Yet at the same time they maintained a tradition of externalizing evil and

146 See Chapter 6 for an extended discussion of these attitudes and their implications for the Salem witch crisis.

so inadvertently promoted recourse to countermagic. Clerical statements about Satan's role in the generation of human sin and suffering could result in the very abdication of responsibility ministers claimed to abhor. Ironically, a particular reading of diabolic mythology could encourage some godly colonists to use magical rituals that others condemned as being diabolical.

4

SINFUL CURIOSITY

ASTROLOGICAL DISCOURSE IN EARLY NEW ENGLAND

Is it not Vanity and Impiety, to attempt the Revelation of Secret Things that belong to the Lord our God?

Christian Lodovick, *The New-England Almanack for the Year of Our Lord Christ 1695*

In 1652, John Cotton, one of the most prominent of the first-generation New England ministers, fell ill and died. That momentous event coincided with the appearance of a comet over New England, a coincidence that did not go unnoticed. The records of the First Church in Boston, where Cotton had served for almost twenty years, contain the following account of the comet's timely course.

> Theire was a starr appeared on the 9th of the 10th month 1652. darke and yet great for Compasse. with Long blaze dim also to the east. and was quicke in the motion. and every night it was less and less till the 22 of the same month and then it did no more appeare, it being the night before our Reverend Teacher mr John Cotton Died, the Greatest starr in the Churches of Christ that we could heare of in the Christian world for opening and unfolding the counssells of Christ to the Churches. and all the Christian world did receive light by his Ministry.[1]

Godly New Englanders paid careful attention to heavenly movement. They believed that celestial bodies were among the subordinate agencies to which God had delegated the task of expressing and carrying out his will: not only did the stars exercise a direct influence over the weather, farming conditions, and physical health, but extraordinary phenomena such as comets and eclipses warned sinners of divine displeasure and urged them to spiritual reawakening. But although Puritans recognized a moral significance in

1 "Records of the First Church in Boston," *Publications of the Colonial Society of Massachusetts,* 39 (1961): 9–10.

heavenly movement, they generally refused to specify that significance, which, they believed, lay beyond the limits of human comprehension. Like other wonders, comets and eclipses were usually assumed to carry a negative message, but the specific content of that message was inscrutable. The official Puritan standpoint regarding astral inquiry was ambivalent: Puritan theologians had no quarrel with astronomy, the study of heavenly movement, or even with astrologers' use of astronomical information to predict natural events, but they would not countenance the application of that information to human affairs or the precise details of divine judgment.

Astrological belief in a direct causal linkage between celestial and terrestrial phenomena bore a close resemblance to belief in image magic, the occult process whereby changes in one object could be reproduced in another related object. This was not the only connection between magic and astrology. Magical divination and astrological prognostication each supplied information about the future that enabled people to negotiate their world more effectively. In terms of both physical process and social value, there was a close affinity between astrology and magic. Not surprisingly, then, Puritan criticism of astrology ran parallel to the Puritan campaign against magic. Controversy over the use of astrology intensified during the last quarter of the seventeenth century, the same time that ministers launched their attack on magic. Thus, there was a chronological as well as a substantive correlation between these two debates.

Astrology attempted to explain all terrestrial events, both natural and human, in the context of astral movement. Whereas astronomers were concerned with heavenly movement itself, astrologers studied the influence celestial bodies exercised over events on earth. The weather, farming conditions, physical health, social interactions, and political events were all believed to be affected by the motion of the stars. According to astrological lore, the influence of the stars was based on a direct link between the four qualities possessed in varying mixtures by the seven known planets, the four elements from which all terrestrial things were made, and the four humors that ruled the human body.

Planetary qualities:	heat	cold	dryness	moisture
Terrestrial elements:	fire	earth	air	water
Bodily humors:	phlegm	melancholy	blood	choler

Astrologers studied the seven planets (Sun, Moon, Saturn, Jupiter, Mars, Venus, and Mercury) as they moved relative to the earth, each other, and the twelve signs of the zodiac. The interplay of planetary and zodiacal influence formed a complex network of permutations that shaped events on earth. *Natural astrology* studied the implications of astral movement for weather conditions, agriculture, and medical treatment; *judicial astrology*, which was much more controversial, predicted human affairs. Contemporaries also distinguished between astrology and *meteorology:* the latter concerned itself with extraordinary celestial phenomena such as comets, blazing stars, rainbows, lightning, thunder, and apparitions in the sky. But in practice, many individuals who called themselves astrologers – and were referred to as such by clients and critics – also studied "meteorological" occurrences.[2]

Astrologers helped their clients to coordinate their actions with heavenly movement by compiling annual forecasts, called *prognostications.* They also provided *horoscopes,* which detailed the planetary configurations for specific points in time. There were three kinds of horoscope. *Nativities* showed the position of the stars at the moment of an individual's birth and could be used to predict the course of his or her life. *Elections* were used to calculate the times at which the stars would favor particular activities, from marrying to sowing seeds to starting on a journey. And finally, astrologers could answer any personal question whatsoever by looking at the position of the stars at the exact moment when the question itself was asked; these were called *Horary Questions.*[3]

Astrologers in early modern England ranged from village cunning folk, who used astral lore to tell fortunes and locate stolen goods, to professional physicians, who found the most appropriate times for medical treatment by casting horoscopes, to full-time consultants, who ran flourishing businesses in the cities and seaports. The knowledge employed by these practitioners varied in its degree of sophistication from the most esoteric of academic treatises to an orally transmitted moon-lore. What united these different levels of inquiry was the fundamental assumption that celestial movements were reflected in earthly events.[4]

2 For an overview of meteorology in the early modern period, see S. K. Heninger, Jr., *A Handbook of Renaissance Meteorology, with Particular Reference to Elizabeth and Jacobean Literature* (Durham, N.C., 1960), chaps. 2 and 3.

3 See Keith Thomas, *Religion and the Decline of Magic* (1971; Middlesex, England, 1973), pp. 338–9, and Bernard Capp, *English Alamanacs, 1500–1800* (Ithaca, N.Y., 1979), p. 16.

4 For detailed discussion of astrology in medieval and early modern England, see Keith Thomas, *Religion and the Decline of Magic,* chaps. 10, 11, and 12, and Bernard Capp, *English Almanacs.* See also Carroll Camden, "Elizabethan Astrological Medicine," *Annals of Medical History,* new ser., 2 (1930): 217–26; Carroll Camden, "Astrology in Shakespeare's Day," *Isis,* 19 (1933): 26–73; Marjorie Nicholson, "English Almanacs and the New Astronomy," *Annals of Science,* 4 (1939): 1–33;

The Christian church had always been critical of astrology, especially when it was used to predict human behavior. Medieval theologians attacked astrologers for offering an explanation of earthly events that conflicted with and diverted attention from the power of God. They condemned the notion that heavenly movement determined human actions as undermining free will. Astrologers were not slow to defend themselves and sought to justify their activities within a broad Christian framework. The stars, they argued, were secondary causes and, as such, merely instrumental: God could overrule them whenever he pleased. They accepted the theological argument that extraordinary celestial phenomena were signs sent by God, often warning of divine displeasure. According to astrologers, the study of heavenly movement glorified God's creation and reinforced religious faith. Many Christians found these arguments persuasive and managed to reach some kind of compromise between religious principle and astrological inquiry. Astrology's reputation as a sophisticated intellectual system and the ease with which the study of astral movement could be incorporated into natural science facilitated its general acceptance.[5]

Christian attacks on judicial astrology renewed in intensity and bitterness during the Reformation. English astrology underwent a revival in intellectual circles during the latter part of the sixteenth century, due in large part to a new interest in applied science. This

Moriz Sondheim, "Shakespeare and the Astrology of His Time," *Journal of the Warburg Institute,* 2 (1939): 243–59; Hugh Dick, "Students of Physic and Astrology: A Survey of Astrological Medicine in the Age of Science," *Journal of the History of Medicine and Allied Sciences,* 1 (1946): 300–15; Hardin Craig, *The Enchanted Glass: The Elizabethan Mind in Literature* (New York, 1950); Marjorie Nicolson, *The Breaking of the Circle: Studies in the Effect of the "New Science" upon Seventeenth-Century Poetry* (Evanston, Ill., 1950); Paul H. Kocher, *Science and Religion in Elizabethan England* (San Marino, Calif., 1953), esp. chap. 10; Genevieve Miller, "A Seventeenth-Century Astrological Diagnosis," in Edgar Ashworth Underwood, ed., *Science, Medicine and History: Essays in the Evolution of Scientific Thought and Medical Practice Written in Honor of Charles Singer,* 2 vols. (New York, 1953), II: 28–33; S. K. Heninger, Jr., *A Handbook of Renaissance Meteorology;* Don Cameron Allen, *The Star-Crossed Renaissance: The Quarrel about Astrology and Its Influence in England* (1941; New York, 1966); Peter French, *John Dee: The World of an Elizabethan Magus* (London, 1973); Derek Parker, *Familiar to All: William Lilly and Astrology in the Seventeenth Century* (London, 1975). For the earlier history of astrology, see Lynn Thorndike, *A History of Magic and Experimental Science,* 6 vols. (New York, 1923–58), and Theodore Wedel, *The Medieval Attitude toward Astrology, Particularly in England* (New Haven, Conn., 1920). Charles Mercier, *Astrology in Medicine* (London, 1914), provides a straightforward guide to astrological medicine.

5 The controversy over astrology in medieval and early modern England is described by Bernard Capp, *English Alamanacs,* pp. 131–44; Keith Thomas, *Religion and the Decline of Magic,* chap. 12, esp. pp. 425–35; and Don Cameron Allen, *The Star-Crossed Renaissance.* See also Richard Kieckhefer, *Magic in the Middle Ages* (New York, 1990), chap. 6, esp. p. 128.

revival coincided with the emergence of a Puritan movement within the reformed church. Puritan evangelists were particularly hostile to astrological inquiry. As staunch providentialists, they believed that God was inherently mysterious and his will utterly inpenetrable; from their perspective, astrology's claim to foreknowledge was both ridiculous and blasphemous. Astrological inquiry was also suspiciously "popish" in character and consequently offensive to the Puritan sensibility: the signs of the zodiac were endowed with human qualities and thus potentially objects of idolatry; the dominion which these signs exercised over different parts of the human body was alarmingly reminiscent of the saints' responsibility for various diseases.[6]

Puritan hostility toward astrology was not due solely to theological considerations: professional rivalry also played a crucial role. The growing popular appeal of astrology in late sixteenth-century England coincided with the process of religious reformation.[7] As Protestant ministers relinquished supernatural powers exercised by their Catholic predecessors on behalf of parishioners, people may well have found a substitute in the services offered by magicians and astrologers. Certainly, the reformed church had great difficulty in persuading its flock to make do without the kind of power that priests, magicians, and astrologers could offer. Puritans were particularly unequivocal in their rejection of such powers and so felt especially threatened by the seductive claims of cunning folk and astrologers.[8]

Thus, a combination of professional and theological impulses drove Puritans to attack astrology. Yet Puritans themselves were extremely interested in the providential significance of heavenly movement and appreciated the difficulties involved in suppressing judicial astrology without discouraging more acceptable branches of astral science. The flipside of this dilemma was that it was difficult to foster an interest in celestial phenomena without encouraging astrology in general. The same kind of tension existed between the Puritans' interest in supernatural incidents they believed to be providential and their specific disavowal of magic as an infringement

6 See Keith Thomas, *Religion and the Decline of Magic,* pp. 435–40.

7 According to Thomas, the popularity of astrology in England rose markedly toward the end of the sixteenth century, just as the impact of the Reformation began to be felt throughout the kingdom. A lull, or at least plateau, in interest characterized the 1620s and 1630s, during which time a revival of ritual under the auspices of Archbishop Laud coincided with a Catholic mission that began in the 1620s. Recourse to astrology increased again during the revolutionary period (Keith Thomas, *Religion and the Decline of Magic,* esp. pp. 341–2, 248–9).

8 See Keith Thomas, *Religion and the Decline of Magic,* chaps. 10 and 11, and Bernard Capp, *English Almanacs,* pp. 20–1, 141–2.

of God's rightful authority. In New England, the orthodox attitude toward astrology was ambiguous. On the one hand, the ministers and their allies, preoccupied with the providential dimensions of their errand into the wilderness, were eager to promote awareness of extraordinary heavenly movement. On the other hand, they fought hard to circumscribe that interest and roundly condemned all forms of judicial astrology. In sermons, treatises and astrological almanacs, a paper war was waged in seventeenth-century New England over the rightful bounds of astrological inquiry.[9]

New England pastors were concerned that their congregations should understand exactly which parts of astral science were theologically acceptable. On 8 February 1656, Jonathan Mitchell, the minister at Cambridge, gave a sermon on the meaning of God's declaration in Genesis 1:14 that the stars were "to be for Signes."[10] Mitchell began by dismissing the notion that the word "Signes" indicated nothing more than constellations: God was referring to "their use [rather] than their frame or figure." Mitchell also rejected the possibility that the stars were intended as "Signes" only insofar as their motions could be used to calculate the time, seasons, and tidal movement. God, Mitchell argued, had a further use for heavenly bodies: the stars indicated when to undertake "many Civill Actions and affairs," including "plowing, sewing, planting, pruning, gathering, reaping" and "taking physick at fit times of the yeare."

> And this appointment of the Lord is his great favour to man, that though he shall not know particular future events (that were not good nor fit for him to know) yet he shall know so much in generall as may guide him in his work and Actions, wherein he may serve and wait upon the providence of god from time to time.

9 For other discussions of early American astrology, see George L. Kittredge, *The Old Farmer and his Almanack* (1904; Cambridge, Mass., 1920); William Stahlman, "Astrology in Colonial America: An Extended Query," *William and Mary Quarterly,* 13 (1956): 551–63; Herbert Leventhal, *In the Shadow of the Enlightenment: Occultism and Renaissance Science in Eighteenth-Century America* (New York, 1976), chap. 1; Marion Stowell, *Early American Almanacs: The Colonial Weekday Bible* (New York, 1977); and Jon Butler, *Awash in a Sea of Faith: Christianizing the American People* (Cambridge, Mass., 1990), chap. 3. Leventhal focuses on the eighteenth century, whereas Kittredge is concerned mainly with late eighteenth-century and early nineteenth-century almanacs. Stowell's study focuses on the almanac as a form of literature. Butler's chapter on "Magic and the Occult" contains valuable astrological material relating to the middle and southern colonies.

10 Jonathan Mitchell, "Continuation of Sermons upon the Body of Divinity, 1655–8" (Massachusetts Historical Society), 8 February 1656.

Mitchell, then, welcomed the use of natural astrology to better understand physical processes such as farming and the influence of the moon upon "Bodily Humours." Such knowledge provided men and women with "generall" rather than "particular" information about "future events" and so did not infringe upon "the providence of god." This was, he argued, "a most worthy, excellent and most commendable Science."

But Mitchell, in common with other New England ministers, harbored many reservations about judicial astrology, the application of astral science to human affairs. Any action that involved a moral decision depended not upon the stars, he advised, but upon human will and, ultimately, divine providence. The use of heavenly movement to predict events contingent upon human will was "vain, presumptuous and groundlesse." Mitchell reminded his congregation that human affairs depended on "the providence and free-pleasure of god (which it were blasphemous to say is determined by the Government of the Starres)." God certainly made use of secondary causes, but did so "with wonderful Liberty and variety, so that how he will please to use and improve and apply the 2d causes to this or that effect is foreknown only to Himself." If the stars did exercise any influence over human events, the nature of their influence was beyond human comprehension, "and so no grounds or certaine prognostications of such things [could] be made by them." Mitchell conceded that extraordinary phenomena such as major eclipses and comets did relate to human affairs: God sent them as "warning to men of His terrour and Judgements" and "men ought to be awakened by them." Yet Mitchell warned that any specific interpretation of such phenomena was unwarrantable: God's will was inherently inscrutable and any attempt to explicate that will was just as inherently blasphemous.

The appearance of comets or other extraordinary celestial phenomena often prompted clerical statements. In these statements, as in Mitchell's sermon, ministers urged layfolk to focus on the "generall" implications of such occurrences and warned against "particular" interpretation. When a comet appeared over the northern colonies in 1664, Samuel Danforth responded with *An Astronomical Description of the Late Comet or Blazing Star*. Danforth's pamphlet concluded with "A Theological Application" in which he reminded his audience that the Bible described comets as "Portentous and Signal of great and notable Changes."[11] Past experience

11 Samuel Danforth, *An Astronomical Description of the Late Comet or Blazing Star* (Cambridge, 1665), p. 16. To support this assertion, he referred to Joel 2:30,31; Luke 21:25; and Acts 2:19,20.

taught that comets were "many times Heralds of wrath to a secure [complacent] and inpenitent World."[12] The warning, however, always came "with an implicite reservation for Gods altering and revoking his threat[e]ned dispensations upon repentance intervening." Danforth refrained from any specific interpretation of the 1664 comet, but did note its "conjunction with diverse other awful Providences and Tokens of Wrath," including earthquakes, the death of several prominent New Englanders, and a series of early frosts. The "Blazing Star," Danforth declared, called upon the people of New England "to awake out of security, and to bring forth fruits meet for Repentance."[13]

In two sermons occasioned by another comet, which appeared in 1680, Increase Mather also warned that such "Signs" were often "tokens of God's anger" and that "men ought to Hear the Voice of God in Signal Providences, especially when repeated and Iterated."[14] New Englanders had cause to fear that "sweeping Judgements" were at hand: the comet had been sent by God to impress those unabashed by recent plague, fire and tempest.[15] Mather urged his congregation to repent and reminded "those that do profanely contemn such signal Works of the most High" of the warning in Psalm 28: "Because they regard not the Workes of the Lord, nor the Operation of his hands, He shall destroy them, and not build them up."[16] The comet was clearly a warning, but it was important, Mather cautioned, not to be too "particular and positive in Interpretations of things of this nature."[17]

> When a fearful Sight appears in heaven, which the whole World cannot but take notice of, now to make a particular and absolute determination that such a place, or such a person, [or] such a Judgement, is certainly intended thereby, is too much boldness.

The specific meaning of this "Latter Sign," Mather declared, should be left "unto God and Time to discover."

Increase Mather and other New England clergymen faced a dilemma: they were anxious that layfolk should not attempt specific interpretations of natural phenomena such as comets and eclipses, since this was to diminish the mystery of divine providence; yet

12 Ibid., pp. 16–17.
13 Ibid., p. 19.
14 Increase Mather, *Heaven's Alarm to the World* (Boston, 1682), p. 14; *The Latter Sign Discoursed Of* (Boston, 1682), p. 6.
15 Increase Mather, *Heaven's Alarm*, pp. 23–4.
16 Increase Mather, *The Latter Sign*, p. 22.
17 Increase Mather, *Heaven's Alarm*, pp. 16–7.

they did not want nature to be stripped of its supernatural significance. In 1683, Mather published a treatise entitled *Kometographia*, the purpose of which was to persuade "the ordinary sort of Reader" that nature could be understood only in supernatural terms.[18] Mather admitted that not all New Englanders agreed with this view. Some argued that since comets had a natural cause, there could be "no speaking voice of Heaven in them, beyond what is to be said of all other works of God." Yet Mather insisted "that many things which m[ight] happen according to the course of nature, [were] portentous signs of divine anger, and prognosticks of great evils hastening upon the world." Thunder, lightning, hail, rain, earthquakes, and comets were all "from natural causes," yet sometimes acted as "signs of God's holy displeasure."[19] Mather argued in *Kometographia* that celestial phenomena were "not only signal but causal" of natural calamities such as droughts, caterpillars, tempests, floods, and sickness.[20] But he rejected the claim that human as well as natural events could be predicted from careful observation of heavenly movement. If "Wars, Commotions, Persecutions, Heresies, the Death of Princes, Changings, and overturnings in the World" often followed the appearance of comets, such heavenly occurrences were "only signal and not causal of such events."[21] Mather lamented "the curiosity and presumption of Judicial Astrologers," who undertook "peremptorily to Prognosticate, what the particular things are, (yea, and the places and persons concerned in them) that shall come to pass after such Configurations and Planetary Aspects." Such predictions were usually shown to be "false and foolish," wherein "God delight[ed] to baffle Judicial Astrologers."[22]

Charles Morton, the minister at Charlestown, Massachusetts, also distrusted those who used extraordinary phenomena such as comets and eclipses to predict specific disasters. Morton held that the primary end of such phenomena was "to raise admiration in the minds of men, . . . to convince us how little we know of the Universe,

18 Increase Mather, *Kometographia* (Boston, 1683), Introduction, p. 2. See Robert Middlekauff, *The Mathers: Three Generations of Puritan Intellectuals, 1596–1728* (New York, 1971), esp. pp. 139–43. Increase Mather, argues Middlekauff, was afraid that contemporary scientific inquiry would diminish awareness of God's power; he sought to reassert the centrality of divine mystery. "Natural explanations sufficed for limited purposes, but for genuine understanding, the final resort had to be to piety" (p. 143). See also Perry Miller, *The New England Mind: From Colony to Province* (Cambridge, Mass., 1953), pp. 438–9.

19 Increase Mather, *Kometographia*, pp. 18–19.

20 Ibid., pp. 132–3.

21 Ibid., p. 133.

22 Ibid., pp. 140–1.

and So to magnifye the Creator."[23] Charles Morton's *Compendium Physicae,* a textbook for the natural sciences adopted by Harvard College in the late 1680s, exemplified Puritan ambivalence toward astrology. Morton had attended Wadham College, Oxford, between 1649 and 1652, at a time when Wadham was the center of experimental science at Oxford. After completing his studies there, he preached in Cornwall and London, opened a dissenting academy in Stoke Newington, a suburb of London, and then crossed the Atlantic to Massachusetts in 1686 at the invitation of the First Church at Charlestown. Morton compiled the *Compendium Physicae* around 1680 and brought the manuscript with him in 1686; it was adopted by Harvard soon after his arrival in the colony and continued to be used as a college text until the late 1720s.

Morton's *Compendium Physicae,* which proclaimed the values of experimental science, affirmed that the stars exerted an influence over "other bodyes," as was "manifest both by Scripture, reason, and Experience." According to Morton, the influence celestial bodies exercised was both direct and indirect. Morton reminded his readers that "Every body by motion and inward fermentations sends forth its Steames of Volatile parts." Planetary "Steames" affected directly "the Air, Meteors, yea Humane bodyes, deseases, etc." They also influenced indirectly "the minds of men" by

> affecting the body, and thereby promoting, or hindering the opperations of the mind.... Therefore it is that we are sometimes Quick, Active, Eager, and at other times Dull, Heavy, Melancholy, according as the Air (that perpetual Ambient Ingredient) is affected by these heavenly Influences.

This influence, direct and indirect, was the basis for astrological inquiry. Morton cautioned that "want of Sufficient Observations to make rational inductions" rendered astrology "very Imperfect and uncertain in its rules." He cited approvingly John Beale's proposal to the Royal Society in London that "a Register [be] kept of all Changes of Weather." This would enable astrologers to predict more accurately through careful observation of prior events and their relationship to astral movement. In other words, "old almanacks were better to be written than new." Morton was convinced that "as to weathers, and temperatures of our bodyes with relation to health or Sickness," much could be learned from the stars "by Good observations of prudent, and Phylosophycal minds." But ju-

23 Charles Morton, "Compendium Physicae," *Collections of the Colonial Society of Massachusetts,* 33 (1940): 93.

dicial astrology (nativities, horary questions, and other calculations "according to the Houses") was not to be taken seriously.[24]

Increase Mather also dismissed judicial astrology as a "fallacious Art." In doing so, he echoed the warnings of other clergymen.[25] Jonathan Mitchell declared in his 1656 sermon that judicial astrology was "not Built upon any Rationall principles or foundations of nature."[26] Thirty-six years later, in *The Wonders of the Invisible World,* Cotton Mather also condemned and derided the "sinful Curiosity" with which "the Prognostications of Judicial Astrology" were "so injudiciously regarded by multitudes among us."[27]

> And altho[ugh] the Jugling Astrologers do scarce ever hit right, except it be in such Weighty Judgements, forsooth, as that many Old men will die such a year, and that there will be many Losses felt by some that venture to Sea, and that there will be much Lying and Cheating in the World: yet their foolish Admirers will not be perswaded but that the Innocent Stars have been concern[e]d in these events.

Judicial astrology was, then, both irrational and blasphemous. It was, wrote Mather, "a disgrace to the English Nation" and "not a little perillous to the Souls of Men" that the "Pamphlets of such idle, futil, trifling Star-gazers" were "so much admired."[28]

Clerical attacks on judicial astrology bore a close resemblance to their fulminations against magic: not only did divination and judicial astrology share an interest in "things secret" that God had "forbidden, and concealed from discovery by lawful means,"[29] but the ministers identified both as the work of the Devil. Mitchell warned his congregation that judicial astrology was "the Devills policie and invention... to draw them from god and His providence and word into an irreligion." Charles Morton suspected that whenever judicial astrologers predicted accurately, "the Divel... had a greater stroak therein than the Art." Using astrology as a snare, the Devil "Animat[ed] these curious impertinents to become perfect wizards, Atheists, Pagans and to think Slight[l]y of God's providence."[30] Information secured via judicial astrology was nei-

24 Ibid., pp. 27–9.

25 Increase Mather, *A Discourse Concerning the Uncertainty of the Times of Men* (Boston, 1697), p. 24.

26 Jonathan Mitchell, "Continuation of Sermons upon the Body of Divinity," 8 February 1656.

27 Cotton Mather, *Wonders of the Invisible World* (1693; Amherst, Wisc., 1862), p. 97.

28 Ibid.

29 John Hale, *A Modest Enquiry Into the Nature of Witchcraft* (1702; Bainbridge, N.Y., 1973), p. 165. See also Samuel Willard, *A Compleat Body of Divinity* (Boston, 1726), p. 17.

30 Charles Morton, "Compendium Physicae," p. 29.

ther natural nor the result of divine revelation. Therefore, argued ministers, it must be diabolical in origin. In a 1689 sermon, Cotton Mather declared that the judicial astrologer was "Cousin-German to a Conjurer" and that his art was equivalent to witchcraft, since all he knew came from the Devil.[31] A decade later, John Hale wrote that the judicial astrologer was informed by "a familiar spirit."[32] Like magical divination, judicial astrology was a form of spiritual apostasy: whether consciously or not, its practitioners and their clients relied upon the services of the Devil.

The ministers' attitude toward astral science required that layfolk make fairly sophisticated distinctions between different kinds of astrological inquiry. Yet doubts abounded among the clergy as to whether layfolk were that discriminating. Similarly, one of their gravest concerns regarding magic was that layfolk sometimes included magical techniques in their otherwise orthodox supernatural armory, thus confounding the godly and the diabolical. Not surprisingly, clerics feared the popularity of astrological experts and their publications in New England. Unfortunately, it is much easier to document the clergy's response to astrology than to gauge the actual appeal of astrological prediction in the northern colonies, but there does survive some direct evidence of astrological activity in seventeenth-century New England.

As noted above, clerics and godly layfolk took a keen interest in extraordinary heavenly movements, but generally described such movements in providential rather than astrological terms. Puritans often characterized eclipses, comets, and other unusual occurrences as portentous, but rarely suggested a causal link between heavenly phenomena and earthly events. When John Cotton became ill in 1652, merchant John Hull recorded in his diary that "A strange comet in the heavens began its motion with [Cotton's] sickness, and ended with his death."[33] The Reverend Samuel Danforth noted in the Roxbury Church records that "There appeared a Comet in the heaven in Orion, which continued its course tow[ar]d the zenith for the space of a fortnight viz. till mr Cottons death."[34] In both descriptions, the precise link between the comet and Cotton's illness was left unspecified, but Hull and Danforth almost certainly understood the comet as God's signal for an event that was laden with significance for the New England community. This perspective is

31 Cotton Mather, *A Discourse on Witchcraft* (Boston, 1689) p. 27.
32 John Hale, *A Modest Enquiry*, pp. 141–2.
33 John Hull, "Diary," *Transactions of the American Antiquarian Society*, 3 (1857): 173.
34 "Roxbury Church Records," in Boston Record Commissioners, *Roxbury Land and Church Records*, 6 vols. (Boston, 1884), VI: 197.

much clearer in the account from the records of the First Church in Boston, quoted at the beginning of this chapter, which described the comet as a fitting symbol for the occasion: after all, Cotton himself was a "starr in the Churches of Christ . . . and all the Christian world did receive light by his Ministry."

Thirty-two years later, in 1684, Peter Thacher, the minister at Milton, Massachusetts, noted in his journal "a great eclipse of the sun," which coincided with another significant death: "this day Mr Rogers, President of Harvard College, died about the time of the suns going out of the eclipse." Thacher's journal entry implies that the two events were connected, although there is no suggestion that one caused the other.[35] Yet not all Puritans believed that heavenly movements were merely "signal." Simon Bradstreet, pastor at New London, Connecticut, recorded in his journal for 1664 that "A great blazing starre appeared in the S: west which continued some monthes." Bradstreet wrote that "the effects appeared much in England, in a great and dreadfull plague that followed the next sum[m]er, in a dreadfull warre by sea with the dutch, and the burning of London the 2d year following." Bradstreet's use of the word "effect" suggests that he did see the "blazing starre" as causal.[36]

Bearing in mind the similarities between divination and astrology, it is hardly surprising that some cunning folk took astrology seriously and read astrological treatises. Katherine Harrison of Wethersfield, Connecticut, boasted to her neighbors that she had read a book by William Lilly, a famous English astrologer.[37] Caleb Powell, a sailor who arrived in Newbury, Massachusetts, toward the end of 1679 and who offered his services as a cunning man to the townsfolk there, claimed to have "understanding in Astrology and Astronomy."[38] Other New Englanders were at least familiar with astrological concepts. In 1692, at the Salem witch trials, Mary Toothaker of Billerica claimed that she had attended witch gatherings where "they used to read many historyes, especially one book that treated of the 12 signes, from which book they could tell a great

35 Peter Thacher, "Journal," in A. K. Teale, *History of Milton, Massachusetts* (Boston, 1887), p. 655.

36 Simon Bradstreet, "Journal," in *New England Historical and Genealogical Society,* 8 (1854): 325.

37 Samuel Willys Collection: Records of Trials for Witchcraft in Connecticut (Connecticut State Library, Hartford), #7, 7 August 1668, testimony of Thomas Waples; and Willys Papers: Records of Trials for Witchcraft in Connecticut (Annmary Brown Memorial, Brown University Library, Providence, R.I.), W–11, 23 September 1668, testimony of Elizabeth Smith.

38 *Records and Files of the Quarterly Courts of Essex County,* 9 vols. (Salem, Mass., 1911–78), VII: 357.

deale."[39] Mary may have seen such a book and was clearly familiar with its purpose.

In 1664, a court sitting at New Haven heard a case that provides an unusually rich and detailed account of one astrologer's pride in his power, a pride matched by the skepticism of his audience. John Browne was brought before the court for "pretending as if he had some art to rayse the divell and acting accordingly": his "art" was that of astrology.[40] Eliakim Hitchcock testified that Browne had come to his house late one night and asked for some food. When he had finished eating, Browne said to Hitchcock, "I have something come into my mind to write . . . prethy helpe me to an inkorne and paper." Hitchcock asked him "what it was he would write," to which Browne replied that "if he should tell him he would not know [understand]." Hitchcock fetched the writing materials and Browne proceeded to write. Then he asked for a pair of compasses, "and haveing them he made a round Circle, and made figures in it, such as [Hitchcock] never saw the like." Browne now asked Hitchcock if he would like to "see the divell raysed." Hitchcock was extremely skeptical and asked what the figures in the circle meant. Browne told him that they referred to "the lords of the 12th house and 2d house etc," terms that Hitchcock "did not understand, never heareing such things before." Hitchcock declared that he did not believe that Browne could use "figures" to raise the Devil, but Browne swore, fittingly, by the stars that he could. He took Hitchcock outside and told him the names of the planets currently in opposition to each other. According to Hitchcock, Browne then pointed to "a place where hung a great deale of indian Corne" and said, "the divell may be there, doe you not see him?" Hitchcock could not see anything. The two men went back inside and Browne threw the paper on which he had drawn the astrological figures into the fire, explaining to Hitchcock that "if he had not done soe, the divell would have come and tore the house downe."

Eliakim Hitchcock's detailed account was corroborated by Nathaniel Hitchcock, Eliakim's brother, who had overheard the dialog from his bed in the next room. Browne himself "granted he was there, and that he had pen and inke and did Cipher but said that the thing he charged him withall about raysing the divell was false." This was not John Browne's first appearance before the New Haven court: he had previously been fined twice for drunkenness. On the

39 Paul Boyer and Stephen Nissenbaum, eds., *The Salem Witchcraft Papers: Verbatim Transcripts of the Legal Documents of the Salem Witchcraft Outbreak,* 3 vols. (New York, 1977), III: 769.

40 Franklin Dexter, ed., *New Haven Town Records,* 2 vols. (New Haven, Conn., 1917), II: 129–31.

first of these occasions, the court had characterized Browne as a "prophaine scorner" and had berated him for his shocking behavior at a recent church meeting: "while his father was acknowledging his evill, that he had not wa[t]ched over him as he should," Browne had walked out of the meeting house, "smileing" as he went. This was, then, a man with a history of "prophaine carriages."[41] The court now warned Browne "of the greatnes of his sin, that he should goe about thus to tempt god," and sent him away "seriously to Consider of his evill." After "some Consideration," Browne returned to "acknowledge his evill, suspecting himselfe that he might [have spoken] more then he now remember[ed]." He admitted "that it was a parcell of folly and madnes in him soe to doe" and promised to be "more watchfull over himselfe, and [his] wayes for the future."

The case of John Browne is significant in several respects. First, Browne's statement that "he had pen and inke and did Cipher" sounds like an admission that he had been using astrological "art," to whatever purpose. Second, unlike Hitchcock, who apparently "did not understand . . . [and] never hear[d] such things before," Browne was familiar with fairly sophisticated astrological concepts and could construct a horoscope. Third, the court evidently saw Browne's offense as serious. And finally, Eliakim Hitchcock's claim that John Browne used astrology to raise the Devil suggests that some New Englanders may have shared or absorbed their ministers' view that astrological knowledge involved some kind of diabolical agency. In 1692, Thomas Brattle, a Boston merchant, reported a widespread rumor that the village of Andover was "much addicted to Sorcery" and "that there were fourty men in it that could raise the Devill as well as any astrologer."[42] Like magicians, astrologers may have been feared as well as valued by their local communities. Katherine Harrison, the Wethersfield fortune-teller who claimed to have read one of William Lilly's astrological volumes, was accused of witchcraft in 1668.

As Eliakim Hitchcock's skepticism suggests, it is extremely dangerous to assume that people paid serious attention to astrological predictions. Yet some New Englanders clearly did. John Winthrop, Jr., made reference in his medical journal to taking a prescribed medicine only after the full moon appeared.[43] Benjamin Lynde, a

41 Ibid., I: 434–35, 490–94.

42 Thomas Brattle, letter to a clergyman, in George L. Burr, ed., *Narratives of the Witchcraft Cases*, p. 181.

43 John Winthrop, Jr., "Medical Journal, 1657–69" (Massachusetts Historical Society). Winthrop had a keen interest in the occult: he transported an enormous alchemical library to America and may have been the author of several alchemical

magistrate of Salem, Massachusetts, noted in his diary entry for 1718 that one of his workers began to mow the bushes on a Monday, "in the last quarter of the moon."[44] Such fragments of evidence can only tantalize, but a fuller sense of the importance of astrology to some colonists emerges from a commonplace book that belonged to the Reverend Seaborn Cotton of Hampton, New Hampshire.[45] The first entries, made when Cotton was a student at Harvard in 1651, were literary extracts. After the young cleric married and settled at Hampton, blank spaces in the book were filled with theological notes, church records, community births, marriages and deaths, genealogical information relating to the Cotton family, and a description of Seaborn Cotton's horse trade. John Cotton, Seaborn's eldest son, inherited the book and also wrote in it, continuing his father's genealogical entries and church records. For the most part, the entries in this book offer no surprises, reflecting the duties and interests of a seventeenth-century New England clergyman. There is, however, an exception. Eighteen pages are devoted to two astrological extracts, "The Nature And Disposition Of The Moone In The Birth Of Children" and "Disposition Of The Planets."

The first extract is structured according to a thirty-day lunar cycle and contains four kinds of astrological information, each based on the phases of the moon: the appropriate times at which to conduct various activities, from marrying to buying servants; the likelihood that a dream would be realized; the future awaiting a newborn child; and the timing of medical treatment. For example:

> the 16 day of the moon to buy and sell is good, to tam[e] oxen and other beasts: a dream is not good, after a long tim[e] it shall not com[e] and it shall be harmfull: to take a wife is good: a child borne shall be of long life but he shall be poore, foresworne and accused: a sick man if he change his place he shall live: to let blood is good.

The second extract begins by describing the general characteristics of the seven planets.

> Saturne is the cause of death, dearth & peace, Jupiter is the cause of long peace, rest and Vertuous Living, Sol is the cause of Life, health and waxing, venus is the cause of Lusty love

treatises published in England during the 1670s under the pseudonym Eirenaeus Philaletha (Jon Butler, *Awash in a Sea of Faith,* pp. 75–6).

44 F. E. Oliver, ed., *Diaries of Benjamin Lynde and Benjamin Lynde, Jr* (Boston, 1880), 10 August 1718, p. 6.

45 Seaborn Cotton, commonplace book (New England Historical and Genealogical Society, Boston, Mass.).

> and treachery, mercury is the cause of much speech, mechindize [trade] and sleightes [trickery], Luna great waters and violent floods.

There follows a much more detailed account of the specific influence each planet exercises during the time of its ascendency and over individuals born under that particular planet.[46] For example:

> Sols houre is the worst of all other houres, no man in this houre may do his will save kings and Lordes and that with great strength: who so in this houre entereth battell shall be dead there: who so hath this star to his planet, hath sharp eyes great speech and wicked thoughts in his heart, he is wicked and avaricious neither white nor black but betwixt both, he hath mark in his face or a wound, a wound in his body by fire, and he is right wicked and grudging in his deeds.

These extracts appear in the handwriting of neither Seaborn Cotton nor his son John: they were transcribed by Seaborn Cotton's first wife, Dorothy Bradstreet Cotton.[47] The two extracts came from a seventeenth-century perpetual almanac entitled *Here Beginnyth The Book Of Knowledge Of Things Unknowne,* compiled by a person known only as Godfridus. This was a substantial collection of astrological lore, including a method for long-range weather forecasts, a section describing the significance of thunder according to the month of the year, and a list of unlucky days. Whereas annual almanacs used precise calculations to make predictions for one year, a perpetual almanac contained no computations. Instead, it offered prognostications that could be applied to any time and never required replacement. Godfridus's almanac was extremely popular: it was first printed in England in 1530, was reissued in 1580, and went through no fewer than thirteen editions during the seventeenth century. It was printed in America for the first time in 1760 and reissued in 1767 and 1772. The Cotton or Bradstreet family must have purchased an English copy.

46 Planetary ascendancy was calculated as follows. Each planet ruled one of the days of the week. On Friday, for example, Venus was most powerful and so ruled the first hour of the day. The following hours were governed by the other planets in order of decreasing influence. After the completion of the seventh hour, power returned to Venus and the cycle began again.

47 This identification was the work of Nancy Spiegal, who wrote on the subject of this commonplace book (Nancy Spiegal, "Sowing Seeds, Taking Wives and Being Born: Beginning by the Light of the Moon in Seventeenth-Century New England," senior thesis, Brandeis University, 1984). The identification was made possible by the discovery of Dorothy's signature on a deed at the Essex Institute. Dorothy had signed as witness to a transaction her husband was conducting with their neighbors.

Madame Dorothy Cotton's extracts represent only a small fraction of the original publication. She edited the extracts as she copied, omitting the daily headings for the lunar cycle, many of which were derived from biblical lore,[48] and also those sections dealing with the sacrament. She was evidently unwilling to allow any confusion of scriptural truth and astrological prognostication. The almanac from which she had chosen to copy was overtly judicial and would have offended many Puritans; Dorothy Cotton must have been aware that these extracts were somewhat anomalous in a Puritan minister's commonplace book. Did she edit the extracts so as to enable the inclusion of the material in her husband's book? Or was she trying to reconcile the astrological material with her own conscience? It seems unlikely that she would have copied such lengthy extracts into a tiny book, in which space was precious, if she did not consider the astrological material valuable in some way. Had the extracts been intended as nothing more than a shocking testimony to the dangers of judicial astrology, the religious references would surely have been retained to underscore the evil of such a combination. All in all, it seems likely that Madame Cotton did take this material seriously. It may not be a coincidence that Dorothy was a sister of Simon Bradstreet, the same Bradstreet whose journal asserted a causal link between the "blazing starre" of 1664 and subsequent earthly events. Dorothy and Simon were children of governor Simon Bradstreet by his first wife Anne, the famous poetess.[49] Two of Anne Bradstreet's poems, "The Four Humours" and "The Four Elements Of Man," address topics relating to astrology. It may be that Dorothy and Simon inherited their interest in astrology from their mother.[50]

A much clearer indication that astrology did appeal to a significant constituency in early New England is the evident popularity of astrological almanacs. The almanac, sometimes called an *ephemeris,* was the principal vehicle for the circulation of astrological information. Cotton Mather remarked in 1683 that these annual publications came "into almost as many hands as" the bible itself.[51] The almanacs produced in seventeenth-century Massachusetts constituted four-fifths of all printed secular literature. Those printed in

48 For example, "The first day Adam created"... "The second day Eve made"... "The third day Caine borne"... "The fourth day Abel borne." The birthdays of biblical figures were believed to confer good or bad luck, according to the moral character of the given figure.

49 *New England Historical and Genealogical Register,* 8 (1854): 312.

50 *The Works of Anne Bradstreet* (Cambridge, Mass., 1967), pp. 18–50.

51 Cotton Mather, *The Boston Ephemeris, an Almanack for the Year of the Christian Aera 1683* (Boston, 1683).

British America during the colonial period as a whole outsold all other books combined, religious and secular. Since imported books had only a limited circulation, and since North America had no newspaper until 1704, the almanac was unquestionably the most widely read nonreligious printed matter in seventeenth-century New England.[52]

Almanacs contained three kinds of information: astronomical data, astrological predictions, and other reference material on matters of local and general interest. All almanacs contained month-by-month tables that listed the times of sunrise and sunset, the quarters of the moon, the sign of the zodiac in which the moon was positioned at noon of a given day, and the changing positions of the planets in the zodiac. Most almanacs also included information unrelated to astronomical or astrological matters. The calendar itself was an important piece of information and many New Englanders used almanacs as diaries. Almanacs often listed the times and places of local courts and fairs. Sometimes they included a chronology of memorable events in the history of New England or even the whole of Christian world history; a table showing the reigns of the Kings and Queens of England; or brief geographical descriptions of the world, of "several chief places in America," or of local highways and roads.[53] Benjamin Harris's *Boston Almanack* for 1692 included a series of formats for legal documents: "A Bill of Obligatory with a Penalty," "A General Release," "An Indenture for an Apprentice," "A Letter of Attorney," and "A Will."[54] But most of the space in early New England almanacs was devoted to astronomical and astrological material.

Whereas the compilers of seventeenth-century English almanacs provided an ambitious range of political, social, and religious predictions, early New England almanacs tended to be descriptive

52 Marion Stowell, *Early American Almanacs,* pp. ix–x, 13–14. Bernard Capp estimates that, in mid-seventeenth-century England, one family in three bought an almanac each year (Bernard Capp, *English Almanacs,* p. 23).

53 For examples of New England chronologies, see Samuel Danforth, *An Almanack for the Year of Our Lord 1648* (Cambridge, Mass., 1648), and Nehemiah Hobart, *An Almanack of Coelestial Motions for the Year of the Christian Era 1673* (Cambridge, Mass., 1673); for a world chronology, see Daniel Leeds, *An Almanack and Ephemerides for the Year of Christian Account 1693* (Philadelphia, 1693). For tables showing the reigns of English monarchs, see Daniel Russell, *An Almanack of Coelestial Motions for the Year of the Christian Aera 1671* (Cambridge, Mass., 1671), and Benjamin Gillam, *The Boston Ephemeris, an Almanack for the Year 1684* (Boston, 1684). For geographical descriptions, see Daniel Russell, *An Almanack of Coelestial Motions for the Year of the Christian Aera 1671;* Daniel Leeds, *An Almanack and Ephemerides for the Year of Christian Account 1693;* and Daniel Leeds, *An Almanack for the Year of Christian Account 1697* (New York, 1697).

54 Benjamin Harris, *Boston Almanack for the Year of Our Lord God 1692* (Boston, 1692).

rather than interpretative in their accounts of heavenly movement.[55] There was a straightforward reason for that restraint. Until 1675, Harvard College possessed the only printing press in the colonies; almanac compilers were mostly Harvard graduates and respected members of the Puritan community. These publications accordingly emphasized astronomy over astrology.[56] Harvard almanacs reflected the intellectual as well as spiritual credentials of their editors and sometimes included well-informed essays on astronomical subjects, such as circular movement in the heavens, the use of planetary movement to calculate the time, and recent discoveries made possible by the invention of the telescope.[57]

Harvard compilers did make occasional excursions into astrological territory. Israel Chauncy's almanac for 1663 included an essay on the disasters portended by eclipses:

1 Eclipses in the fiery Triplicity Menace sharp Wars, mutuall grudges between the more Noble and Ignoble, Pestilent diseases, Famine, etc, especially in those places subject to the Sign Eclipsed.

2 When there shall happen an Eclipse of either Luminary in the Earthly or Humane Triplicity, there follows scarcity of fruits and Corne . . .

3 In the airy and humane Triplicity, it presageth Famine and Pestilent Diseases, and commonly brings Tempestuous and stormy Winds.

4 In the watery Triplicity it shews the death of common and ignoble people, daily motions of Wars by Sea and Land, etc. . . .[58]

Jeremiah Shepard's *Ephemeris of the Coelestial Motions* for 1672 discussed the nature and qualities of the twelve signs of the zodiac in

55 For a discussion of political and social prognostication in English almanacs, see Bernard Capp, *English Almanacs,* chaps. 3 and 4. For the incorporation of astrology into the English apocalyptic tradition, see ibid., pp. 164–79.

56 English theologian William Perkins had recently underscored Puritan hostility toward astrology in *A Resolution to the Countryman, Proving It Utterly Unlawfull to Buy or Use Our Yearely Prognostications* (Cambridge, England, 1618). Perkins criticized astrologers for distracting their audience from a providential understanding of events. As David D. Hall points out, Perkins's critique and the debate it stimulated in England "was background to the making of the first New England almanacs" (David D. Hall, *Worlds of Wonder, Days of Judgment: Popular Religious Belief in Early New England* [New York, 1989], p. 59).

57 Thomas Shepard, *An Almanack for the Year of Our Lord 1656* (Cambridge, Mass., 1656); Samuel Cheever, *An Almanack for the Year of Our Lord 1660* (Cambridge, Mass., 1660); and Nathaniel Mather, *The Boston Ephemeris, an Almanack of Coelestial Motions of the Sun and Planets, with Some of the Principal Aspects for the Year of the Christian Aera 1685* (Boston, 1685).

58 Israel Chauncy, *An Almanack of the Coelestial Motions for the Year of the Christian Aera 1663* (Cambridge, Mass., 1663).

relation to the four elements.[59] But Chauncy and Shepard were exceptions: most Harvard compilers shunned interpretative speculation. Comets, wrote Alexander Nowell in 1665, did "oft proceed preternatural effects," but only the misguided would "desire to be certified of the event" or "presume prophetically to specificate from general truths."[60] John Sherman, minister at Watertown, Massachusetts, remarked in the introduction to his almanac for 1674 that "the too great predominancy" of Mercury and Mars portended "no small evil," but declined to engage in more detailed discussion of the portent.[61] Two years later, Sherman refused to interpret planetary movements for the coming year: "What these signify I shall not say, but leave their Effects to Gods providence and mans observance."[62] In 1677, Sherman reminded his readers that the stars were never "intended for windows, through which poor mortals might peep and steal a look into the sacred Decrees, and secret Counsels of the most High."[63]

If New England almanacs eschewed prognostication, they did share with their English counterparts an extremely religious tone. Seventeenth-century English almanacs included a large quantity of religious material. English compilers used almanacs both to instruct their readers in the rudiments of faith and to engage in religious polemic. Not surprisingly, the doctrinal content of this material was much more heterogeneous than in the colonies.[64] The frontispieces of colonial almanacs frequently included scriptural quotations sanctioning the study of heavenly movement. For example:

> Psalms 8.3,4. When I consider thy Heavens: the work of thy Fingers, the moon and the stars which thou hast ordained: what is man that thou art mindful of him? and the Son of man, that thou visitest him?[65]

59 Jeremiah Shepard, *An Ephemeris of the Coelestial Motions for the Year of the Christian Epocha 1672* (Cambridge, Mass., 1672). See also John Foster, *An Almanack of Coelestial Motions for the Year of the Christian Epocha 1679* (Boston, 1679).

60 Alexander Nowell, *An Almanack of Coelestial Motions for the Year of the Christian Epocha 1665* (Cambridge, Mass., 1665). John Josselyn quoted Nowell's essay in his *Account of Two Voyages to New-England* (Boston, 1672).

61 John Sherman, *An Almanack of Coelestial Motions, viz. of the Sun and Planets, with Some of Their Principal Aspects, for the Year of the Christian Aera 1674* (Cambridge, Mass., 1674).

62 John Sherman, *An Almanack of Coelestial Motions of the Sun and Planets, with Some of Their Principal Aspects, for the Year of the Christian Aera 1676* (Cambridge, Mass., 1676).

63 John Sherman, *An Almanack of Coelestial Motions of the Sun and Planets, with Some of Their Principal Aspects, for the Year of the Christian Aera 1677* (Cambridge, Mass., 1677).

64 See Bernard Capp, *English Almanacs*, pp. 144–63.

65 John Sherman, *An Almanack of Coelestial Motions of the Sun and Planets, with Some*

Almanac editorials often contained remarks that reflected the author's Puritan sensibility. In 1666, Josiah Flint's edition condemned the use of "Heathenish Language" in astrological discourse. Flint was referring to the use of pagan names for the planets and calendar months."[66] Twenty years later, in 1686, Samuel Danforth's *New-England Alamanack* apologized for bowing to "cruel Customs Laws" in retaining "The Names Impos[e]d by old Idolatry On Months and Planets."[67] Some almanacks included brief essays or compositions with a religious theme. The almanac for 1646 explained the Puritan position on holy days.[68] Nathaniel Chauncy's 1662 edition included a poem that associated the signs of the zodiac with Christian motifs:

> Thy RAM for clothing is the lamb of God:
> Thy OX, unmuzled that thy Corne out-trod:
> Thy TWINS, the Loving Saints Communion is.
> Thy CRABBS, thy turning back from whats amisse:
> Thy LYON eke, thy fortitude and Faith:
> Thy VIRGIN undefiled worship hath:
> Thy BALLANCE Justice is, the wicked's terrour,
> Thy SCORPION, is Truth's Antidote 'gainst errour:
> Thine ARCHER to the last end's aiming right:
> Thy HORNED GOATES, against the World to fight:
> Thy WATERMAN Sobriety would breed.
> Thy FISH with Temperance thy selfe should feed.[69]

Cotton Mather himself compiled an almanac in 1683 and affirmed in his editorial that "the Readers of an Almanack" could also be "Christian Men."[70]

During the last quarter of the seventeenth century, some compilers became much more willing to engage in interpretative speculation. For several decades, Harvard's printing monopoly had ensured the conformity of New England almanacs to Puritan teaching on the legitimate bounds of astral science. But that monopoly

of Their Principal Aspects, for the Year of the Christian Aera 1677 (Cambridge, Mass., 1677).

66 Josiah Flint, *An Almanack of Astronomical Calculations of the Most Remarkable Celestial Revolutions etc. Visible in Our Horizon, for the Ensuing Year 1666* (Cambridge, Mass., 1666).

67 Samuel Danforth (1666–1727), *The New-England Almanack for the Year of Our Lord 1686* (Cambridge, Mass., 1685).

68 Samuel Danforth (1626–74), *An Almanack for the Year of Our Lord 1646* (Cambridge, Mass., 1646).

69 Nathaniel Chauncy, *An Almanack for the Year of Our Lord 1662* (Cambridge, Mass., 1662).

70 Cotton Mather, *The Boston Ephemeris, an Almanack for the Year of the Christian Aera 1683* (Boston, 1683).

came to an end in 1675, when John Foster (author, printer, and engraver) set up the first Boston printing press and began to produce almanacs independently of Harvard. Some of these almanacs were explicitly astrological in their content. The 1676 edition included a diagram to show which parts of the body were controlled by particular signs of the zodiac.[71] Seventeenth-century medical practice relied heavily on astrological assumptions, particularly the dominion of the signs of the zodiac over different parts of the human body. The "Anatomy" or "Man of Signs" was a standard feature in English almanacs and could be used to determine astrologically appropriate medical treatment for various bodily ailments. The Anatomy was probably the only reference tool available to many nonprofessional physicians and was accessible even to the semiliterate. Foster himself was an amateur doctor. The inclusion of the Anatomy was an important innovation, but medical astrology was not actually heterodox: Morton's *Compendium Physicae* recognized that heavenly movements affected the human body, although he doubted the ability of astrologers to gauge that influence accurately. Even Foster's almanacs avoided any form of judicial prognostication and the content of most New England almanacs prior to the late 1680s remained largely astronomical. Samuel Danforth spoke for most almanac compilers when he declared in his 1686 edition that he practiced only "Harmless Astronomy" and "much abominate[d]" judicial astrology.[72]

That consensus came to an end with the appearance of John Tulley's controversial almanac series, beginning in 1687. Tulley was born in England and settled in Connecticut; he was not a Harvard graduate. Tulley's almanacs described in copious detail the implications of heavenly movement for the weather, medical treatment, and human affairs. The month-by-month tables included weather predictions for specific dates. Tulley informed his readers that these predictions were "guessed at from the Signs, Planets and their Aspects." He warned that "ancient Writers ha[d] been often deceived about the Weather" and "desire[d] a charitable censure concerning it."[73] In the 1687 edition, an essay called "Prognostica Georgica: Or The Countryman's Weather-Glass" showed how general observation of the heavens could be used to predict impending weather:

71 John Foster, *An Almanack of Coelestial Motions for the Year of the Christian Aera 1676* (Boston, 1676).
72 Samuel Danforth (1666–1727), *The New-England Almanack for the Year of Our Lord 1686* (Cambridge, Mass., 1685).
73 John Tulley, *An Almanack for the Year of Our Lord 1688* (Boston, 1688).

> Redness of the Skie in the morning, is a token of Wind, or Rains, or both: if the circles that appear about the Sun, be red and broken, they portend wind: if thick and dark, Winds, Snow, or Rain.[74]

The 1690 edition detailed the kinds of weather portended by rainbows, thunder and lightning.[75] In 1692, Tulley discussed the effect of the planets and their aspects on the weather.[76]

Tulley's publications gave credence to both medical and judicial astrology. In his 1689 edition, Tulley described which parts of the body were governed by particular signs of the zodiac and which of these signs were favorable for bleeding.[77] Each of his almanacs from 1693 to 1697 included a Man of Signs. The 1694 edition contained a description of when to purge and bleed.

> Good to let the Sanguine blood when the Moon is in Pisces. To let the Cholerick blood when the Moon hath her course in Cancer or Pisces. To let the Melancholly blood when the Moon is in Libra, Aquarius or Pisces. To let the Phlegmatic blood when the Moon is in Sagitarius or Aquarius.

Tulley also advised his readers to "cut the Hair of the Head or the Beard, when the Moon is in Libra, Sagitarius, Aquarius or Pisces," to "Set, Sow Seeds, Graft and Plant, the Moon being in Taurus, Virgo, or in Capricorn," to "Shear Sheep at the Moon's increase," and to "kill fat Swine for Bacon the better to keep their fat for boiling about the Full Moon." This same edition included an astrological discourse on the French king's nativity and an essay relating the year's eclipses to human affairs. Tulley explained that the particular significance of an eclipse depended upon the zodiacal house in which it occurred: the ninth, for example, signified "Religion," the tenth "all sorts of Magistracy, and Officers in Authority."[78] Tulley's series, then, not only provided specific astrological predictions relating to the weather and medical treatment, which ministers suspected on grounds of accuracy, but also included judicial prognostications, which they condemned as a usurpation of divine authority.

It is no coincidence that these overtly astrological almanacs first appeared during the late 1680s. In 1662, the General Court of Massachusetts had issued an order stipulating that all material had

74 John Tulley, *An Almanack for the Year of Our Lord 1687* (Boston, 1687).
75 John Tulley, *An Almanack for the Year of Our Lord 1690* (Boston, 1690).
76 John Tulley, *An Almanack for the Year of Our Lord 1692* (Cambridge, Mass., 1692).
77 John Tulley, *An Almanack for the Year of Our Lord 1689* (Boston, 1689).
78 John Tulley, *An Almanack for the Year of Our Lord 1694* (Boston, 1694).

to be submitted to the government for licensing before it could be published. The order was repealed in 1663, but then reenacted in 1665.[79] Thus, even after Harvard's printing monopoly came to an end in 1675, official censorship ensured that almanac compilers remained cautious in their choice of material. But after the establishment of the Dominion in 1686, New England was ruled by Edmund Andros, who was an Anglican. Anglicans were more relaxed about astrology than were Puritans,[80] and so the Andros regime, followed by the confusion of revolution and the eventual establishment of a more tolerant form of government, provided a favorable environment for the production of more openly astrological almanacs. Tulley was extremely sensitive to the predilections of officials in the Dominion government. In his 1688 edition, he included Anglican saint days in the calender and referred to Oliver Cromwell as a "Tyrant" in a chronology of significant historical events.[81] Yet Tulley was not writing exclusively for Anglicans and royalists. The hallmark of his series was its overtly astrological format; Tulley retained that format long after the royalists' departure from Massachusetts. Indeed, his almanacs became even more astrological in content during the early 1690s. Tulley must have sensed a popular demand for such material. Changes in the political climate made it possible for him to respond to that demand much more fully than would have been conceivable in the days of the Harvard monopoly and strict Puritan censorship.

Year after year, Tulley continued to produce his astrological almanacs, presumably because they were popular and sold well. Other compilers followed Tulley's example and began to include weather predictions, medical advice, and even judicial prognostication in their editions. Harvard graduate Henry Newman's *Ephemeris* for 1690 gave general information on the weather likely to result from particular planetary configurations.[82] In 1691, Newman incorporated specific weather predictions into the monthly tables themselves, as did the *Boston Almanack* for 1692, the *New-England Almanack* for 1700, and Daniel Leeds's series for Philadelphia and New York through the 1690s.[83] Leeds, formerly a Quaker but now

79 Nathaniel Shurtleff, ed., *Records of the Governor and Company of Massachusetts Bay in New England*, 5 vols. (Boston, 1853–4), IV (pt. 2): 62, 73, 141.

80 See Keith Thomas, *Religion and the Decline of Magic*, pp. 438–9.

81 John Tulley, *An Almanack for the Year of Our Lord 1688*.

82 Henry Newman, *Harvard's Ephemeris, or Almanack, Containing an Account of the Coelestial Motions, Aspects, etc., for the Year of the Christian Empire 1690* (Cambridge, Mass., 1690).

83 Henry Newman, *News from the Stars, an Almanack Containing an Account of Coelestial Motions, Aspects, etc., for the Year of the Christian Empire 1691* (Boston, 1691); Benjamin Harris, *Boston Almanack for the Year of Our Lord God 1692* (Boston,

an Anglican, included in his almanacs charts showing which parts of the body were governed by particular signs, a tabular equivalent of the Anatomy.[84] He also gave the astrologically appropriate times for gathering herbs. "Tis the Opinion of Astrological Physicians," wrote Leeds in 1697, "as also my belief, that all Herbs are stronger, and of greater virtue, if gathered when the Planet that governs them is well fortified."[85] Leeds's 1693 Philadelphia almanac contained a selection of past predictions made by judicial astrologers across the Atlantic.[86]

This trend was not without its opponents. During the years that followed the appearance of Tulley's almanac series, ministers attacked "the prognostications of Judicial Astrology" and lamented that these were "so injudiciously regarded by multitudes among us."[87] As noted above, the apparent concentration in the 1680s and 1690s of clerical attacks on magic and astrology may be partly an illusion created by the expansion of the printing industry during the latter part of the century; but ministers do seem to have become more hostile toward astrology and magic as their fears for the moral future of New England deepened. Clerical attacks on judicial astrology may have been prompted more specifically by the appearance of overtly astrological almanacs during the last quarter of the century.

Yet for all the ministers' supposed influence within the community, it was only when certain branches of astrology came under attack from rival almanac compilers that criticism began to have an impact. Almanacs had a larger circulation than did theological works, and so almanac editorials were more effective as instruments for influencing public opinion than published sermons or theological treatises. Once almanac compilers themselves began to attack their rivals' excesses on scientific and theological grounds, their colleagues had no choice but to take notice. In 1694, Harvard astronomer William Brattle's almanac "purposely omitted" any

1692); Samuel Clough, *The New-England Almanack, for the Year 1700* (Boston, 1699); Daniel Leeds, *An Almanack and Ephemerides for the Year of Christian Account 1693*, *An Almanack for the Year of Christian Account 1694* (New York, 1694), *An Almanack for the Year of Christian Account 1695* (New York, 1695), *An Almanack for the Year of Christian Account 1696* (New York, 1696), *An Almanack for the Year of Christian Account 1697*, and *An Almanack for the Year of Christian Account 1698* (New York, 1698).

84 For Leeds's change in religious affiliation, see Marion Stowell, *Early American Almanacs*, p. 66.

85 Daniel Leeds, *An Almanack for the Year of Christian Account 1697*.

86 Daniel Leeds, *An Almanack and Ephemerides for the Year of Christian Account 1693*.

87 Cotton Mather, *Wonders of the Invisible World*, p. 97. See also Cotton Mather, *A Discourse on Witchcraft*, p. 27; Increase Mather, *A Discourse Concerning the Uncertainty of the Times of Men*, p. 24; and John Hale, *A Modest Enquiry*, pp. 141–2.

reference to "the weather and other Astrological Predictions." According to Brattle, these were "very Arbitrary and fallible," serving "onely to Delude and Amuse the Vulgar."[88] In the following year, an almanac compiled by physician Christian Lodovick launched a blistering attack on John Tulley's use of astrology. Lodovick's editorial offered "some seasonable Cautions against certain Impieties and Absurdities in Tulley's Almanacks, giving a truer Account of what may be expected from Astrological Predictions."[89] According to Lodovick, Tulley was guilty of both "Vanity and Impiety" in having attempted "the Revelation of Secret Things that belong to the Lord our God." The "direct tendency" of such predictions was clear:

> to withdraw Persons from a holy Reliance in God's Will and Providence, and to precipitate the minds of such as are lovers of specious Novelties, into a sinfull love of that Soul-bewitching Vanity of Star-Prophecy, commonly called Astrology, the foundations of which are meer Chimaeras.

Lodovick was particularly shocked by Tulley's discussion of the French king's nativity, which he condemned as "Impious . . . and Irrational." The "Fictions of Astrologers, about the Vertues and Qualities of the twelve Zodiacal Signs" were "but groundless Speculations," and the "imaginary Circle" on which the zodiac was based had been "but at pleasure (for Doctrine sake) Geometrically divided into 12 signs." Tulley's "conceipts of the Dominion of the Moon in Man's body, as it passeth under the 12 signs," along with his advice about purging and bleeding, were, declared Lodovick, "things disclaimed by the greatest part of Physicians."[90] On one point, Lodovick's position was rather ironic. Like Brattle, he argued that weather predictions based on heavenly movement were "meerly Conjectural," yet he included weather predictions in his own month-by-month tables. Lodovick may have been courting the godly in his editorial and yet responding to public demand in the almanac itself.

The next year, Tulley defended himself against Lodovick's at-

88 William Brattle, *Almanack of the Coelestial Motions, Aspects, and Eclipses, etc., for the Year of Our Lord God 1694* (Boston, 1694).

89 Christian Lodovick, *The New-England Almanack for the Year of Our Lord Christ 1695* (Boston, 1695).

90 Lodovick did offer nonastrological medical advice underneath each monthly table. For example: "For the Yellow Jaundice. Take one dram of Castle-soap, or of some other soap (the older the better), dissolved in warm Milk, sugared, once or twice a day. Or, boil 2 or 3 ounces of Hempseed in Milk, drink it warm, renewing it, if need, for some dayes."

tack.[91] He claimed that the astrological account of the French king's nativity had been included against his will. He assured his readers that he would not have sanctioned the inclusion of any material which he "did really apprehend or think might be displeasing to God, whatever it were to man." Tulley claimed that the various predictions contained in his almanacs were compiled "according to the several Rules to each of them prescribed by the Authors of these Arts; which Arts for many years ha[d] been and still [were] practised and allowed of in England." His weather predictions were based on "the common Rules of Meteorology." Yet Tulley admitted that such predictions were as likely "to fail, as to hit right." The reason Tulley gave for the unreliability of astrological predictions indicated a change in his editorial style:

> For the only Wise and All-knowing God that Created the Heavens and the Earth, and the Sun and Moon and Stars, may and many times doth so order it, that all Signs shall fail, as well upon other accounts, as this about the Weather, and therefore as I have said heretofore, I expect a Charitable censure concerning it.

Tulley had indeed remarked in his 1688 editorial that astral science was not always dependable, but the providentialist context in which he now placed the need for caution represented a dramatic shift in tone. The following year, Tulley again warned that weather predictions and other forms of prognostication were "according to Second Causes and therefore not Infalable, for He that is the first Cause, ordereth all Second Causes according to the Counsel of His own Will."[92]

Tulley's new emphasis on the secondary and dependent nature of heavenly movement was matched by a general caution in his subsequent almanacs. In his 1698, 1699, and 1700 editions, he

91 John Tulley, *An Almanack for the Year of Our Lord 1696* (Boston, 1696).

92 John Tulley, *An Almanack for the Year of Our Lord 1697* (Boston, 1697). A more restrained exchange of views took place in New York almanac literature a few years after the attack on Tulley in Boston. John Clapp's *Almanack for the Year 1697* (New York, 1697) warned against the assumption that God ordained eclipses as "Presages of direful Effects." Clapp reminded his readers that "God alone knows what he has to do with us." Thus, it was best "not from Natural Causes [to] draw unnatural Consequences." Humankind's "lamentable state and condition" gave ample cause "to lament, fear and tremble at [God's] Judgements," without any resort to questionable interpretations of heavenly phenomena. Daniel Leeds responded to this argument in *An Almanack for the Year of Christian Account 1698*. He agreed with Clapp as to "the particular effects of Eclipses being hid from us mortals," but disagreed with the notion that "they have no Effects because they are natural." Like Increase Mather, Leeds believed that natural phenomena could carry supernatural meaning.

offered no Anatomy; in 1701, he gave equivalent information in a nonpictorial form. His final edition in 1702 again had no Anatomy, but did give advice on the astrologically appropriate times for bloodletting. In 1699, Tulley included an essay written by Cotton Mather that drew attention to recent earthquakes and plagues, the darkening of the sun, and strange weather. Mather offered "A General Admonition":

> Expect the speedy arrival of some Further and Greater CHANGES upon the World; and prepare for those Changes, that will come as a Snare upon the Earth. In the mean Time, Let any one Reader of this our Almanack, tell if he can, Whether this year may not bring upon himself in particular the greatest Change that ever befel him? Even that of his Mortality.

This "General Admonition" was notably unspecific, as one would expect from a cleric who had recently attacked judicial astrology. Tulley's inclusion of the essay by Mather was extremely canny: what better way to reaffirm the godly credentials of his almanac series? In these later editions, Tulley still provided the astronomical information that readers could use for astrological purposes, but he now declined to offer specific predictions himself.[93]

Other almanac compilers had also become much more cautious and defensive. Much of the information that enabled astrological prediction could be presented as astronomical data, but the Man of Signs and weather predictions were obviously astrological and compilers became increasingly unwilling to include such material. In his edition for 1700, Samuel Clough insisted that "the times and seasons are in the Hand of God alone, and He charges them as He pleaseth." Clough protested that he offered weather predictions with great reluctance:

> it is against my mind to put any such thing in, but considering the People have been us[e]d to it in the Almanacks of late, I have set it down to gratify those that desire it.[94]

Three years later, Clough again claimed that his inclusion of the Anatomy was a concession to popular demand:

93 John Tulley, *An Almanack for the Year of Our Lord 1698* (Boston, 1698), *An Almanack for the Year of Our Lord 1699* (Boston, 1699), *An Almanack for the Year of Our Lord 1700* (Boston, 1700), *An Almanack for the Year of Our Lord 1701* (Boston, 1701), and *An Almanack for the Year of Our Lord 1702* (Boston, 1702). See also Cotton Mather, *Diary*, ed. Worthington C. Ford, 2 vols. (1911; New York, 1957), I: 276.

94 Samuel Clough, *The New-England Almanack, for the Year 1700.*

The anatomy must still be in
Else th'Almanack's not worth a pin:
For Countrymen regard the sign
As though 'Twere Oracle Divine.[95]

In the aftermath of Lodovick's attack, Tulley and Clough sought to negotiate between orthodox strictures and the demands of the marketplace. According to Clough, the public had become accustomed to the inclusion of overtly astrological material in their almanacs and demanded that this format be continued. But compilers had to exercise caution in responding to such demands: a quarter-century after the end of Harvard's monopoly, "the Hand of God" still hovered, albeit less steadily, over the printing presses of New England.

New England almanac makers offered no deliberate challenge to Puritan orthodoxy. Even those who took an interest in judicial prognostication did not see themselves as the enemies of religion. Astrology was an inclusive system; many of its practitioners and constituents considered its use to be compatible with religious faith. Some colonists who practiced astrology were far from godly: John Browne, for example, was a "prophaine scorner." But others drawn to astrology, such as Dorothy Cotton, were respected members of the godly community. Madame Cotton was the wife of a minister; her brother Simon Bradstreet, who also seems to have believed in the influence of the stars over human events, was himself a clergyman. Bradstreet may have been an anomaly: after all, other New England ministers condemned judicial astrology as diabolical. Yet the popularity of almanac literature in seventeenth-century New England indicates that many layfolk were willing to experiment with an "art" that promised to make the world a more predictable and manageable place. Puritan leaders condemned fortune-telling and astrology as a blasphemy against the mystery of God's design. Yet predestinarian theology, which insisted that men and women could not foresee their own destinies, required a degree of uncertainty about the future that not all believers were able or willing to endure. Fortune-telling and astrological prediction provided an antidote to that uncertainty.

The controversy surrounding astrological inquiry in late seventeenth-century New England should be understood in the context of a broader crisis. It coincided with not only a rising concern within the New England clergy about popular recourse to magic, but also

95 Samuel Clough, *The New-England Kalendar, Or An Almanack for the Year of Our Lord 1703* (Boston, 1702).

the Andros regime's espousal of Anglicanism and a new wave of conversions to Quakerism in the wake of an evangelical tour by Englishman George Keith, who crossed the Atlantic in 1688. Judicial astrology, magical practice, the Andros regime's Anglican tendencies, and the spread of Quakerism each threatened to corrupt the New-English Israel. Hostility toward magic, astrology, and dissent were closely related: together, they represented a surge of orthodox sensitivity to all competing supernatural agencies, whether magical, astrological, or sectarian. Meanwhile, another problem emanating from the supernatural world resolved itself in a manner far from comforting to New England ministers during the last quarter of the century: this related to the credibility of witch trials and affected a broad spectrum of the community, clerical and lay, godly and less than godly. The next two chapters examine the difficulties involved in trying witches as criminals, and the consequences for all concerned.

5

INSUFFICIENT GROUNDS OF CONVICTION

WITCHCRAFT, THE COURTS, AND COUNTERMAGIC

> If any man or woman be a Witch, that is, hath or consulteth with a familiar spirit, they shall be put to death. Exod.22.18. Lev.20.27. Deut.18.10,11.
>
> General Lawes and Libertyes Concerning the Inhabitants of the Massachusetts

In 1661, William Holmes of Marshfield, Plymouth Colony, brought a legal complaint against his neighbor Dina Silvester for declaring in public that Holmes's wife was a witch.[1] Summoned to court, Silvester swore that Goodwife Holmes had recently appeared to her, "about a stones throw from the higheway," in the shape of a bear. In Silvester's opinion, this ability to assume animal form was a sure sign that Goodwife Holmes was indeed a witch. But the magistrates wanted proof of the Devil's involvement in Holmes's transformation; as far as they were concerned, witchcraft was an inherently diabolical phenomenon. The magistrates asked Silvester "what manor of tayle the beare had," presumably hoping for a forked tail. Silvester answered that "shee could not tell, for his head was towards her." The court, frustrated by Silvester's failure to provide any indication of a demonic presence, refused to take her story seriously and found her guilty of defamation. Silvester was

1 Thirty-eight known slander cases in seventeenth-century New England involved an accusation of witchcraft. The plaintiffs in these cases filed defamation suits against individuals who had accused them of witchcraft. The objective was to secure a public retraction of the accusation. Twenty-six of these cases are listed in John Demos, *Entertaining Satan: Witchcraft and the Culture of Early New England* (New York, 1982), pp. 402–9. There were at least twelve other cases, involving the defamation of Jane James (1646, *Records and Files of the Quarterly Courts of Essex Country*, 9 vols. [Salem, Mass., 1911–78], I: 108); [?] Sawyer (f; 1650, ibid., I: 202); Jane Collins (1653, ibid., I: 274); John Godfrey (1664, ibid., III: 120–2; 1669, ibid., IV: 152–5); Susannah Martin (1669, ibid., IV: 129, 133); William Thomson (1676, ibid., VI: 237–8); Elizabeth Hooper (1678, ibid., VI: 387); [?] Philips (f; 1678, ibid., VI: 387); Jane Walford (1648, Nathaniel Bouton, ed., *Documents and Records Relating to the Province of New Hampshire*, 5 vols. [Concord, N.H., 1867–80], I: 38; 1670, ibid., I: 258); and [?] Tope (f; 1674, ibid., I: 304).

required to sign a statement "freely acknowlidg[ing]" that she had "wronged" her neighbor.[2]

Dina Silvester's confrontation with the General Court of Plymouth Colony was not an isolated incident. Throughout the seventeenth century in New England, legal proceedings relating to witchcraft were plagued by the disjunction between official demands for proof of diabolical complicity and popular testimony that failed to mention the Devil. Since the concerns of townsfolk accusing witches were primarily practical rather than theological, one would expect accusers to be less preoccupied with the Devil's involvement than were ministers and magistrates. However, the almost complete absence of references to the Devil in popular testimony points to a dissimilarity in conception as well as agenda. It was in the courtroom that the difference between magical and theological interpretations of witchcraft became most apparent.

Afflicted New Englanders who blamed illness or misfortune on witchcraft often wanted to punish the witch responsible. Some victims used countermagic to identify and injure the malefactor; but others who already thought they knew the witch's identity might turn instead to legal action. These two forms of retaliation were not mutually exclusive: some victims used countermagic successfully against a suspect and then related the experiment in court as evidence against the supposed witch; they hoped to inflict additional, official, and capital punishment.[3] Others may have prosecuted after trying unsuccessfully to harm the suspect by way of countermagic: the failure of a countermagical experiment might be due to the practitioner's incompetence or the target's self-protective skill, and did not necessarily mean that the suspect was innocent.[4] Whatever their reasons for doing so, a significant number of witchcraft victims did seek redress through legal channels. Even omitting the Salem prosecutions, there were at least sixty-one trials for witchcraft in seventeenth-century New England.[5]

Trying a witch, however, involved defining witchcraft. In dealing with witchcraft cases, the courts followed theological principles:

2 Nathaniel Shurtleff and David Pulsifer, eds., *Records of the Colony of New Plymouth in New England,* 12 vols. (New York, 1968), III: 207, 5 March 1660–1.

3 See, for example, Margaret Garrett's testimony against Elizabeth Seager (Willys Papers: Records of Trials for Witchcraft in Connecticut [Annmary Brown Memorial, Brown University Library, Providence, R.I.], W–4, 17 June 1665).

4 See Richard Weisman, *Witchcraft, Magic, and Religion in Seventeenth-Century Massachusetts* (Amherst, Mass., 1984), p. 40.

5 For a listing of cases that went to trial and came to final judgment, see Appendix A. This figure is certainly an underestimate. There can be no doubt that more legal actions occurred than are reported in surviving documents. In particular, there are many gaps in the records of the Massachusetts Court of Assistants, which decided capital cases, including witchcraft.

they wanted proof that the witch was in league with the Devil. Yet most of those who brought complaints against witches made no mention of any external agency, diabolical or otherwise: they apparently believed that the accused acted independently. It seems almost inconceivable that these layfolk had not been exposed to a diabolical view of the crime; indeed, they may have believed on some theoretical level that Satan was involved in witchcraft. But when dealing with witchcraft in practice, their attitude does not appear to have been informed by a theological perspective. Indeed, accusers hardly ever referred to the Devil in their testimony. This made legal conviction extremely difficult. The courtroom became a battleground on which New Englanders contested the meaning of witchcraft; cases involving accusations of witchcraft thus revealed the limits of shared culture in early New England.

In Europe, England, and New England alike, theologians saw witchcraft as a form of heresy: the witch, they believed, had repudiated Christianity and entered the service of Satan; in return for obedience, the Devil perpetrated evil deeds on the witch's behalf. Many layfolk, however, understood witchcraft simply as a misuse of occult power: they emphasized its practical impact, not the agency that made it possible; whether the Devil or any other supernatural being assisted the witch was of peripheral concern. Whereas theologians emphasized diabolical complicity, popular accusations of witchcraft focused on *maleficium* (the doing of evil) and showed little interest in diabolical compact.[6] This disjunction between theological and popular perceptions of witchcraft mattered most when people turned to the legal system for protection against witches. European, English, and colonial courts had to negotiate between these two views of witchcraft and determine what kinds of evidence should justify conviction.

6 Richard Kieckhefer argues that most European villagers who accused their neighbors of witchcraft did so for "essentially practical reasons." They attacked witches as "noxious creatures who were undermining their health and welfare." A minority did mention the Devil, but these deponents "generally left unspecified" the nature of his involvement: they did not allege any ritual or devotional relationship between witch and Devil; the latter appeared in depositions as a shadowy, folkloric figure, not as the focus of an organized cult. Kieckhefer shows that charges of devil-worship arose, for the most part, only in cases adjudicated by ecclesiastical courts. In general, there was a clear correlation between the degree of clerical involvement and the likelihood of diabolical implication in the witches' crimes (Richard Kieckhefer, *European Witch Trials* [Berkeley, 1976], pp. 36–7). See also Alan Macfarlane, *Witchcraft in Tudor and Stuart England* (London, 1970), p. 189, and Keith Thomas, *Religion and the Decline of Magic,* (1971; Middlesex, England, 1973) p. 531. Thomas writes that, "for most contemporaries, the essence of witchcraft was not its affiliation with the Devil, but its power to inflict damage by occult means, acquired or inherited, upon lives, bodies and property."

Medieval legislation against witchcraft had focused on the practical harm perpetrated by witches, but during the early modern period, European laws came to embody the theological view of witchcraft. This change originated in a combination of evangelical fervor and political expediency. Religious reformers, eager to convert and educate the European peasantry, allied with centralizing governments in a campaign to establish control over outlying communities that were as yet virtually autonomous and only nominally Christian. Evangelists identified popular conceptions of magic and witchcraft as the most striking expression of a distinct and thus threatening supernatural tradition. They translated popular witch beliefs into diabolical terms and then set about converting people to their own theological perspective. This attempt to superimpose diabolism on popular tradition became the focus for an international campaign to acculturate the European peasantry.[7]

Wholesale legal reform was crucial to this process of conversion. During the sixteenth and seventeenth centuries, most European countries adopted the inquisitorial system, thereby shifting the initiative in bringing a legal action from accuser to state officials and also removing most restrictions against the use of torture. The courts took suspects and witnesses who saw witchcraft in terms of maleficium rather than diabolical compact and then used torture

7 Recent scholarship has emphasized the role played by evangelism in early modern witch trials. See Robert Muchembled, "Witchcraft, Popular Culture, and Christianity in the Sixteenth Century with Emphasis upon Flanders and Artois," in Robert Forster and Orest Ranum, eds., *Ritual, Religion and the Sacred* (London, 1982), pp. 213–36; Christina Larner, *Enemies of God: The Witch-Hunt in Scotland* (Baltimore, 1981); Marie-Sylvie Dupont-Bouchat, "La Répression de la sorcellerie dans le duché de Luxembourg aux XVIe et XVIIe siècles," in Marie-Sylvie Dupont-Bouchat, Willem Frijhoff, and Robert Muchembled, eds., *Prophètes et Sorciers dans les Pays-Bas: XVIe–XVIIe siècle* (Paris, 1978), pp. 41–154; Robert Muchembled, "Sorcières du Cambresis: L'Acculturation du monde rural aux XVIe et XVIIe siècles," in Dupont-Bouchat, Frijhoff, and Muchembled, eds., *Prophètes et Sorciers*, pp. 155–261; and Jean Delumeau, *Catholicism between Luther and Voltaire*, trans. J. Moiser (London, 1977), pp. 154–74. See also Stuart Clark, "Protestant Demonology: Sin, Superstition, and Society," in Bengt Ankarloo and Gustav Henningsen, eds., *Early Modern European Witchcraft: Centres and Peripheries* (Oxford, 1990), esp. pp. 72–4.

The literature on witchcraft in early modern Europe is extensive. Recent work is reviewed by David D. Hall, in "Witchcraft and the Limits of Interpretation," *New England Quarterly*, 58 (1985): 253–81; H. C. Erik Midelfort, "Witchcraft, Magic, and the Occult," in Stephen Oxment, ed., *Reformation Europe: A Guide to Research* (St. Louis, 1982), pp. 183–209; Christina Larner, *Enemies of God*, chap. 2; and E. William Monter, "The Historiography of European Witchcraft: Progress and Prospects," *Journal of Interdisciplinary History*, 2 (1972): 435–51. For two excellent surveys of this vast subject, see Brian Levack, *The Witch-Hunt in Early Modern Europe* (New York, 1987), and Joseph Klaits, *Servants of Satan: The Age of the Witch Hunts* (Bloomington, Ind., 1985); both volumes have thorough bibliographies.

to extract the kind of evidence that would justify conviction on theological terms. Through the use of coercive techniques and the public reading of forced confessions, the authorities disseminated their own view of witchcraft.[8] As propagandists taught the peasantry to recast their traditions in a Christian mold, popular witch beliefs began to transform during the sixteenth and seventeenth centuries. This in turn enhanced the authority of the early modern state, which claimed to be an instrument of divine will and used Christian ideology to legitimize its actions.[9]

In most European countries, witch trials played an important role in the assertion of political control: the witch was all that a good citizen ought not to be. But in England, the political system was, by contemporary standards, highly centralized and relatively secure, so that there was no reason to launch a major offensive against popular culture. Legal initiative remained in the hands of the accuser and the use of the jury system ensured that the resolution of a legal action against witchcraft reflected popular as much as official belief.[10] English law defined witchcraft as a hostile act rather than as heresy. The witchcraft statutes of 1542 and 1563 made no reference whatsoever to diabolical compact. The statute of 1604 did condemn "covenant[ing] with . . . any evil and wicked spirit," but it rejected the theological view that all forms of magic involved a diabolical covenant: the legislators made a clear distinction between malefic witchcraft and less harmful forms of magic such as divination, for which the penalties were much lighter.[11] Toward the end of the sixteenth century, the courts did become better informed about continental demonology and showed an increasing interest in devil-related evidence. A combination of clerical propaganda and judicial pressure began to affect the content of popular testimony, especially confessions, which by the early seventeenth century often included descriptions of diabolical compact. Yet most deponents still focused on maleficium and insisted on

8 For further discussion of legal reform and the use of torture in early modern Europe, see Joseph Klaits, *Servants of Satan,* chap. 6, and Brian Levack, *The Witch-Hunt in Early Modern Europe,* pp. 63–77.

9 See Christina Larner, *Witchcraft and Religion: The Politics of Popular Belief* (Oxford, 1984), pp. 113–26; and Stuart Clark, "Inversion, Misrule, and the Meaning of Witchcraft," *Past and Present,* 87 (1980): 98–127.

10 This is not to suggest that the judicial process embodied only popular beliefs and concerns. As Clive Holmes points out, witch trials involved "a complex series of transactions between various elite and popular elements" (Clive Holmes, "Popular Culture? Witches, Magistrates, and Divines in Early Modern England," in Steven L. Kaplan, ed., *Understanding Popular Culture: Europe from the Middle Ages to the Nineteenth Century* [New York, 1984], p. 87).

11 The English statutes against witchcraft are available in E. L'Estrange Ewen, *Witch Hunting and Witch Trials* (London, 1929), pp. 15–21.

distinguishing between good and evil magic. In England, there was no fundamental transformation of popular belief.[12]

The legal definition of witchcraft in early modern England was broadly compatible with popular tradition and so facilitated legal process. New England courts, on the other hand, were uniquely ill-equipped to deal with witchcraft cases. The laws passed against witchcraft in the northern colonies were biblically inspired and followed theological principles. Plymouth, Massachusetts, New Hampshire, and Connecticut laws defined a witch simply as "any man or woman . . . [who] hath or consulteth with a familiar spirit [a devil]."[13] Yet New England courts had no legal recourse to torture as a way to extract diabolical evidence from individuals whose perception of witchcraft was at odds with that of the law. Like European courts, they were operating according to laws that did not coincide with the popular view of witchcraft. Unlike European courts, they had no way to bridge the gap between legal prescription and popular belief. Because those who gave testimony in such cases tended to describe witchcraft in terms of maleficium, their evidence rarely justified a conviction. The only occasion on which a New England court was able to secure extensive evidence of diabolical witchcraft was at Salem in 1692; this was also the only known occasion on which the authorities used torture to extract confessions.[14] Of the sixty-one known prosecutions for witchcraft in seventeenth-century New England, omitting the Salem trials, sixteen at most (perhaps only fourteen) resulted in conviction and execution, a rate of 26.2 percent.[15] In Essex, England, the conviction rate between 1560 and 1680 was 44.3 percent; the execution rate was 25.4 percent.[16] For the continent, one recent estimate puts

12 See Keith Thomas, *Religion and the Decline of Magic,* chap. 14, and Clive Holmes, "Popular Culture? Witches, Magistrates, and Divines in Early Modern England," esp. pp. 92–3.

13 John D. Cushing, ed., *The Laws of the Pilgrims . . . 1672 and 1685* (Wilmington, Del., 1977), 1671:4 and 1685:10; Thomas G. Barnes, ed., *The Book of the General Laws and Libertyes Concerning the Inhabitants of the Massachusetts* (1648; San Marino, Calif., 1975), p. 5; John D. Cushing, ed., *Acts and Laws of New Hampshire, 1680–1726* (Wilmington, Del., 1978), p. 205; John D. Cushing, ed., *The Earliest Laws of the New Haven and Connecticut Colonies, 1639–1673* (Wilmington, Del., 1977), p. 83. New Haven colony also based its witchcraft law on scriptural injunction (John D. Cushing, ed., *The Earliest Laws of the New Haven and Connecticut Colonies,* p. 18). In contrast, Rhode Island cited the English law of 1604, which, as noted above, defined witchcraft rather differently (John Bartlett, ed., *Records of the Colony of Rhode Island and Providence Plantations in New England, 1636–1663,* 10 vols. [Providence, R.I., 1856–65], I: 166).

14 See Chapter 6 for a discussion of physical and psychological torture in 1692.

15 Four of the convicted individuals confessed, which made the court's job much easier. If these are omitted, the conviction rate falls to 19.7 percent.

16 At the Essex Assizes, 291 people were accused: 129 were found guilty; 74 were executed (Alan Macfarlane, *Witchcraft in Tudor and Stuart England,* p. 57).

the execution rate at 54.5 percent; the conviction rate was probably higher.[17]

Judicial policy on witchcraft in the northern colonies followed guidelines laid down by two English legal experts, William Perkins and Richard Bernard, both of whom were also divines. During the sixteenth and seventeenth centuries, English writers produced a vast body of literature discussing witchcraft from spiritual, medical, and legal perspectives. These publications represented a broad spectrum of opinion. At one extreme, materialists such as Thomas Hobbes questioned the Devil's very ability to intervene in human affairs on a physical plane. Hobbes rejected as self-contradictory the notion of an incorporeal substance and argued that devils could neither assume bodily form nor occupy a human being. According to Hobbes, the Devil's power over humankind was purely spiritual.[18] A much larger and more widely regarded group of authors did not question the Devil's physical power, but rejected many of the traditions that underlay continental demonology, including the witches' sabbath, on the grounds that they had no biblical foundation. According to these writers, the European image of demonic witchcraft was a hodge-podge of pagan superstition and popish invention.[19] Yet authors such as Joseph Glanvill and Richard Baxter, situated at the opposite end of the spectrum from the materialists, reaffirmed traditional witch beliefs. They sought to refute skeptics by presenting numerous "relations" of supernatural incidents that, according to Glanvill and Baxter, proved conclusively the reality of witchcraft.[20]

A number of English authors focused on the difficulties involved in proving witchcraft as a crime. Medical authorities such as John Cotta stressed the need to distinguish carefully between natural

17 Brian Levack, *The Witch-Hunt*, p. 21. Levack estimates that there were approximately 110,000 witch prosecutions and 60,000 executions. As Levack points out, these figures are conservative compared with many earlier estimates.

18 Thomas Hobbes, *Leviathan* (London, 1651), chaps. 34, 44, and 45. See also Lodowick Muggleton, *A True Interpretation of the Witch of Endor* (London, 1669), and Muggleton, *The Acts of the Witnesses* (London, 1699).

19 See, for example, Reginald Scot, *The Discoverie of Witchcraft* (London, 1584); Samuel Harsnett, *A Declaration of Egregious Popish Impostures* (London, 1603); Thomas Ady, *A Candle in the Dark* (London, 1656); John Wagstaffe, *The Question of Witchcraft Debated* (London, 1669); and John Webster, *The Displaying of Supposed Witchcraft* (London, 1677).

20 Joseph Glanvill, *Saducismus Triumphatus* (London, 1681); Richard Baxter, *The Certainty of the World of Spirits* (London, 1691). Increase Mather was to employ a similar strategy in his *Essay for the Recording of Illustrious Providences* (Boston, 1684). Indeed, Baxter was a friend of Mather, to whom he dedicated his *Glorious Kingdom of God* (London, 1691). For further discussion of both skeptical and affirmative literature, see Keith Thomas, *Religion and the Decline of Magic*, chap. 18.

disease and supernatural affliction. Cotta also argued that confessions should not be admissable in witchcraft cases, since the accused might be ill and suffering from hallucinations.[21] The two most influential studies of witchcraft as a legal problem were William Perkins's *Discourse on the Damned Art of Witchcraft* and Richard Bernard's *Guide to Grand-Jury Men,* published in 1608 and 1627 respectively.[22] Perkins's *Discourse* spearheaded a campaign by Protestant commentators to cleanse witch prosecutions of both "pagan" and "popish" error. Perkins and Bernard wanted to establish a straightforward procedure for trying witches that would rely on a few, unexceptionable criteria. They sought to discredit traditional folk practices such as "ducking": this involved submerging a suspect witch in water to see if she or he floated; many believed that water would refuse to accept a witch, so that buoyancy was proof of guilt. Critics such as Perkins and Bernard argued that there was neither biblical nor scientific foundation for trial by water.[23]

The legal procedure favored by these commentators centered on the need to prove a direct link between the accused witch and the Devil. Unlike John Cotta, Perkins and Bernard argued that confessions should be admissable. However, if the witch did not confess, conviction was justifiable only if two or more reliable witnesses testified to having seen the witch either invoking the Devil or performing deeds which unquestionably relied upon a diabolical agency. There had to be at least two witnesses for each incriminating incident. Circumstantial evidence about illness or misfortune in the aftermath of an argument with the accused, the most common form of evidence against witches on both sides of the Atlantic, did not justify a conviction.[24]

New England ministers were well aware of this procedural literature and played a crucial role in transmitting its recommendations across the Atlantic. Increase Mather, for example, referred to Perkins's strictures against ducking in his *Essay for the Recording of Illustrious Providences.* Mather assured his readers that ducking had "no foundation in nature, nor in Scripture."[25] Magistrates deal-

21 John Cotta, *The Triall of Witchcraft* (London, 1616). See also Meric Casaubon, *A Treatise Concerning Enthusiasme* (London, 1655).

22 For the impact of Perkins and Bernard's work on other seventeenth-century commentaries, see Richard Weisman, *Witchcraft, Magic, and Religion,* p. 99.

23 See, for example, Richard Bernard, *Guide to Grand-Jury Men* (London, 1627), p. 214.

24 Protestant legal experts all over Europe were insistent in their demands for judicial rigor and caution in prosecuting witches. See Stuart Clark, "Protestant Demonology," pp. 75–6.

25 Increase Mather, *An Essay for the Recording of Illustrious Providences,* p. 281. For further discussion of the Mathers' response to this literature and also to the medical works by Cotta and Casaubon, see Robert Middlekauff, *The Mathers:*

ing with witchcraft cases often consulted ministers who were well-read on the subject.[26] But not all magistrates relied on the clergy to keep them abreast of current literature; some did their own research as well. William Jones, deputy governor of Connecticut, was particularly conscientious: he took detailed notes from an unnamed author's description of the correct procedure in witchcraft cases.[27] According to these notes, which Jones seems to have kept for future reference, the author condemned traditional methods for proving guilt, such as ducking suspects in water, forcing them to pick up a hot iron, or putting their hands into scalding water, as "superstitious and unwarantable." Moreover, the testimony of a diviner, "who pretend[ed] to show the face of the witch . . . upheld in a glass," was "diabolicall and dangerous" since "the divill may represent a person inocent."

The text that Jones was using specified seven grounds for examining a witch: "Notoreous defamation by the Comon report of the people"; "death or at least mischiefe" following a curse delivered by the suspect; "personal mischiefe" after a quarrel with the suspect; incriminating testimony provided by another witch; kinship or close association with a "knowne or Convicted" witch; the Devil's mark; and finally, contradictions in the suspect's answers when first questioned. Each of these constituted "ground of suspicion," but none were "sufficient for Conviction or Condemnation." This distinction between grounds for "suspicion" and those for "Conviction or Condemnation" may have been an attempt to placate public opinion by according some legitimacy, albeit limited, to popular tradition.[28] In practice, it probably had quite the opposite effect, since it raised and then dashed public spirits by admitting cases in which there was no hope of conviction.

Having enumerated these categories of "insufficient" evidence, Jones summarized the author's discussion of legitimate grounds for conviction. A court of law, the author wrote, should convict an accused witch only if the suspect confessed, or if two reputable witnesses testified that the accused had either "made a le[a]gue with the Divill" or "don[e] som Knowne practices of witchcraft." In either case, the witnesses must prove either that "the party hath invocated the divill for his help," or that "the party hath entertained a familiar spirit in any forme," or that "the party hath don[e] any accon

Three Generations of Puritan Intellectuals, 1596–1728 (New York, 1971), pp. 155–9.

26 See, for example, the cases of Elizabeth Clawson, Mercy Disborough, and Katherine Harrison, discussed below.

27 Willys Papers, W–38: Grounds for Examination of a Witch.

28 See Richard Weisman, *Witchcraft, Magic, and Religion*, p. 100.

[action] or work w[hi]ch inforc [enforce] the C[ovenan]t wth the divill." This "accon or work" could consist of "show[ing] the face of a man in a glass, or us[ing] inchantm[en]ts or such feates, divineing of things to Come, raising tempests, or Causing the forme of a dead man to appeare, or the like." Ironically, the only admissable evidence likely to be produced by witnesses related to forms of magic townsfolk actually valued: divination, charms, and so on. Witnesses offered such evidence only because it showed the suspect's possession of occult skills that could be used for malevolent as well as benevolent purposes, not because they believed these particular types of magic to be reprehensible. The author whose recommendations Jones was noting so carefully admitted that proving witchcraft was not easy. Yet, the author added reassuringly, the Devil's "Malice towards all men" was such that he often allowed witches to be exposed. Meanwhile, wrote Jones, "the Author warn[ed] Jurors etc not to Condemne suspected persons on bare presum[p]t[i]ons without good and sufficient proofes."

The rigorous standards which New England courts applied in witchcraft cases derived from theological commitment rather than from any lack of enthusiasm for the prosecution of witches. The authorities were well informed about new developments in witchcraft investigation across the Atlantic and encouraged courts to experiment with the latest methods for proving witchcraft. In 1648, when Margaret and Thomas Jones of Charlestown, Massachusetts, were accused of witchcraft, the General Court gave orders that "watching" be used in the investigation. This method, developed by Matthew Hopkins during the English witch hunt of 1645, involved the careful observation of suspects over an extended period of time in the hope that a diabolical familiar would appear. The assembly instructed that "a strict watch be set about [Margaret Jones] every night, and that her husband be confined to a privat[e] roome, and watched also." Fortunately for Margaret and Thomas Jones, no familiar appeared.[29]

Not all witch prosecutions were undermined by problems of evidence. In sixteen cases prior to the Salem witch trials, New England courts felt justified in convicting witch suspects. Four suspects confessed to diabolical witchcraft. Rebecca Greensmith of Hartford, Connecticut, tried for witchcraft in 1662, claimed that she "had had familiarity with the Devil." Greensmith had not yet signed a diabolical covenant, but "the Devil [had] told her that at Christmas

29 Nathaniel Shurtleff, ed., *Records of the Governor and Company of Massachusetts Bay in New England*, 5 vols. (Boston, 1853–4), II: 242, III: 126. See also Matthew Hopkins, *The Discovery of Witches*, ed. Montague Summers (1647; London, 1928), p. 54.

they would have a merry Meeting, and then the Covenant between them should be subscribed." Meanwhile, she had "promised to go with him when he called, which accordingly she had sundry times done." Greensmith also told the court that local witches held "Meetings at a place not far from her house."[30] These sixteen convictions indicate that the courts did sometimes elicit from suspects and witnesses a view of witchcraft consistent with that recognized by colonial laws. New England courts were quite willing to convict if there was direct proof of diabolical allegiance. Yet most of those who gave testimony in witchcraft cases never mentioned the Devil, so that courts had no choice but to acquit. The theological stance of New England laws against witchcraft and the rigor exercised by New England courts in implementing those laws made it extremely difficult to take effective legal action against witches.

The richly documented cases of Elizabeth Clawson and Mercy Disborough illustrate the difficulties inherent in this situation. Clawson and Disborough were tried together in 1692 at Stamford, Connecticut.[31] That spring, Katherine Branch, a seventeen-year-old French servant who lived in Stamford, had begun to suffer strange fits. Katherine worked in the household of selectman Daniel Wescott, an eminently respectable citizen who had represented Stamford in the General Court for several years and was also a sergeant in the local militia. These fits, which terrified Katherine, included "pinching and pricking at her breasts" and "ratling in her throat." Katherine soon became so ill that Wescott sent for a local midwife, Sarah Bates. (Stamford had no resident physician at that time.) Bates thought that the illness "might be from som[e] naturall cause" and advised the Wescotts "to burn feathers under her nose and other menes [means] that had dun good in fainting fits."[32] Katherine, however, claimed that she had been bewitched and named two women, Elizabeth Clawson and Mercy Disborough, as her principal tormenters.[33] Clawson lived near the Wescotts in

30 Increase Mather, *An Essay for the Recording of Illustrious Providences,* pp. 137–8. See also John Whiting to Increase Mather, *Collections of the Massachusetts Historical Society,* 4th ser., 8 (1868): 466–9.

31 For the legal documents relating to these two cases, see Samuel Willys Collection: Records of Trials for Witchcraft in Connecticut (Connecticut State Library, Hartford), #18 through #37; and Willys Papers, W–19 through W–39. See also Ronald Marcus, *Elizabeth Clawson ... Thou Deservest to Dye* (Stamford, Conn., 1976).

32 Willys Papers, W–24, 13 Sept 1692, testimony of Sarah Bates.

33 In addition to Clawson and Disborough, Katherine Branch also accused Mary and Hannah Harvey, Mary Staples, and Goody Miller, all of Fairfield. Miller fled to New York and so could not be brought to trial. Charges against the other three women were dropped once it became clear that there was virtually no

Stamford with her husband Stephen; Disborough, who was also married, lived at Compo, a small community just within the formal boundaries of Fairfield, the county town. When the remedies prescribed by Sarah Bates failed to produce any lasting improvement in Katherine's condition, Wescott concluded that his servant was indeed bewitched and complained to the authorities on her behalf.

On 27 May, a court of inquiry began hearings in the meeting house at Stamford. It soon became clear that there was "a multiplicity of witnesses" against Clawson and Disborough.[34] In addition to Katherine Branch herself, townsfolk from Stamford and the surrounding communities came forward to testify against the two women; they provided a substantial body of evidence incriminating Clawson and Disborough as witches. Yet there was hardly any evidence in these depositions that pointed to a direct link between the accused and the Devil. This placed the court in an extremely awkward position.

Most of the witnesses who appeared before the court of inquiry described quarrels with Clawson and Disborough which had been followed by illness or misfortune; they believed that the accused had bewitched them as a direct consequence of these arguments. Wescott himself testified that he and his wife, Abigail, had argued with Goodwife Clawson over the weight of some flax that she had spun for them. Henceforth, Clawson "took occation uppon any frivoulous matter to be angry and pick a quarrill" with the Wescotts. Shortly after their breach with Clawson, the Wescotts' daughter Johannah "was taken suddenly in the night, schreching [screeching] and Crying out, there is a thing will catch me."[35] The Wescotts suspected that Clawson was responsible for Johannah's affliction and decided to confront her. Daniel Wescott accordingly paid Clawson a visit "and had severall discourses with goody Clawson: about several of her actions: and about [his] girle being Bewitcht."[36] That evening, Johannah "was handled with fitts more violently then shee had bin of late." Wescott did not believe that this was a coincidence.

Many other townsfolk came forward with similar stories. Thirty-three-year-old John Finch claimed to have had "a Considerable difference" with Goody Clawson. Soon afterward, his child "in an eveninge was taken very violently with screaminge and Cryinge . . .

evidence against them save for Katherine Branch's accusation. See Willys Papers, W–39.

34 J. Hammond Trumbull and Charles J. Hoadly, eds., *The Public Records of the Colony of Connecticut,* 15 vols. (Hartford, Conn., 1850–90), IV: 76–7.

35 Willys Papers, W–29, 15 September 1692, testimony of Daniel Wescott. See also Willys Papers, W–29, 12 September 1692, testimony of Abigail Wescott.

36 Willys Papers, W–28, 7 June 1692, testimony of Daniel Wescott.

and so it Continued very wrestless about the space of a fortnight and then died."[37] Mary Newman, also in her early thirties, argued with Clawson and "angry words past betweene them." The next day, three of the Newmans' sheep died suddenly. The Newmans examined the sheep carefully and could not find any natural cause of death. Some of their neighbors concluded that the animals had been "bewicht."[38]

Several witnesses believed that Mercy Disborough could "unbewitch." During the previous summer, twenty-seven-year-old Ann Godfrey "had A sow very sick and said Mercy Cam[e] bye and she called to her and bad[e] her on-bewitch her sow . . . and soon after that her sow was well and eat her meal."[39] John Gamman, Sr., told the court that he had been staying at Compo with his wife and child about five years back when his child became ill suddenly for no apparent reason. Gamman's nephew, Thomas Benit, was convinced that Mercy Disborough had caused the illness and told Gamman "to go and scould at Mercy." When Gamman demurred, Benit "went out and called s[ai]d Mercy and bad[e] her unbewitch his Unkles Child . . . or else he would tear her hart out." According to Gamman, Disborough immediately "came over to the child and stroaked it and s[ai]d god forbad that shee should hurt the child and soon after the Child was well." Both Gamman and Benit believed that Disborough caused as well as removed the affliction.[40]

Disborough was not alone in her ability to "unbewitch." Thirty-nine-year-old Henry Grey had used countermagic against Disborough and now reported the results for use as evidence against her. Witnesses in witchcraft cases often described countermagical experiments in which they had engaged and which, they believed, incriminated the accused. Countermagic was valuable to victims of witchcraft not only as a form of independent retribution, but also as a means to procure evidence against a witch suspect for use in a court of law. Some people may have resorted to countermagic with that specific objective in mind. In early June, Henry Grey appeared before the court of inquiry with a remarkable story about the recent illness of his heifer. Grey had quarreled with the Disboroughs on a number of occasions and so suspected that Mercy had bewitched the animal. He decided to verify his suspicions by

37 Willys Papers, W–32, 28 October 1692, testimony of John Finch.
38 Samuel Willys Collection, #20, 30 June 1692, testimony of Mary Newman. See also Willys Papers, W–33, 6 June 1692, testimony of Thomas Benit and Henry Grey.
39 Willys Papers, W–33, 6 June 1692, testimony of Ann Godfrey.
40 Willys Papers, W–33, 6 June 1692, testimony of John Gamman and Thomas Benit.

way of countermagic. First, he cut off a piece of the heifer's ear, but that did no good. Then, "he sent for his Cart whip and gave the Cow a stroak with it." Not surprisingly, the animal "Arose suddenly and Ran from him." Grey followed the heifer and struck it again several times. Within an hour, the animal recovered from its illness. Meanwhile, the injury was apparently translated back onto the witch responsible: next morning, Mercy Disborough "Lay on the bed and stretht [stretched] out her arme and said . . . I am allmost kild." The court duly transcribed Grey's account and added it to the other testimony against Disborough.[41]

Once the initial hearings at Stamford had come to an end, Clawson and Disborough were moved to the county jail in Fairfield. On 22 June, the General Court appointed a special legal commission to deal with the case. The trial itself, which took place in Fairfield, began on 14 September. From a legal viewpoint, the depositions before the court were far from compelling. Of all the evidence offered against Clawson and Disborough, only two testimonies gave any indication of a link between the accused and the Devil. Katherine Branch, the servant whose illness had prompted the investigation, now claimed that she was "possessed with the devill." Satan apparently wanted her to become a witch; "and if she would not he would tear her in pieces."[42] The Devil appeared to her in a number of forms: as a creature "with a great head and wings and noe body, and All Black," "in the hen house in the shape of a black calf," and another time "in the shape of a white dogg." He also came to her "in the shape of . . . goody clason [Clawson] . . . and the woman at Compo [Disborough]." Neighbor Joseph Gamsy, who was at the home of Daniel Wescott when Katherine made this claim, asked her "how she knew that it was the devill that appeared in the shape of these . . . women." "He tould me so," she answered.[43]

But why did Katherine Branch implicate the Devil in her troubles? One of Katherine's many confrontations with her spectral tormentors provides an important clue. On this particular occasion, Katherine told the spirits afflicting her that "their portion was hell fyr to all Eternity," and that two ministers, John Bishop of Stamford and Thomas Hanford of Norwalk, "had tould her shee must not yeald to them."[44] Bishop and Hanford had recently visited Kath-

41 Willys Papers, W–33, 6 June 1692, testimony of Henry Grey and Ann Godfrey.

42 Samuel Willys Collection, #30, date unspecified, testimony of Joseph Gamsy.

43 Samuel Willys Collection, #30b, date unspecified, testimony of Joseph Gamsy; Willys Papers, W–21, 28 June 1692, report of Jonathan Selleck. See also Willys Papers, W–22.

44 Willys Papers, W–22, 29 June 1692, letter from Jonathan Selleck to Nathan Gold. See also Willys Papers, W–21.

erine and had spoken to her at length. They may have persuaded Katherine to see her condition as a diabolical assault. Significantly, there is no evidence of her having mentioned the Devil as the source of her troubles at any time prior to their visit. The court itself became increasingly suspicious of Katherine's testimony. Lidia Penoir, the niece of Katherine's mistress, Abigail Wescott, reported a conversation in which Katherine actually denied having said that she was "posest with the Devil." Penoir also informed the court of her aunt Abigail's remark that Katherine "was such a lying gairl that not any body Could beleive one word what shee said."[45]

Apart from Katherine Branch, only one other witness raised the issue of the accused witches' allegiance to the Devil. Ann Godfrey, the young woman who believed that Mercy Disborough had "onbewitch[ed]" her cow, told the court about a conversation she had with Disborough in which the accused said that an unnamed woman had recently come to her, "reviled her . . . [and] tould her that her god was the Devill."[46] Once imprisoned, Disborough herself claimed to be tormented by the Devil "and also sed before this Cort she believed that there was devination in all her troubles."[47] Disborough was probably trying to defend herself by claiming that she too was bewitched in some way, although the precise meaning of her remark is unclear.

In addition to Katherine's testimony and the many depositions provided by townsfolk, two other kinds of evidence were available to the court: ordeal by water, or ducking, and the Devil's mark. When Daniel Wescott first accused Elizabeth Clawson of bewitching his daughter, he threatened to have her ducked. Clawson responded that "if Mr Bishop and the authority sayd it was Reeliable shee would, but if not shee would not."[48] It is not clear whether John Bishop, the minister at Stamford, did approve of ducking, but when Mercy Disborough actually asked to be ducked, the local officials at Fairfield were willing to oblige. On 2 June, both suspects underwent ordeal by water: neither Clawson nor Disborough sank; the water's rejection of them pointed to their guilt.[49] Fortunately for the accused, ducking was extremely controversial. The authorities at Fairfield may have agreed to ordeal by water in this case because one of the accused had specifically requested it. But the special court that presided over the trial itself was unlikely to

45 Samuel Willys Collection, #31, 24 August 1692, testimony of Lidia Penoir.
46 Willys papers, W–33, 6 June 1692, testimony of Ann Godfrey.
47 Willys Papers, W–34, 15 September 1692, testimony of Thomas Halliberch, jailkeeper.
48 Willys Papers, W–28, 7 June 1692, testimony of Daniel Wescott.
49 For accounts of the two duckings, see Samuel Willys Collection, #22, #39.

take the test seriously. The magistrates were leading figures in the Connecticut government: the governor and deputy governor, the secretary, and four assistants. These men were much more likely than the local officials at Fairfield to have read the recent literature on legal procedure, or at least to be aware of its recommendations. Indeed, the deputy governor was William Jones, the person who had taken careful notes from a text on witch trials, perhaps in preparation for this trial. Jones's notes would have reminded him that ducking was "superstitious and unwarantable."

No less controversial as a form of evidence was the Devil's mark, an abnormal outgrowth of flesh which the Devil or an animal familiar used to drink the witch's blood. The initial court of inquiry had given orders for both Clawson and Disborough to be examined for such marks. The committee of women examining Clawson "founde nothing, save [a] wort on one of her arms." Disborough, however, had marks "not Common in other women, and for w[hi]ch they [could] give no natural reason."[50] New England courts often had witch suspects examined for the Devil's mark, but the examiners usually had difficulty in distinguishing between natural and supernatural excrescences.[51] The magistrates presiding over this case evidently had doubts about the reliability of such evidence: they had both Clawson and Disborough searched a second time and later recalled individual members of the examination committee to confirm their findings.[52] Even if Disborough did have seemingly "preternatural" marks on her body, this did not establish her guilt in a court of law. Seventeenth-century legal manuals categorized "the Divills mark" as grounds for suspicion but not conviction. Again, Jones could consult his notes for clarification on this point.[53]

The evidence before the court, although substantial, was hardly sufficient to prove that either Clawson or Disborough was guilty of "familiarity with Satan, the grand enemie of God and man."[54] The jury was unable to reach a verdict for either of the accused,

50 Willys Papers, W–19, 28 May 1692, reports of the examination committee.

51 See, for example, the cases of Goodwife Knapp (Charles J. Hoadly, *Records of the Colony or Jurisdiction of New Haven*, 2 vols. [New Haven, Conn., 1857–8], II: 80–4) and Rebecca Nurse (Paul Boyer and Stephen Nissenbaum, eds., *The Salem Witchcraft Papers: Verbation Transcripts of the Legal Documents of the Salem Witchcraft Outbreak*, 3 vols. [New York, 1977], II: 606–7).

52 Willys Papers, W–31, 24 and 26 October 1692, further reports on the examination of Elizabeth Clawson.

53 For further discussion of the Devil's mark, see Clive Holmes, "Popular Culture? Witches, Magistrates, and Divines in Early Modern England," pp. 98–9; and Keith Thomas, *Religion and the Decline of Magic*, p. 530.

54 Willys Papers, W–39, 14 September 1692, indictments of Elizabeth Clawson and Mercy Disborough.

perhaps because its members were torn between the legal criteria for conviction and their own instincts, and so the magistrates referred the case to the General Court. Meanwhile, a group of prominent clergymen met at Hartford to discuss the case. The magistrates may themselves have suggested the meeting in an attempt to resolve some of the issues with which they and the jurors were grappling. In October 1692, the ministers submitted a four-point written "Opinion." First, they agreed "with the generallity of divines that the Endeavour of conviction of witchcraft by Swimming [was] unLawfull and Sinfull." Second, they argued that the court should not allow the Devil's mark as evidence "without the Approbation of some able physicians." Third, the ministers doubted that Katherine Branch was a trustworthy witness: they submitted that some of her testimony "carr[ied] a suspition of her Counterfeiting" and also warned that spectral evidence was "very uncertain and fallable, from the easy deception of her senses and [the] Subtile devices of the devill." Fourth, "as to the other Strange accidents as the dying of cattle etc," they "apprehend[ed] the applying of them to these women as matters of witchcraft to be upon very slender and uncertain grounds."[55] In effect, the report challenged the legitimacy of almost all the evidence before the court. The ministers were evidently unwilling to sanction a conviction for witchcraft unless there was direct and unequivocal proof of diabolical complicity.

There is no record of the magistrates' response to the ministers' report, although subsequent events suggest that its cautionary tone was not without effect. The General Court met in October, heard an account of the court proceedings in Fairfield, and instructed the jury to come to a definite verdict.[56] Later that month, the jury acquitted Clawson, but found Disborough guilty and sentenced her to death. Not only was the sheer quantity of evidence against Disborough much greater than that against Clawson, but Clawson's friends had been extremely active on her behalf. No less than twenty-six individuals, some of them elected Stamford officials, had signed a document attesting to her good character. Supporters of Disborough now submitted a petition pointing out that one of the original jurors had been absent from the second session of the court. A committee of magistrates appointed by the General Court to look into this claim concluded that the second half of the trial had indeed been illegal. But the committee members went on to suggest another reason for reprieving Disborough. None of the

55 Willys Papers, W–30, 17 October 1692, Ministers' Opinion.
56 *The Public Records of the Colony of Connecticut,* IV: 79.

evidence against her, they claimed, satisfied the criteria for conviction laid down by theologians and legal experts:

> namely 1st Confession (this there was none of) 2ndly two good wittnesses proveing som[e] act or acts done by the Person which Could not be but by help of the devil.

The influence of the ministers' "Opinion" was apparent in the committee's report. With regard to "the Common things of spectral evidence, ill events after quarels or threates, teates, water tryalls and the Like," these were "al discarded and som[e] of them abominated by the most Judicious as to be convictive of witchcraft."[57] Clawson and Disborough both went free.

The acquittal of Elizabeth Clawson and Mercy Disborough must have shaken many people in Fairfield county. Men and women from Stamford and its environs had flocked to give what they believed to be damning testimony against the two accused women. Yet that testimony proved to be inadequate in a court of law. The Fairfield trials embodied a fundamental disjunction between popular and legal perceptions of witchcraft. The presiding magistrates could not recommend conviction unless there was clear proof of a link between the accused and the Devil, yet most witnesses did not interpret the incidents which they described in diabolical terms; they made no mention of the Devil in their testimony. Rigorous enforcement of legal criteria was almost bound to result in acquittal. The court's decision cannot have pleased local citizens. They had given evidence against Clawson and Disborough because they were convinced of their guilt and because they hoped to secure official redress against them. Such redress was not forthcoming.

The debacle at Fairfield was not an isolated incident. In 1668, Katherine Harrison of Wethersfield, Connecticut, also escaped conviction for witchcraft after a prolonged controversy about the evidence brought against her.[58] Harrison had left England in 1651; she spent two years as a servant in Hartford, Connecticut, and then came to live in Wethersfield. After the death of her husband in 1666, Harrison became involved in a number of lawsuits: these related to conflicting property claims and Harrison's purported slandering of her neighbors. Harrison was not a popular woman and the local jury entered verdicts against her in all of these cases. It

57 Willys Papers, W–36, 12 May 1693, Reasons for reprieving Mercy Disborough.

58 For the testimony against Katherine Harrison, see Samuel Willys Collection, #6 through #17, and Willys Papers, W–10 through W–18. See also John Demos, *Entertaining Satan,* pp. 355–65, and Carolyn Langdon, "A Complaint against Katherine Harrison, 1669," *Bulletin of the Connecticut Historical Society,* 34 (1969): 18–25.

was in the context of increasingly overt local hostility toward Harrison that her trial for witchcraft took place.[59]

Harrison had been suspected of witchcraft for many years. Indeed, some of the evidence used against her in 1668 referred to incidents which had taken place during her stay in Hartford during the early 1650s. The townsfolk from Hartford and Wethersfield who came forward to testify against Harrison claimed that she had been active in both communities as a fortune-teller and healer. Harrison's possession of occult skills had made her position as a servant in John Cullick's household problematic: when Cullick turned Harrison "out of his service, one matter or cause was because the saide Catherin tould fortunes."[60] Townsfolk from Hartford and Wethersfield believed that Harrison had used her "cunning" for malevolent as well as benevolent purposes. A number of deponents described arguments with Harrison, each of which had been followed by illness or misfortune, apparently inflicted by Harrison in response to the quarrel. Others testified to the appearance of specters in Harrison's form and her generally odd behavior. However, the only witness to make any mention of the Devil was Mary Hale, a young woman of Wethersfield, who claimed to have been visited by Harrison's apparition. According to Hale, the specter had come to her in the night, tortured her, and told her that it had a commission from God to kill her. Mary had replied that God would not give a commission to kill and that "theirefor it must be from the divle."[61]

As in the cases of Elizabeth Clawson and Mercy Disborough, the evidence against Harrison was substantial but not legally compelling. The jury decided to acquit her, but Harrison's enemies in Wethersfield and Hartford refused to accept the decision and renewed the charges against her in May 1669. The jury again refused to convict, and the court was adjourned until October. Meanwhile, thirty-eight townsmen signed a complaint objecting to Harrison's having been set at liberty until then. When the court reconvened, the jury finally found her guilty, perhaps under pressure from

59 Carol Karlsen argues that Harrison's status as a financially independent widow, which violated established patterns of inheritance, made Harrison a fit candidate for persecution as a witch (Carol Karlsen, *The Devil in the Shape of a Woman: Witchcraft in Colonial New England* [New York, 1987], pp. 84–9).

60 Willys Papers, W–11, 23 September 1668, testimony of Elizabeth Smith. It is not clear why Cullick disapproved of Harrison's fortune-telling: he may have been one of those who objected to such practices on principle, insisting that they were diabolical; or he may have feared only the abuse of occult skill. In either case, he probably wanted to avoid association with the suspicions attached to Harrison herself.

61 Willys Papers, W–17, 25 May 1669, testimony of Mary Hale.

their fellow citizens, but the magistrates were reluctant to accept the verdict and referred the case to a group of ministers. The clergymen were asked to consider three specific questions: first, whether "a plurality of witnesses be necessary, legally to evidence one and the same individuall fact"; second, whether "apparitions of a person, legally proved, be a demonstration of familiarity with the devill"; and third, whether "foretelling some future event, or revealing of a secret, be a demonstration of familiarity with the devill."

In their response, the ministers emphasized that each piece of evidence against the accused must be corroborated by two or more witnesses. Their "Opinion," unlike that delivered in the case of Disborough and Clawson, did accept the legitimacy of spectral evidence, on condition that the apparition was "legally proved": in other words, there had to be "a plurality of witnesses" for each spectral appearance. Furthermore, the ministers declared that Harrison's fortune-telling "argue[d] familiarity with the Devill, in as much as such a person, doth thereby declare his receiving of the Devills testimony, and yeeld up himself as the devills instrument to comunicate the same to others." But here again, there had to be at least two witnesses for each incriminating incident. The ministers' "Opinion" was less cautious than that offered by their counterparts at the trial of Clawson and Disborough. But even so, their repeated insistence upon "a plurality of witnesses" strengthened the magistrates' hand in opposing public pressure for a conviction.[62] After having read the report, the magistrates overturned the jury's verdict and released Harrison, on condition that she leave Wethersfield, both for her own safety and for her neighbors' peace of mind.[63]

There are, unfortunately, few cases as well documented as those of Elizabeth Clawson, Mercy Disborough, and Katherine Harrison. Yet other fragments of evidence convey the same message: that courts found it difficult to convict on the basis of the evidence before them, and that townsfolk were infuriated by the courts' attitude. Locals were not always willing to accept a court's decision. They conferred with their neighbors, gathered new evidence against the suspect, and then renewed legal charges. John Godfrey of Andover, Massachusetts, was prosecuted and acquitted on charges of witchcraft on three separate occasions: in 1659, 1662, and 1665. After the first and second of these trials, Godfrey sued his accusers for slander. He won both cases, yet on neither occasion did this deter

62 Willys Papers, W–18, 20 October 1669, Ministers' Opinion.
63 *Public Records of the Colony of Connecticut,* II: 132, 12 May 1670.

his enemies from mounting a sequel prosecution.[64] Eunice Cole of Hampton, Massachusetts, was tried and acquitted in 1656, again in 1673, and a third time in 1689. Elizabeth Seager of Hartford, Connecticut, was acquitted twice, in January and July of 1663. Two years later, Seager was finally convicted, but the governor of Connecticut, John Winthrop, Jr., had grave doubts about the evidence against her and intervened to delay sentencing. In 1666, the Court of Assistants met to discuss the case at Winthrop's request and released Seager on the grounds that the jury's verdict did "not legally answer the inditement."[65]

Five other individuals each appeared in court twice on charges of witchcraft: Mary Parsons of Northampton, Massachusetts (1651, 1674); Jane Walford of Portsmouth, Massachusetts (1656, 1669); Mary Hall of Setauket, Connecticut (1664, 1665); Mary Hale of Boston, Massachusetts (1681, 1691); and Winifred Benham of Wallingford, Connecticut (1692, 1697). With the fleeting exception of Elizabeth Seager, none of these accused witches were ever convicted.[66] The recurrence of repeat prosecutions suggests widespread public dissatisfaction with the courts' handling of witchcraft cases. Traveling to court in order to give testimony was often inconvenient and expensive. That people were ready to do so despite an earlier acquittal testifies to their unshaken confidence in the witch's guilt and their determination to secure a conviction.

In their judgments, the courts sometimes tried to appease townsfolk by recognizing that legal innocence did not necessarily mean actual innocence. In 1665, the Court of Assistants found John Godfrey "suspitiously Guilty of witchcraft, but not legally guilty, according to lawe and evidence . . . received."[67] A similar decision was given at the trial of Eunice Cole in 1673: "not Legally guilty according to Inditement butt Just ground of vehement suspissyon of her haveing had famillyarryty with the devil."[68] When Winifred Benham appeared in court on a charge of witchcraft in 1692, the decision was as follows:

> The Court having heard and considered all the evidence against the said Winifred Benham and not finding sufficient

64 *Records and Files of the Quarterly Courts of Essex County,* II: 157, III: 120–2.

65 Richard Tomlinson, *Witchcraft Trials of Connecticut* (Hartford, Conn., 1978), pp. 32, 34–9.

66 See Appendix A.

67 John Noble and John F. Cronin, eds., *Records of the Court of Assistants of the Colony of Massachusetts Bay, 1630–1692,* 3 vols. (Boston, 1901–28), III: 151–2.

68 Massachusetts Archives (Columbia Point, Boston, Mass.), vol. 135, #16. Mary Hale of Boston and James Fuller of Springfield were also found "Not Guilty according to Inditement" (*Records of the Court of Assistants,* I: 189, 228).

> grounds of conviction for further prosecution ... do therefore at this time dismiss the business, yet advising the said Winifred Benham solemnly to reflect upon the case, and grounds of suspicion given in and alleged against her, and told her if further grounds of suspicion of witchcraft, or fuller evidences should appear against her by reason of mischief done to the bodies or estate of any by any preternatural acts proved against her, she might justly fear and expect to be brought to her trial for it.

The court recognized the "grounds of suspicion given in and alleged against" Benham and warned her not to treat her acquittal as a personal vindication. These "grounds of suspicion" probably comprised the kinds of evidence most witnesses believed to be ample proof of witchcraft, whereas the lack of "sufficient grounds of conviction" indicated the absence of any proof of diabolical allegiance. The court wanted the people of Wallingford to believe that it took their testimony seriously, even though that testimony could not justify a conviction.[69]

Unfortunately for the accused, official statements of this kind did not guarantee public equanimity in the aftermath of an acquittal. Mary Webster of Hadley, Massachusetts, was tried for witchcraft in 1683 and duly acquitted. Yet the following year, when one of Webster's neighbors fell ill, she was held responsible. A gang of young men now took the law into their own hands: they visited Webster's home one night and brutally assaulted her; Webster barely escaped with her life.[70] On one occasion, the General Court of Connecticut exerted its authority in an attempt to diffuse local tension surrounding a released witch suspect. In 1658, Elizabeth Garlick of Easthampton, Connecticut, was tried for witchcraft. Garlick was a middle-aged woman of humble rank who had moved to Easthampton from Massachusetts. The jury found her not guilty, but the presiding magistrates realized that acquittal was not going to end public hostility toward Garlick and so referred the case to the General Court. In a letter to the people of Easthampton, the General Court confirmed that "there did not appeare sufficient evidence to prove her guilty," but "well approve[d] and commend[ed] the Christian care and prudence of those in Authority ... in searchinge into that case, according to such just suspicion as appeared." The General Court instructed the people of East-

69 New Haven County Court Records (Connecticut State Library, Hartford, Conn.), I: 202.

70 Samuel Drake, *Annals of Witchcraft in New England* (1869; New York, 1972), p. 179.

hampton to "car[r]y neighbourly and peaceably, without just offence, to Joseph Garlick and his wife." The Garlicks "should doe the like."[71]

Townsfolk serving as jurors in witchcraft cases found themselves in an extremely difficult position, torn between the legal requirements by which they were expected to abide, the determination of their neighbors to secure a conviction, and their own confusion when presented with evidence that was sometimes utterly perplexing. The jury responsible for Elizabeth Seager's trial in January 1663 was divided and baffled by the testimony before the court. Most of the evidence against Seager was circumstantial: she was apparently "Intimat[e]" with several other women accused of witchcraft and had further incriminated herself by denying her "familiarity" with them. Seager had also made a number of shocking references to the Devil in recent conversations with her neighbors, but these offered no conclusive proof of diabolical compact.[72] When the jurors met to determine their verdict, half of them voted to convict her, but the remainder were "deeply suspicious, and . . . at a great loss." In their confusion, the undecided jurors "stagger[ed]" back and forth between conviction and acquittal. Eventually, the jury decided to acquit. The surviving records do not explain why they did so, but as the foreman pointed out when he delivered the verdict, their decision could have gone either way.[73]

It should be emphasized that half the jurymen responsible for Elizabeth Seager's fate were convinced of her guilt, and that the remainder came close to voting with them. On a number of occasions, juries determined to convict witches on the basis of evidence that did not prove demonic allegiance. In such instances, the jury sided with popular instinct rather than legal restraint.[74] This

71 "Records of the Particular Court of Connecticut," in *Connecticut Historical Society Collections*, 22 (1928): 188; *Public Records of the Colony of Connecticut*, I: 572–3.

72 When questioned about "triall by swiming," Seager had said, "the divill that caused me to com[e] heare can keep me up" (Willys Papers, W–2). When told by Goodwife Garrett that she was "under suspicion for a witch," Seager "did adventure to bid satan go and tell them she was no witch." Goody Garrett, who was understandably shocked by this remark, asked Seager "why did she not bese[e]ch God to tell them she was no witch." Seager replied, "because satan knew she was no witch" (Willys Papers, W–4). On another occasion, Seager apparently told Goodwife Migatt that "god was Naught, it was very good to be a witch and desired her to be one, she should not ned [need] fare [fear] going to hell, for she should not burne in the fire" (Willys Papers, W–3).

73 Willys Papers, W–2.

74 Clive Holmes characterizes the jury's role in English law "as the embodiment of local sentiment and knowledge rather than as a neutral evaluator of evidence under the direction of the judge" (Clive Holmes, "Popular Culture? Witches, Magistrates, and Divines in Early Modern England," p. 89).

could lead to open conflict between judges and jurymen. When Hugh Parsons of Springfield, Massachusetts, was tried for witchcraft in 1651, the jury found him guilty, but the magistrates refused to accept the decision and brought the case before the General Court. "On perusal of the evidences bought in against him," the assembly ruled that Parsons was "not legally guilty of witchcraft."[75] Ann Hibbens of Boston, Massachusetts, a contentious woman who had been excommunicated from her church for quarrelsome and abusive behavior, appeared before the Court of Assistants on a charge of witchcraft in 1656. The jury found her guilty, but the magistrates disagreed and appealed to the General Court. On this occasion, the assembly confirmed the jury's verdict.[76]

A similar controversy took place twenty-four years later, in 1680, when Elizabeth Morse of Newbury, Massachusetts, was convicted on charges of witchcraft by a jury at the Court of Assistants and then granted a reprieve by governor Simon Bradstreet and the Assistants. According to John Hale's account of the trial, the Assistants "were not satisfyed that a Specter doing mischief in her likeness should be imputed to her person as a ground of guilt." Moreover, they "did not esteem one single witness to one fact, and another single witness to another fact" as equivalent to "two witnesses against the person in a matter Capital."[77] This decision was incomprehensible to the House of Deputies: the members submitted a formal objection to the reprieve, in which they declared that they did "not understand the reason why execution of the sentence given against her" had not been carried out. The magistrates, however, refused to give way under pressure from the Deputies, and Morse was eventually released.[78] The Deputies' protest against Morse's reprieve provides yet another indication of the gulf between legal policy and nonjudicial opinion on the subject of witchcraft.

Like their European counterparts, New England courts viewed witchcraft from a perspective radically different from that of witchcraft victims. Unlike their European counterparts, New England courts operated within a legal system that forbade the use of torture as a way to bridge the gap between different perceptions of the crime; as a result, they could only reject popular testimony. Witchcraft laws in England embodied popular belief in their treatment of witchcraft as an antisocial act that did not necessarily involve

75 Nathaniel Shurtleff, ed., *Records of the Governor and Company of Massachusetts Bay*, III: 273.
76 Ibid., IV (pt. 1): 269.
77 John Hale, *A Modest Enquiry*, pp. 21–2.
78 Massachusetts Archives, vol. 135, #18.

diabolical allegiance. But New England laws defined witchcraft as diabolical heresy: since most witnesses against accused witches provided no evidence of diabolical involvement, colonial courts found it extremely difficult to justify a conviction. Witchcraft trials often ended in confusion, dissension, and public frustration. The jurymen dealing with Elizabeth Seager's case ("deeply suspicious," "at a great loss," and "staggering" back and forth) provide a fitting image of the New England legal system as it struggled with the deadly but elusive crime of witchcraft.

New England ministers saw witchcraft in the same theological light as did colonial law, yet the ministers were ambivalent about witchcraft prosecutions. Ideally, they taught, people who believed that they were bewitched should focus on their own spiritual failings as the ultimate cause of all suffering: bewitchment was a punishment from God; only sincere repentance would secure its removal. Yet ministers also recognized that witches could not be allowed to roam free: their presence constituted not only a public menace, but also a serious embarrassment in light of New England's claim to spiritual purity. Therefore, the clergy conceded that prosecution should be available to those who became convinced that a particular individual was afflicting them. After all, scriptural injunction on this subject was clear: "Thou shalt not suffer a witch to live."

But sanctioned legal channels only rarely provided effective redress against witchcraft. The difficulty of securing a legal conviction for witchcraft became increasingly apparent as the years passed: of the sixteen convictions prior to 1692, eleven took place in the 1640s and 1650s; apart from the four convictions at Hartford, Connecticut, in 1662–3, there were no further convictions for witchcraft until Goodwife Glover's confession in 1688. It is not clear why the rate of conviction declined, but colonists responded by turning less frequently to the legal system for action against witch suspects. The number of witch prosecutions in New England fell dramatically during the 1670s and 1680s: there were nineteen such prosecutions during the 1660s, but only six during the 1670s and eight during the 1680s.[79] A decline in the number of witch prosecutions did not mean a decline in popular fear of witchcraft. Jasper Danckaerts, a Dutch visitor to Boston in 1680, remarked that he had "never been in a place where more was said about witchcraft and witches."[80] The people of New England feared witchcraft and

79 See Appendix A. For further discussion of the changing incidence of witch trials through the seventeenth century in New England, see John Demos, *Entertaining Satan*, chap. 12, and Carol Karlsen, *The Devil in the Shape of a Woman*, pp. 14–45.

80 Jasper Danckaerts, "Journal of a Voyage to New York and a Tour of Several

needed some form of redress against witches. Interestingly enough, it was during the 1680s that New England ministers first voiced their anxiety about popular recourse to countermagic. This may not have been a coincidence. As it became clear that witchcraft could not be punished through legal channels, it is possible that New Englanders turned to countermagic instead.

The ministers' campaign against countermagic during the last two decades of the century perhaps reflected a changing reality: the clergy may have been responding to a rise in the use of countermagic as the public became disillusioned with legal prosecution (just as clerical attacks on astrology in the late 1680s and 1690s were prompted in part by the appearance of an openly astrological almanac literature). Thus, the ministers' growing hostility toward various kinds of supernatural competition arose not only from their own increasing concern about the spiritual prospects of New England, but also, in all likelihood, from an actual rise in occult practice. Ironically, the rigorous implementation of God's law may have driven people to an alternative strategy that the clergy condemned as diabolical. In their sermons, the ministers urged the afflicted of New England to abandon countermagic in favor of prayer, but such entreaties were unrealistic. People turned to the law or informal channels such as countermagic because they were not willing to leave a malefactor's punishment to God. If another human being was responsible for their condition, they wanted to know who it was, and they wanted revenge.

of the American Colonies in 1679–1680," trans. H. C. Murphy, in *Memoirs of the Long Island Historical Society*, I (1867): 419.

6

RAPE OF A WHOLE COLONY

THE 1692 WITCH HUNT

> The mind is its own place, and in it self
> Can make a Heav'n of Hell, a Hell of Heav'n.
>
> John Milton, *Paradise Lost,* I, 254–5

In 1692, a witch panic of epidemic proportions swept through the county of Essex in Massachusetts. The panic began in Salem Village, spread rapidly through the neighboring communities, and soon engulfed the entire county. During that year, townsfolk and villagers brought formal charges of witchcraft against one hundred and fifty-six people. These accused witches came from twenty-four towns and villages.[1] By early October, when governor William Phips halted the trials, nineteen people had been hanged, one man had died under interrogation, and over one hundred suspects were languishing in jail. The witch hysteria was most intense in Salem Village and Andover: over half of the accusations originated in these two communities. Yet the special court appointed to deal with the crisis presided over cases from all over the county.

The panic began in the early winter months of 1692, when several girls in Salem Village began to suffer strange "fits" and "distempers." The local physician, William Griggs, examined the girls and concluded that they were "under an Evil Hand."[2] Samuel Parris, minister at Salem Village, was the father of one afflicted girl and uncle of another; clearly, the villagers would look to Parris for an appropriate response. For over a month, Parris pursued a regimen of prayer and fasting. His fellow ministers had advised him to "sit still and wait upon the Providence of God."[3] But in late February, possibly under pressure from neighbors and church members, Parris changed his strategy: he now instructed his daughter and niece to name their tormentors and encouraged his neighbors to do

1 For a list of formal witch accusations in Essex County during 1692, see Appendix B.

2 John Hale, *A Modest Enquiry into the Nature of Witchcraft* (1702; Bainbridge, N.Y., 1973), p. 23.

3 Ibid., p. 25.

likewise. The girls' accusations immediately became public knowledge and the local magistrates issued warrants for the arrest of three women: Tituba, a Caribbean slave in Parris's service; Sarah Good, a homeless and destitute woman who had been begging for food and shelter in the village; and Sarah Osborne, a native of Watertown who had come to live in the village thirty years before. A few weeks later, the afflicted girls began to denounce other villagers. Accusations now proliferated with amazing speed and soon spread from Salem Village itself to neighboring communities and beyond. Before long, the entire county had become involved in the crisis.[4]

Throughout the spring, summer, and fall of 1692, the afflicted girls and their convulsive fits gripped the imagination of Essex County. The girls' torments were the focus of attention both inside and outside the courtroom. John Hale, a close observer of the witch crisis, wrote the following description of their ordeal:

> These Children were bitten and pinched by invisible agents: their arms, necks and backs turned this way and that way, and returned back again, so as it was impossible for them to do of themselves, and beyond the power of any Epileptick Fits, or natural Disease to effect. Sometimes they were taken dumb, their mouths stopped, their throats choaked, their limbs wracked and tormented so as might move a heart of stone to sympathise with them.[5]

Whenever an accused witch appeared before the court, the magistrates had the girls brought into the courtroom to see if they would be struck down by the accused. Even when dealing with suspects who lived in communities far removed from Salem Village itself, the court questioned the girls as to whether the accused had ever tormented them. Indeed, the people of Andover arranged for the girls to be transported thither for use in identifying witches there.[6] Despite the fact that hundreds of people became accusers during 1692, the tormented girls remained the focus of public interest. Not only did their vulnerability offer a convenient way to ascertain the innocence or guilt of the accused, but their fits epitomized the experience of Essex County as a whole. Like the afflicted

4 For detailed narratives of these events, see Paul Boyer and Stephen Nissenbaum, *Salem Possessed: The Social Origins of Witchcraft* (Cambridge, Mass., 1974), pp. 1–21, and Chadwick Hansen, *Witchcraft at Salem* (New York, 1969).

5 John Hale, *A Modest Enquiry*, p. 24.

6 Thomas Brattle, letter to a clergyman, in George L. Burr, ed., *Narratives of the Witchcraft Cases* (1914; New York, 1952), pp. 180–81; Robert Calef, "More Wonders of the Invisible World," in ibid., pp. 371–2.

girls themselves, the county was "wracked and tormented" by the ordeal of 1692.

The Salem witch crisis sheds light on the relationship between witchcraft, magic, and Puritanism in two significant respects. First, the underlying causes of witch hysteria in 1692 reaffirm the crucial link between accusations of witchcraft and a predisposition to blame suffering on external rather than internal causes. Just as the ministers' ambiguity on the subject of liability permitted layfolk throughout the seventeenth century to locate blame for their misfortunes outside the self, so a series of events that befell the northern colonies during the last quarter of the century caused New Englanders to obsess about outside threats, creating an atmosphere conducive to witch accusations on a massive scale. The collapse of the trials in late 1692 constitutes a second link with earlier witch accusations. Apart from the afflicted girls and those accused witches who confessed, both of which groups came under increasing suspicion, hardly any of those who appeared before the court at Salem mentioned the Devil or sought to implicate him in the witches' activities. As on previous occasions, the disjunction between theological and magical conceptions of witchcraft undermined the legal process.

Why did a witch panic of this magnitude break out in 1692? Actions against witchcraft, legal or otherwise, were an ongoing part of New England life. Indeed, the Salem witch trials did not constitute the only witch hunt in seventeenth-century New England. During that same year, a wave of accusations in Stamford, Connecticut, endangered the lives of Elizabeth Clawson and Mercy Disborough, both of whom were eventually acquitted. Thirty years earlier, in 1662, a series of witch trials in Hartford, Connecticut, had led to three (perhaps four) executions.[7] Nevertheless, the scale of the witch hunt at Salem and the intensity of witch hysteria that the prosecutions expressed were altogether exceptional. The events of 1692 demand particular explanation.

The number of witch prosecutions in New England had fallen dramatically during the two decades prior to 1692, as townsfolk realized the difficulty of securing a legal conviction for witchcraft. The magistrates now had to deal with a backlog of witchcraft incidents: much of the evidence presented at Salem referred to events that had taken place several years before, in some cases a decade

7 For a list of historical accounts and source materials relating to the Hartford trials, see John Demos, *Entertaining Satan: Witchcraft and the Culture of Early New England* (New York, 1982), p. 509 n60.

or more. But why did so many New Englanders come forward with depositions against witch suspects in response to events in Salem, despite the failure of most previous trials to result in convictions? Why were they so eager to express witch-related fears at that particular point in time? The answers to these questions are bound up with a series of events that shook the colony of Massachusetts during the two decades prior to 1692. Only by placing the witch hunt in its immediate historical context can we understand why the people of Essex County reacted so strongly to the afflictions in Salem Village.[8]

Until 1675, the northern colonies had enjoyed relative peace, stability, and prosperity. Over the previous fifty years, the English colonists had transformed a patchwork of scattered and vulnerable settlements into a well-organized and seemingly permanent colonial society. The New Englanders lived in peace, albeit an uneasy peace, with the Dutch in New York and the French in Canada. Since 1636, their conflicts with the native Americans had been sporadic and minimally disruptive. The settlers had constructed an efficient and representative political system that gave loyal support to an entrenched but responsive leadership. Religious and civil institutions had succeeded in enforcing at least a facade of Puritan orthodoxy; for all the ministers' concern about the future, New England's spiritual mission was apparently intact. The achievements of the last fifty years were, then, impressive. But the events of the next two decades would demonstrate just how fragile many of those achievements really were.

During the final quarter of the seventeenth century, a series of disasters convulsed the northern colonies and brought New England to the brink of destruction. The first of these disasters was Metacomet's War (sometimes called King Philip's War) of 1675–6. Relations with the native Americans had deteriorated over the two decades previous to the war. Continued English appropriation of native land, the colonial government's insistence that native Americans acknowledge English laws, and the settlement of several thousand native converts to Christianity in "praying Indian" towns had gradually convinced native Americans that the English settlers posed a fundamental threat to their survival as autonomous peo-

8 Richard Weisman argues that during the Salem crisis, judges "replaced the community as the locus for legal initiatives against witchcraft" (Richard Weisman, *Witchcraft, Magic, and Religion in Seventeenth-Century Massachusetts* [Amherst, Mass., 1984], p. 132). Although it is true that the magistrates were assiduous, even fanatical, in their prosecution of witch suspects, there was also broad-based popular support for a witch hunt, exemplified by the enormous number of depositions submitted against the accused.

ples. In 1675, a court at Plymouth Colony convicted and executed three members of the Wampanoag tribe for the murder of a "praying Indian" called Sassoman. The Wampanoags' chief, Metacomet, responded by ordering his tribesmen to attack the colony. From June to December 1675, native Americans ravaged the interior of Massachusetts and Plymouth Colony. Guerrilla warfare continued through 1676 and at one point Metacomet's forces came within twenty miles of Boston itself. The English eventually defeated and dispersed the Wampanoags and their allies, but not before they had sustained terrible losses. One in every sixteen men of military age died as a result of the war. Many other men, women, and children were either killed in raids, carried off into captivity by the native Americans, or died of starvation and exposure. Hundreds more fell victim to a smallpox epidemic in 1677–8.[9] By the end of the war, twelve towns had been completely destroyed and half the towns in New England badly damaged. The war cost almost one hundred thousand pounds and all but crippled the colonial economy. By any standards, this was a catastrophe for New England.[10]

If Metacomet's assault brought into question the very survival of the northern colonies, the imperial government in London became a no less fundamental threat to the colonists' way of life during the decade following. In the late 1670s and early 1680s, the English crown tried to establish a closer control over the affairs of its American colonies, particularly in matters of trade. None of the colonies were eager to cooperate with the government's wishes, but Massachusetts was particularly stubborn in its refusal to compromise over the exercise of royal authority within its boundaries. This recalcitrance infuriated the rising imperialist faction within the En-

9 See John Demos, *Entertaining Satan,* p. 521 n17.

10 The most detailed account of the 1675–6 war remains Douglas Edward Leach, *Flintlock and Tomahawk: New England in King Philip's War* (New York, 1958). For contemporary narratives of the war, see John Easton, "A Relacion of the Indyan Warre," in Charles Lincoln, ed., *Narratives of the Indian Wars* (1913; New York, 1952), pp. 7–17; Nathaniel Saltonstall, *The Present State of New-England with Respect to the Indian War* (London, 1675); Saltonstall, *A Continuation of the State of New-England* (London, 1676); Saltonstall, *A New and Further Narrative of the State of New-England* (London, 1676); Increase Mather, *A Brief History of the War with the Indians in New-England* (Boston, 1676); Benjamin Tompson, *New England's Crisis, or, A Brief Narrative of New-England's Lamentable Estate at Present, Compar'd with the Former (but Few) Years of Prosperity* (Boston, 1676; reprinted in Richard Slotkin and James K. Folsom, eds., *So Dreadfull a Judgment: Puritan Responses to King Philip's War, 1676–7* [Middletown, Conn., 1978], pp. 213–33); Thomas Wheeler, *A Thankefull Remembrance of God's Mercy to Several Persons at Quabaug or Deerfield* (Cambridge, Mass. 1676); William Hubbard, *A Narrative of the Troubles with the Indians* (Boston, 1677); Richard Hutchinson, *The War in New-England Visibly Ended* (London, 1677); Mary Rowlandson, *The Sovereignty and Goodness of God, Together with the Faithfulness of His Promises Displayed* (Cambridge, 1682); and Thomas Church, *Entertaining Passages Relating to Philip's War* (Boston, 1716).

glish government. Eventually, London lost patience with Massachusetts and decided to abandon negotiation in favor of a more radical and draconian solution. In 1684, the English crown revoked Massachusetts' charter. Two years later, it incorporated all eight colonies stretching northward from New Jersey into a new imperial structure, the Dominion of New England.

The Dominion took power away from colonists and placed it in the hands of royal officials. New Englanders would no longer elect their own governor and ruling council; these would now be royal appointments. There would be no representative assembly. Town meetings would take place only once a year, and then only for the election of local officials. Perhaps most ominous of all in light of recent English history, the government could levy taxation without popular consent. The New Englanders had placed democratic procedures at the very center of their public life; the dismantling of representative institutions that now ensued constituted nothing less than a political revolution. The new regime's land policy was no less radical in its implications. Hitherto, each township had itself controlled the distribution of land within its boundaries. Royal officials now announced that all land grants except for those given by the General Court and bearing the colony's official seal were invalid; all those whose deeds were in doubt had to petition the new government for a legitimate patent. In other words, landowners were to become formally dependent upon the crown for the titles to their land.

Edmund Andros, governor of the Dominion, epitomized the authoritarian spirit of the new regime. Andros, a career soldier who had spent many years as governor of New York, was temperamentally as autocratic as his royal master James II. The governor's personal style was domineering and offensive, as was the administration of which he was the head. Andros not only behaved like a Stuart, but he also looked the part. The governor dressed like a London courtier and shocked Bostonians by attending a Harvard commencement wearing a scarlet coat and flowing wig.

Not only did the Andros regime emasculate local government and threaten property rights, but it also failed to protect the frontier settlements from native American attacks. The governor's attempts to negotiate a peace with the native Americans collapsed and his costly military expedition to Maine in the winter of 1688–9 was a dismal failure. Indeed, native American tribesmen were so successful in evading the governor's forces that some colonists began to suspect a secret alliance between their new master and the native Americans. Andros had now lost all credibility. When news of James II's downfall reached northern America in 1689, New Englanders responded with uncharacteristic unanimity and overthrew the Dominion. On 18 April 1689, the people of Boston arrested Andros and his supporters in a bloodless coup. Both the royal fort on Castle Island and the royal frigate moored in Boston harbor surrendered on the following day. A month later, delegates from all over Massachusetts convened in Boston and instructed an interim government to administer the colony according to the old charter. The colonists requested that Increase Mather, who was already in London protesting against the Dominion, now negotiate a permanent settlement with the royal government.[11]

No sooner had New Englanders thrown off the shackles of the Dominion than they had to face another threat in the form of renewed native American attacks. With the accession of William and Mary to the English throne, Louis XIV of France declared war on England and its colonies. The war in northern America took the form of French-inspired native American raids along the New England frontier, no part of which was left unthreatened. These were dark years for the northern colonies. Their expedition against Quebec in 1690 was a disastrous failure. The unruliness of returned soldiers, the heavy losses sustained by merchants who had helped to finance the expedition, and the general economic effects of curtailed trade with France spread fear and despondency throughout New England. In late 1690, another smallpox epidemic ravaged Massachusetts and morale there reached a new low.[12] It was at this point that the native Americans launched a series of attacks on the Massachusetts backcountry. Until 1691, they had concentrated their efforts on the northern reaches of New England, but in the summer of that year, native Americans attacked Lancaster, Brookfield, and Billerica.[13]

The native American assault on Massachusetts in 1691 coincided with the appearance of yet another major threat. The new charter, ratified that year, gave freedom of worship to all dissenters from Congregationalism. During his brief tenure as governor of the colony, Edmund Andros had taken initial steps toward the dises-

11 For more detailed accounts of the Dominion and its downfall, see Richard Johnson, *Adjustment to Empire: The New England Colonies, 1675–1715* (New Brunswick, N.J., 1981), chaps. 1 and 2; David Lovejoy, *The Glorious Revolution in America* (New York, 1972); Timothy Breen, *The Character of a Good Ruler* (New Haven, Conn., 1970), chap. 4; Michael G. Hall, *Edward Randolph and the American Colonies, 1676–1703* (Chapel Hill, 1960); Viola F. Barnes, *The Dominion of New England: A Study in British Colonial Policy* (New York, 1923).

12 John Demos, *Entertaining Satan*, p. 522 n22.

13 Philip Haffenden, *New England in the English Nation, 1689–1713* (Oxford, 1974), chap. 3. See also Cotton Mather's account of these years in *Decennium Luctuosum* (Boston, 1699).

tablishment of Congregationalism in New England. Andros had forced the South Church in Boston to let Anglicans hold weekly services there. He also appropriated a plot of common land for the construction of a separate Anglican chapel. These measures scandalized Congregationalists. When the Dominion collapsed in 1689, New England Puritans hoped that they could now put behind them the governor's unwelcome experiment in liberty of conscience. But the charter of 1691 gave its blessing to public heterodoxy and enfranchised dissenting groups such as Quakers and Anglicans. This was a direct blow to the Congregationalists' privileged position within the community.[14]

New England, then, was under attack – physically, politically and spiritually – during the last quarter of the seventeenth century. The degree to which these different threats affected people's lives depended on their geographical location. Those who lived in or around Boston would have been much more aware of the political changes wrought by Andros than those living out on the frontier. Yet colonists settled in outlying areas were in greater danger from native American attacks and the failure of the Andros government to provide adequate defense. Wherever New Englanders lived during these years, they experienced fear and uncertainty. Whereas earlier crises such as the Antinomian controversy and the struggle over the halfway covenant had originated within the colonial community, the dangers that faced New England toward the end of the century intruded upon the colonies as emissaries of a hostile outside world.[15] In close and deadly succession, a series of external forces had assaulted the colonists, imperiling not only their integrity as a political and spiritual community but even their very survival. This chain of crises had a cumulative impact, constituting for New

14 For studies of Quakerism in early New England, see Carla Gardina Pestana, *Quakers and Baptists in Colonial Massachusetts* (New York, 1991); Jonathan Chu, *Neighbors, Friends, or Madmen* (Westport, Conn., 1985); Christine Heyrman, *Commerce and Culture: The Maritime Communities of Colonial Massachusetts, 1690–1750* (New York, 1984), chap. 3; Arthur Worrall, *Quakers in the Colonial Northeast* (Hanover, N.H., 1980); George Selleck, *Quakers in Boston: 1656–1964, Three Centuries of Friends in Boston and Cambridge* (Cambridge, Mass., 1976); J. William Frost, *The Quaker Family in Colonial America: A Portrait of the Society of Friends* (New York, 1973); Frederick Tolles, *Quakers and the Atlantic Culture* (New York, 1960); Rufus Jones, *The Quakers in the American Colonies* (London, 1911); Richard Hallowell, *The Quaker Invasion of Massachusetts* (Boston, 1883).

15 See John Demos, *Entertaining Satan*, p. 380. Kenneth Silverman also argues that "a mentality of invasion" took hold in New England during the last quarter of the century (Kenneth Silverman, *The Life and Times of Cotton Mather* [New York, 1984], chap. 3). The discussion that follows lends support to the interpretations put forward by Demos and Silverman. See also James E. Kences, "Some Unexplored Relationships of Essex County Witchcraft to the Indian Wars of 1675 and 1689," *Essex Institute Historical Collections*, 120 (1984): 194.

Englanders a common trauma, which they expressed in a common language.

During the months that followed the collapse of the Dominion, "Gentlemen," "Merchants," and other "Inhabitants of Boston" penned and published a number of tracts to justify their rebellion. The language these writers used to describe the Dominion emphasized the alien, invasive, and oppressive character of the Andros regime. The tracts condemned Edmund Andros's policy as "a Treasonable Invasion of the Rights which the whole English Nation lay claim unto."[16] Just as James II's government in England "had invaded both the Liberty and Property of English Protestants," so Andros "did Invade the Property as well as Liberty of the Subject" in New England.[17] Andros had loaded preferments upon "such Men as were strangers to and haters of the People."[18] His high sheriff was "a Stranger in the Country, and one that had no Estate there." He appointed as jurors other "Strangers who had no Freehold."[19] Before Andros came to Boston, he had been governor of New York. The anti-Andros tracts now declared that New Englanders had been "squeez'd by a Crew of abject Persons fetched from New York, to be the Tools of the Adversary."[20] It was surely no coincidence that New England Puritans also called Satan "the Adversary." Nor was Andros the only representative of the imperial government to be described in diabolical terms: according to Samuel Sewall, Boston mariners referred to Colonel Percy Kirke, the ruthless governor of Tangier, whom Charles II had selected as governor of Massachussets in 1685 (but whose appointment was cancelled after the king's death), as "the Devil Kirk[e]."[21]

The Andros tracts located their description of the Dominion within a framework of anti-French and anti-Catholic sentiment. The seventeenth-century English tended to associate autocratic government with the French monarchy and Roman Catholicism. Many believed that any attempt to impose authoritarian government must originate with one or both of these alien powers. There was some empirical basis for such an association. The Stuart mon-

16 "An Account of the Late Revolutions in New-England" (1689), in William Whitmore, ed., *The Andros Tracts,* 3 vols. (Boston, 1868–74), II: 192.
17 "The Revolution in New-England Justified" (1691), in *The Andros Tracts,* I: 72, 87.
18 "Declaration of the Gentlemen, Merchants and Inhabitants of Boston" (1689), in *The Andros Tracts,* I: 13.
19 "The Revolution in New-England Justified," in *The Andros Tracts,* I: 112.
20 "Declaration of the Gentlemen, Merchants and Inhabitants of Boston," in *The Andros Tracts,* I: 13.
21 Samuel Sewall, *Diary,* ed. M. Halsey Thomas, 2 vols. (New York, 1973), I: 108, 15 April 1686.

archs had repeatedly sought French support for their experiments in nonrepresentative government. Charles I was an Arminian and married a Catholic; James II was himself a Catholic. When Charles II had moved to secure James's position as heir, the government's enemies denounced this as the latest stage in a "popish plot." The anti-Andros tracts now claimed that the revocation of the colonial charters had been "one of the most considerable Branches of the late Popish Plot."[22] Andros had insisted on complete liberty of conscience and worship for Anglicans within the Dominion. New Englanders, many of whom saw Anglicanism as crypto-popery, accused Andros and his associates of being "intoxicated with a Bigotry inspired into them by the great Scarlet Whore."[23] According to the pamphleteers, Andros had determined "to destroy the Fundamentals of the English and to Erect a French Government."[24] That "French design" was "an Essay or Specimen of what was intended for the whole English Nation."[25]

Not only did these writers associate Andros with French authoritarianism and the spiritual corruptions of Roman Catholicism, but they also linked him to a much more immediate despoiler of English life and liberty: the Indian. According to his enemies, Andros had supplied native Americans with ammunition and had encouraged them to make war against the colonists.[26] In the past, the French in Canada had often inspired or encouraged native American attacks and there were suspicions that Andros had made a secret pact with the French.[27] Both literally and figuratively, the colonists were in danger of being "given away to a Forreign Power."[28] By invading the liberty and property of the colonists, by usurping control over their affairs, and by imposing an external authority, Edmund Andros and his government had "commit[ted] a Rape on a whole Colony."[29]

A significant symmetry emerges here: the anti-Andros tracts described the Dominion in much the same terms used to characterize witchcraft. In the same year that these political essays began to appear, Cotton Mather published in *Memorable Providences* his ac-

22 "An Appeal to the Men of New-England" (1689), in *The Andros Tracts,* III: 192.
23 "Declaration of the Gentlemen, Merchants and Inhabitants of Boston," in *The Andros Tracts,* I: 12.
24 "The Revolution in New-England Justified," in *The Andros Tracts,* I: 79–80.
25 Ibid., I: 87; "An Appeal to the Men of New-England," in *The Andros Tracts,* III: 194.
26 See especially "The Revolution in New-England Justified," in *The Andros Tracts,* I: 101–11.
27 Timothy Breen, *The Character of a Good Ruler,* p. 149.
28 "Declaration of the Gentlemen, Merchants and Inhabitants of Boston," in *The Andros Tracts,* I: 19.
29 "The Revolution in New-England Justified," in *The Andros Tracts,* I: 128.

count of a 1688 Boston witchcraft case that had resulted in the execution of Goodwife Glover, an Irish Catholic. Glover had apparently bewitched the children of John Goodwin, a pious mason who belonged to Mather's congregation. Mather appended to his account a sermon on witchcraft he had delivered in Boston during the winter of 1688–9. Mather's description of witchcraft in this sermon bore a close resemblance, both in language and tone, to the anti-Andros tracts' description of the Dominion regime. According to Mather, witches and their confederate Devils sought to "break the hedge of . . . Providence" that protected New Englanders against the "Assaults" of Satan's minions. Just as Andros had "Invade[d] the Property as well as Liberty of the Subject," so witches "invaded" and "plunder[ed]" their victims' bodies and possessions, ever anxious to "exert their Devillish and malignant Rage upon their Neighbours."[30] Like Andros's "Crew of abject Persons fetched from New York, to be the Tools of the Adversary," Goodwife Glover was an outsider, marginalized by both ethnicity and religious faith. Alien, invasive, and oppressive: the affinities between the two descriptions are unmistakable.[31]

Native American raids constituted a much more literal form of invasion and were perceived as such by New Englanders. Despite English attempts to convert and acculturate neighboring tribes, most of the native Americans had clung to their own way of life; they remained as alien as ever. In the aftermath of Metacomet's War, English colonists had every reason to see the native Americans as a deadly threat. English accounts of the war described recent hostilities in terms of native American invasion. "The Boar out of the Wood," wrote William Hubbard, "hath broke into the Vineyard."[32] During the war itself, in September 1675, the Council of Massachusetts had called for a day of humiliation,

> we having greatly incensed [God] to stir up many Adversaries against us, not only abroad, but also at our own Doors, causing the Heathen in this wilderness to be as Thorns in our sides, who have formerly been, and might still be a wall unto us therein.

The councilors chose to evoke the war through a series of specific images, each of which related to intrusion. The "Heathen[s]," formerly a "wall" against the French, were now "Thorns" in the "sides"

30 Cotton Mather, *A Discourse on Witchcraft* (Boston, 1689), pp. 6, 10, 18, 21.

31 John Demos notes that "untoward and unwanted intrusiveness" was a recurring element in descriptions of witches (John Demos, *Entertaining Satan*, pp. 178–9).

32 William Hubbard, *A Narrative of the Troubles with the Indians*, The Epistle Dedicatory, p. ii. Hubbard was minister at Ipswich, Massachusetts.

of the English. They threatened English settlers "not only abroad" but even at their "own Doors."[33] Increase Mather, writing in 1676, described the war as a fulfillment of God's warning in Leviticus 26:31:

> I will send wild Beasts among you, which shall rob you of your Children, and destroy your Cattle, and make you few in number, and if you will not be reform'd by these things, I will bring your Sanctuaryes to Desolation, and I will not smell the sweet Savor of your Odours.

To the language of invasion Mather added the potent image of "wild Beasts," violating "Sanctuaryes" and bringing them to utter "Desolation." Mather described the "Epidemical Diseases" that accompanied the war in similar language, as "breaches . . . upon divers of the colonies of New-England."[34]

The twin images of invasion and bestial violation dominate both clerical and lay narratives of native American raids during 1675–6 and after 1689. These narratives often described the attacks as "assaults"[35] and referred to the native Americans themselves as "beasts of prey" and "brutish wolves."[36] The literally invasive character of these attacks surfaces again and again in English accounts. Town after town and, perhaps more significantly, home after home fell to the native Americans. It is through detailed descriptions of raids on individual homes that we can see most clearly the impact of the war on those "assaulted" by native forces. Mary Rowlandson, who was taken captive in February 1676, wrote an account of the attack on her home in Lancaster, Massachusetts:

> It is a solemn sight to see so many Christians lying in their blood, some here, and some there, like a company of Sheep torn by Wolves. All of them stripped naked by a company of

33 Declaration of Massachusetts Council, 17 September 1675, quoted by Increase Mather in *A Brief History of the War*, pp. 15–16.

34 Increase Mather, *A Brief History of the War*, pp. 17, 32.

35 See, for example, Mary Rowlandson, *The Sovereignty and Goodness of God*, p. 13; Josiah Winslow and Thomas Hinckley, "A Brief Narrative of the Begining and Progresse of the Present Trouble between Us and the Indians," in Nathaniel Shurtleff and David Pulsifer, eds., *Records of the Colony of New Plymouth in New England*, 12 vols. (New York, 1968), X: 364; Nathaniel Saltonstall, *A New and Further Narrative*, pp. 2, 3, 4, 10; Increase Mather, *A Brief History of the War*, pp. 12, 23, 24, 29, 30, 33, 37, 41, 48; and Cotton Mather, *Decennium Luctuosum* (Boston, 1699), pp. 33, 45, 90, 91, 144.

36 Nathaniel Saltonstall, *A New and Further Narrative*, p. 8; Benjamin Tompson, *New England's Crisis*, p. 219. See also Increase Mather, *An Earnest Exhortation to the Inhabitants of New-England to Hearken to the Voice of God in His Late and Present Dispensations* (Boston, 1676), p. 6; and Cotton Mather, *Decennium Luctuosum*, pp. 25, 123.

> hell-hounds, roaring, singing, ranting, and insulting, as if they would have torn our very hearts out.[37]

Benjamin Tompson's verse narrative of the war, *New England's Crisis* (published in 1676), is equally vivid, though poetically inept, in its evocation of individual responses to native American attack:

> Poor people spying an unwonted light,
> Fearing a martyrdom, in sudden fright
> Leap to the door to fly, but all in vain,
> They are surrounded with a pagan train;
> Their first salute is death, which if they shun
> Some are condemned the gauntelet to run;
> Death would a mercy prove to such as those
> Who feel the rigor of such hellish foes.
> . . . .
> Here might be seen the infant from the breast
> Snatched by a pagan hand to lasting rest:
> The mother, Rachel-like, shrieks out "My child."
> She wrings her hands and raves as she were wild.
> The brutish wolves suppress her anxious moan
> By cruelties more deadly of their own.
> Will she or nill the chastest turtle must
> Taste of the pangs of their unbridled lust.
> From farms to farms, from towns to towns they post,
> They strip, they bind, they ravish, flay, and roast.[38]

Tompson was not alone in accusing native American attackers of sexual assault. Nathaniel Saltonstall claimed that raiders "defile[d]" English women, forcing them "to satisfie their filthy lusts" before killing them.[39] Collectively, individually, and sexually, then, the New Englanders saw themselves as having been the victims of native American "invasion" and "assault."

Just as incursions of imperial authority were described by New Englanders in much the same language used to characterize assaults by witchcraft, so colonists linked native Americans to witchcraft. But in this case, the association was explicit. Many of the English settlers had either seen or heard about the native medicine-men and their mysterious rituals. New Englanders tended to equate native American supernaturalism with witchcraft. At a New Haven

37 Mary Rowlandson, *The Sovereignty and Goodness of God,* p. 5.

38 Benjamin Tompson, *New England's Crisis,* pp. 219, 221. "Turtle" refers to turtledove.

39 Nathaniel Saltonstall, *The Present State of New-England,* p. 6; Saltonstall, *A New and Further Narrative,* p. 14.

slander hearing in 1653, Goodwife Atwater was said to have claimed that Elizabeth Godman was a witch and that Habbamock, a native spirit, was her husband.[40] When Nicholas Disborough of Hartford, Connecticut, became afflicted ("things being thrown at him and his boy, night and day, in house and feilde"), the first suspect was a native American who worked for neighbor Richard Lord.[41] In the early 1650s, Mary Staples of Fairfield, Connecticut, came under suspicion for witchcraft partly as a result of a story circulating the neighborhood about a native American who, it was claimed, had visited Staples's house and offered her "two little things brighter than the light of the day . . . Indian gods, as the Indian called them." When questioned by neighbors, Staples apparently admitted that the visit had taken place, but claimed that she had refused the proffered gift, a claim some townsfolk were reluctant to believe.[42] Any association with native Americans, however tenuous and whether or not connected with native religion, could be used to incriminate a witch suspect. As we will see, accusers at the Salem witch trials in 1692 not only detailed the connections between suspects and native Americans as indicative of their guilt, but also claimed that the Devil looked like a native American.

Puritans were convinced that New England and its native inhabitants had belonged to the Devil until the arrival of God's chosen, namely, the English.[43] It is, then, hardly surprising that ministers and godly layfolk referred to the native Americans in diabolical terms. Cotton Mather described them as Satan's "most devoted and resembling children."[44] Writing in 1689, Mather claimed that "Evil spirits" were at work in "the Wigwams of Indians, where the pagan Powaws often raise[d] their masters, in the shapes of Bears and

40 Charles J. Hoadly, ed., *Records of the Colony or Jurisdiction of New Haven,* 2 vols. (New Haven, Conn., 1857–8), II: 31, 4 August 1653. The native Americans believed that Habbamock entered certain individuals and resided in their bodies as guardian and familiar. Habbamock was not the only spirit to do this; sometimes, several spirits would occupy the same person. Humans into whom spirits entered derived special powers from their guardians and became "pow-wows," or shamans. Puritans claimed that Habbamock and the other guardian spirits were devils, and that pow-wows were possessed witches (see William S. Simmons, "Cultural Bias in the New England Puritans' Perceptions of Indians," *William and Mary Quarterly,* 38 [1981]: 60–2).

41 John Russell to Increase Mather, 2 August 1683, *Collections of the Massachusetts Historical Society,* 4. ser., 8 (1868): 86–7.

42 Charles J. Hoadly, ed., *Records of the Colony or Jurisdiction of New Haven,* II: 80, 86.

43 See, for example, Cotton Mather, *Wonders of the Invisible World* (1693; Amherst, Wisc., 1862), p. 74.

44 Cotton Mather, *Magnalia Christi Americana,* 2 vols. (1702; New York, 1967), I: 213.

Snakes and fires."[45] These "powaws" were apparently "horrid Sorcerers, and hellish Conjurers, and such as Conversed with Daemons."[46] Mary Rowlandson accused the native Americans of "devilish cruelty to the English" and described one native camp as "a lively resemblance of hell."[47] Benjamin Tompson's verse narrative characterized the native Americans as "hellish foes."[48] Metacomet, like Andros, was described in terms also used to characterize Satan: the sachem was a "grand Rebel" who harbored "inveterate malice and wickedness against the English."[49] Like Satan and his indefatigable minions, the native Americans constituted "an Ever-Approaching and Unapproachable Adversary."[50] Their reputation for witchcraft and diabolism reinforced their impact as an invasive threat. Native American raids during the years following 1689 confirmed and deepened the psychological effects of the Dominion experience.

Many colonists perceived heresy as yet another alien force that had invaded and now threatened to subvert the New England community. In the late 1650s, a number of Quakers had crossed the Atlantic in a bid to purify New England of its spiritual corruption. Needless to say, Congregationalists did not appreciate this attention. The Quakers' refusal to abide by norms of social deference and their generally bizarre behavior made them appear threatening even to those who were less concerned about their spiritual beliefs. The General Court in Massachusetts was not slow to take action against the Quaker mission. In a bid "to prevent the intrusions of the Quakers," the court ordered that all visiting Friends be ejected, and that all resident converts to Quakerism be banished.[51] Initial responses to Quakerism within the colony often used invasive imagery to describe the Friends. John Norton, a Puritan cleric who was commissioned by the General Court to write a tract refuting Quaker doctrine, compared the Friends to "the wolfe which ventures over the wide Sea, out of a ravening desire to prey upon the sheep, when landed."[52] In 1658, twenty-five laymen submitted a

Quakers

45 Cotton Mather, *Memorable Providences* (Boston, 1689), Introduction, p. ii.

46 Cotton Mather, *Decennium Luctuosum*, p. 103. See also Increase Mather, *Angelographia* (Boston, 1696), To the Reader, p. x.

47 Mary Rowlandson, *The Sovereignty and Goodness of God*, pp. 6, 62.

48 Benjamin Tompson, *New England's Crisis*, p. 221.

49 William Hubbard, *A Narrative of the Troubles with the Indians*, pp. 103–4.

50 Cotton Mather, *Decennium Luctuosum*, p. 79. English commentators often complained that the native Americans' stealth and tendency to attack at night made them as inscrutable as they were deadly (see, for example, Nathaniel Saltonstall, *A New and Further Narrative*, p. 8).

51 Nathaniel Shurtleff, ed., *Records of the Governor and Company of Massachusetts Bay*, IV. pt 1, 346, 19 October 1658; and pt 2, 2–3, 22 May 1661.

52 John Norton, *The Heart of New-England Rent at the Blasphemies of the Present*

petition to the General Court, demanding severer laws against the Quakers, who had, claimed the petitioners, "audaciously intruded themselves" upon the colonists.[53] Governor John Endecott, writing to Charles II on behalf of the General Court in order to explain its punitive actions toward the Quakers, described the Friends as "breaking in upon us."[54] The General Court itself referred to the Quakers' "arrogant, bold obtrusions."[55] The court also used images of disease and even of sexual subversion in describing the Quaker threat: the Friends had "infected and seduced . . . diverse . . . inhabitants."[56]

Images of invasion reappeared in two anti-Quaker tracts published in the early 1690s. Both pieces were written in response to the evangelical efforts of George Keith, an itinerant Quaker preacher who had arrived in New England in June 1688. The first piece, published in 1690 and written by three prominent New England ministers (James Allen, Joshua Moodey, and Samuel Willard), maintained that the Church of God had "in all ages undergone the Batteries of a various assault." Heresy was foremost among these "Batteries." According to Allen, Moodey, and Willard, no heresy posed so grave a threat to the New-English Israel as did Quakerism, "this great Choak-weed of the Christian and Protestant Religion, taking root in the Borders of New England."[57] A year later, Cotton Mather also warned against "the assaults of Quakerism" and recommended that the godly arm themselves with an array of spiritual "Weapons" to "keep off the Quakers with." Mather, like Norton, saw the Friends as "Grievous Wolves" who sought to devour the "Little Flocks" of New England Congregationalists.[58]

Anti-Quaker polemic linked the Friends to threats from the invisible as well as visible world. Puritans believed that there was a close connection between heresy, diabolism, and witchcraft. The Friends were particularly susceptible to such associations, partly as a result of their reliance upon revelation. Congregationalists re-

Generation, or, A Brief Tractate Concerning the Doctrine of the Quakers (Cambridge, Mass., 1659), p. 54.

53 "Petition for Severer Laws against the Quakers," October 1658, Massachusetts Archives, X: 246.

54 *Records of the Governor and Company of Massachusetts Bay,* IV: pt. 1, 451, 19 December 1660.

55 Ibid., IV: pt. 1, 346, 19 October 1658. See also IV: pt. 1, 383, 18 October 1659.

56 Ibid., IV: pt. 1, 346.

57 James Allen, Joshua Moodey, and Samuel Willard, *The Principles of the Protestant Religion Maintained* (Boston, 1690), Preface, pp. i, iii.

58 Cotton Mather, *Little Flocks Guarded against Grievous Wolves* (Boston, 1691), p. 100. See also ibid., p. 57. For more references to Quakers as wolves, see James Allen et al., *The Principles of the Protestant Religion Maintained,* Preface, p. vi; p. 152.

fused to accept that the Quakers received "inner light" from God: as John Norton put it, Quaker revelation was "in pretence divine, but indeed diabolical."[59] Increase Mather assured his readers that Quakers were "under the strong delusions of Satan" and that "some of them [were] undoubtedly possessed with Evil and Infernal Spirits, and acted [upon] in a more than ordinary manner by the inmates of Hell."[60] The General Court condemned Quaker doctrine as "devilish" and "diabollicall."[61] The Friends' tendency to "quake" when receiving revelation strengthened their association with Satan in Puritan minds, since their physical convulsions bore a close resemblance to possession. "The quaking and shaking motions of the Quakers," wrote Roger Williams, "cannot be imagined to proceed from the Holy Spirit of God, but from Sathan."[62] John Norton claimed that it was Satan's "ancient and known manner . . . when he inspired his Enthusiasts, to afflict the bodyes of his instruments with paines and those often in their bowells, and to agitate them with Antick and uncouth motions, and in particular with this of quaking and trembling."[63] According to Cotton Mather, "Diabolical Possession was the thing which did dispose and encline men unto Quakerism."[64]

In both England and New England, Quakers were vulnerable to accusations of witchcraft.[65] In 1656, when two Quaker missionaries, Ann Austin and Mary Fisher, arrived in Massachusetts, magistrates instructed a group of midwives to search the two women for witch marks.[66] Magistrates and ministers were not alone in associating Quakers with witchcraft. When Friend Mary Thompkins disrupted a church service in Portsmouth, members of the congregation threw her down a flight of stairs; Thompkins survived the fall, and the disappointed townsfolk attributed this to her being a witch.[67] Caleb Powell, the seaman who offered his services as a cunning man to townsfolk in Newbury, Massachusetts, and who was subsequently

59 John Norton, *The Heart of New-England Rent*, p. 6.

60 Increase Mather, *An Essay for the Recording of Illustrious Providences* (Boston, 1684), pp. 345, 347.

61 *The Records of the Governor and Company of Massachusetts Bay*, IV (pt 1): 278, 321.

62 Roger Williams, "George Fox Digg'd Out of His Burrowes," ed. J. Lewis Diman, in *The Complete Writings of Roger Williams* (New York, 1963), pp. 44–5.

63 John Norton, *The Heart of New-England Rent*, pp. 5–6.

64 Cotton Mather, *Memorable Providences*, p. 67.

65 See Keith Thomas, *Religion and the Decline of Magic* (1971; Middlesex, England, 1973), pp. 580–1; and Amelia Mott Gummere, *Witchcraft and Quakerism: A Study of Social History* (Philadelphia, 1908), pp. 30–5.

66 Humphrey Norton, *New England's Bloody Ensigne* (London, 1659), p. 7; George Bishop, *New England Judged by the Spirit of the Lord*, Part One (London, 1661), p. 12.

67 George Bishop, *New England Judged by the Spirit of the Lord*, Part Two (London, 1667), p. 82.

accused of witchcraft, claimed to have learned his craft from Francis Norwood, a Quaker who lived in Gloucester.[68] In 1688, when John Goodwin's four children became bewitched, they derived great comfort from any mention of Quakerism. One of them was unable to read the bible, but could read "a Quaker's Book." Another fell into fits if his parents tried to take him to a Congregationalist meeting, but felt much better when his father spoke of going to a Quaker assembly. The Goodwin children's attraction to Quaker writings and meetings whilst bewitched horrified those around them, but it cannot have come as a surprise.[69]

As in the case of the native Americans, the Quakers' association with witchcraft intensified the psychological impact of their intrusion into the officially sanctioned community after 1691. Cotton Mather drew a direct connection between the Quaker and native American threats:

> While the Indians have been thus molesting us, we have suffered Molestations of another sort, from another sort of Enemies, which may with very good Reason be cast into the same History with them. If the Indians have chosen to prey upon the Frontiers, and Out-Skirts, of the Province, the Quakers have chosen the very same Frontiers, and Out-Skirts, for their more Spiritual Assaults; and finding little Success elsewhere, they have been Labouring incessantly, and sometimes not unsuccessfully, to Enchant and Poison the souls of poor people, in the very places where the Bodies and Estates of the people have presently after been devoured by the Salvages.

According to Mather, native American and Quaker "Assaults" could "be cast into the same History." Both had "prey[ed] upon the Frontiers, and Out-Skirts, of the Province." The Quakers had "Labour[ed] . . . to Enchant and Poison the souls" of those very people whose "Bodies and Estates" were then "devoured by the Salvages."[70] Mather was not alone in making this association. John Norton compared Quaker palpitations to "the custome of the Powwows or Indian Wizards, in this Wilderness; whose bodies at the time of their diabolicall practises, are at this day vexed and agitated in a strange, unwonted and dreadfull manner."[71] Edmund Batter, a merchant of Salem Town, testified in court that Elizabeth Kitchen was a Friend, having met her "betim[e]s in the morning

68 *Records and Files of the Quarterly Courts of Essex County*, 9 vols. (Salem, Mass., 1911–78), VII: 357.
69 Cotton Mather, *Memorable Providences*, pp. 22, 43.
70 Cotton Mather, *Decennium Luctuosum*, p. 162.
71 John Norton, *The Heart of New-England Rent*, p. 6.

comeing as he supposed from a quaking meeting." Batter referred to Quakerism as "apawawing."[72]

All of these interrelated, alien, and intrusive forces, which the colonists equated with witchcraft, converged on a local level in Essex County. In particular, Salem Village and Andover, the two principal sources of witch hysteria in 1692, were prey to threatening, invasive forces. When France declared war on England in 1689 and persuaded the native Americans to attack New England, native forces converged initially on the northern areas of English settlement. Not until 1691 did Massachusetts become a target, with one significant exception. On 14 August 1689, native Americans attacked Andover, killing John and Andrew Peters, the sons of a distiller.[73] Andover was the only settled community in Massachusetts to suffer a native raid during the first two years of the war. The anxieties caused by the raid of 1689 revived and intensified in 1691 as the native Americans launched a major attack on western Massachusetts. The following year, Andover produced more cases of witchcraft than any other community.[74]

Salem Village faced less literal but equally disturbing forms of invasion. The village, legally subordinate to nearby Salem Town, had no civil government of its own and no independent church. Salem Town maintained careful control over the village's internal affairs and showed remarkable insensitivity to the villagers' concerns. Some of the villagers were eager to secure legal independence from the town; others, who had economic ties with the town and identified with its interests, resisted independence.[75] The conflict between village and town, which became increasingly bitter as the years passed by, was, in effect, a microcosm of the troubled rela-

72 *Records and Files of the Quarterly Courts of Essex County,* II: 219, 26 June 1660.

73 Sarah Loring Bailey, *Historical Sketches of Andover* (Boston, 1880), p. 179.

74 The Andover cases are often underplayed in historical accounts of the 1692 crisis. See Chadwick Hansen, "Andover Witchcraft and the Causes of the Salem Witchcraft Trials," in Howard Kerr and Charles Crow, eds., *The Occult in America: New Historical Perspectives* (Urbana, Ill., 1983), pp. 38–57.

75 See Paul Boyer and Stephen Nissenbaum, *Salem Possessed.* Boyer and Nissenbaum argue that the divisions within Salem Village over the issue of autonomy were closely bound up with economic circumstance. As Salem Town became more prosperous, the farmers who lived in the surrounding countryside were encountering serious economic difficulty. Population growth and the diminished availability of land led to smaller units of ownership and a consequent decline in individual wealth. Those Salem Village farmers who lived closest to the town were in a much stronger position than those who lived at the other end of the village: not only was their land of a higher quality, but their proximity to the town gave easier access to its markets. These farmers tended to see the growth of the town as an exciting opportunity, whereas those who lived further west feared and resented the town.

tionship between Massachusetts and England. In 1689, the same year in which the Dominion collapsed, those in favor of autonomy from the town secured the ordination of Samuel Parris as minister of an independent congregation. Henceforth, Parris and his church became the focus for conflict within the village. In his sermons, Parris translated factional division into a cosmic struggle between the forces of good and evil. Parris made an explicit connection between his enemies and the legions of Hell: there was, he declared in 1690, "a lamentable harmony between wicked men and devils, in their opposition of God's kingdom and interests."[76] Sectarian as well as political forces threatened Salem Village: between the village and Salem Town itself was located the largest Quaker community in all of Essex County.[77] As the villagers looked eastward, they saw a doubly threatening world just beyond the village boundary.[78]

The pattern of witch accusations in 1692 suggests an intense preoccupation with invasion in the minds of Salem Villagers. Of those villagers who became actively involved in witchcraft cases, most accused witches and their defenders lived on the side of the village nearest to Salem Town, whereas most accusers lived on the other side of the village.[79] Many of the accused also lived in close proximity to the Quaker community situated between village and town.[80] In other words, the direction of witch accusations expressed fears aroused by the alien forces, both political and spiritual, which threatened the integrity of the local community.[81]

76 Samuel Parris, "Sermons 1689–1695" (Connecticut Historical Society), 12 January 1690.

77 See Richard Gildrie, *Salem, Massachusetts, 1626–1683: A Covenant Community* (Charlottesville, N.C., 1975), pp. 117, 130–7. See also Jonathan Chu, *Neighbors, Friends, or Madmen.*

78 John Demos notes that the "strains" that engendered a "sense of crisis" throughout New England in the early 1690s were "powerfully evident at Salem, perhaps more so than in any other New England community" (John Demos, *Entertaining Satan,* p. 385).

79 See Paul Boyer and Stephen Nissenbaum, *Salem Possessed,* p. 34.

80 See Christine Heyrman, *Commerce and Culture,* p. 114.

81 David Konig argues that the people of Massachusetts were particularly sensitive to the violation of boundaries during the years leading up to the witch hunt; the depositions of 1692 referred frequently to animals intruding on private property. Konig places this sensitivity in the context of general insecurity caused by the breakdown of the legal system during the political crisis of 1684–92. According to Konig, fences and other boundaries "stood as symbols of local regulation" (David Konig, *Law and Society in Puritan Massachusetts: Essex County 1629–92* [Chapel Hill, 1979], p. 180). Kai Erikson pursues a similar line of argument in *Wayward Puritans: A Study in the Sociology of Deviance* (New York, 1966). Social and political change had removed many of the boundaries according to which the colonists had defined themselves: "Most of the familiar landmarks of the New England Way had become blurred by changes in the historical climate, like signposts obscured in a storm . . ." (p. 140). The colonists, "bewildered by the loss of their old destiny but not yet aware of their new one,"

Salem Villagers were not alone in using witch accusations to express hostility toward Quakers. In Andover, Gloucester, and other towns throughout Essex County, a significant number of the accused had close Quaker associations. In the aftermath of the new charter's imposition of religious toleration, Congregationalists could no longer have Quakers fined for espousing heretical doctrines or refusing to attend orthodox church meetings. Attacking Quakers as witches was equally unacceptable: the beliefs and palpitations that made Friends vulnerable to such accusations were now, at least officially, unexceptionable. However, the direction of witch accusations against the relatives and friends of Quakers offered an alternative way to express anxieties aroused by their invasion of the orthodox community. A significant number of the accused were connected to Quakers by ties of kinship or friendship.[82] Rebecca and Francis Nurse had acted as the guardians of Samuel Southwick, the orphaned son of a local Quaker farmer. Elizabeth Proctor's family, the Bassets, included a large number of Quakers. Thomas Farrar was father of a leading Lynn Friend; the Wardwells and Hawkes also had Quaker connections.[83] Job Tookey, another accused witch, was reputed to be the son of "an Annybaptisticall Quakeing Rogue that for his maintainence went up and down England to delude Soules for the Divell."[84]

Just as the direction of witch accusations reflected a fear of sectarian invasion, so court depositions expressed acute anxiety about native American invasion. Essex County, situated in northern Massachusetts, was uncomfortably close to New Hampshire and Maine, where most of the attacks occurred. The county had suffered heavy losses during the war of 1675–6 and must have feared for the worst now that hostilities had resumed, especially after the raid on Andover in 1689.[85] Since the beginning of the war, refugees from the northern stretches of New England had resettled in Massachusetts; their presence must have intensified local fear and uncertainty. Mercy Short, a seventeen-year-old servant who was afflicted by specters following an argument with one of the accused, had been

used the witch hunt "to discover some image of themselves..." (159). See also Larzer Ziff, *Puritanism in America: New Culture in a New World* (New York, 1973), pp. 244–5.

82 This paragraph is much indebted to Christine Heyrman, *Commerce and Culture*, chap. 3. Heyrman argues that "the witchcraft outbreak... constituted in part a counteroffensive against the Quaker heresy under the conditions imposed by the new Massachusetts charter" (p. 123).

83 These examples are drawn from Christine Heyrman, *Commerce and Culture*, pp. 112–14.

84 *Records and Files of the Quarterly Courts of Essex County*, VIII: 336, 27 June 1682.

85 James E. Kences, "Some Unexplored Relationships of Essex County Witchcraft to the Indian Wars of 1675 and 1689," p. 181.

captured by native American forces in 1690. Until 18 March 1690, Mercy had lived with her family in Salmon Falls, Maine, but that day the native Americans launched a surprise attack against the settlement. Thirty-four people were killed, including Mercy's parents, one brother, and one sister; fifty-four were taken prisoner, including Mercy, who was carried north to Canada by her captors and then brought to Boston after having been redeemed. Perhaps not surprisingly, she described the Devil as being "a Tawney, or an Indian colour."[86] Mary Toothaker of Billerica, an accused witch, also claimed that the Devil appeared to her "in the shape of a Tawny man." Toothaker had recently been "troubled w[it]h feare about the Indians, and used often to dream of fighting with them." The Devil, she confessed on 30 July, persuaded her to become a witch by promising to keep her safe from native Americans.[87] That Toothaker had good reason to be worried about the possibility of an attack was demonstrated six days later, on 5 August, when native American forces raided the Toothaker farm in Billerica.[88] Abigail Hobbs, who confessed to witchcraft, had lived in Maine until driven south by native attacks. In her confession, Hobbs declared that she had first seen the Devil in the woods near Casco, Maine.[89]

Other testimony presented to the court in 1692 linked accused witches and the Devil to native Americans. One confessing witch told the court that French Canadians and native Sagamores had attended the "Cheef Witch-meetings," hoping "to concert the methods of ruining New England."[90] In mid–1692, just after the outbreak of witch hysteria in Andover, a number of townsfolk at nearby Gloucester claimed to have seen native Americans and Frenchmen lurking on Cape Ann.[91] Sarah Osborne, a witch suspect from Salem Village, testified that she "either saw or dreamed that shee saw a thing like an indian all black which did pinch her in her neck and pulled her by the back part of her head to the dore of

86 Douglas Leach, *Arms for Empire: A Military History of the British Colonies in North America, 1607–1763* (New York, 1973), p. 88; Cotton Mather, "A Brand Pluck't Out of the Burning," in George L. Burr, ed., *Narratives of the Witchcraft Cases,* pp. 259, 261.

87 Paul Boyer and Stephen Nissenbaum, eds., *The Salem Witchcraft Papers: Verbatim Transcripts of the Legal Documents of the Salem Witchcraft Outbreak,* 3 vols. (New York, 1977), III: 767–8.

88 Samuel Adams Drake, *The Border Wars of New England* (1897; Williamstown, Mass., 1973), p. 107.

89 *Salem Witchcraft Papers,* II: 405.

90 Cotton Mather, "A Brand Pluck't Out of the Burning," pp. 281–2. Cotton Mather suspected that the witch conspiracy had "some of its Original among the Indians" (Cotton Mather, *Decennium Luctuosum,* p. 103).

91 Ibid., pp. 243–7. See also Christine Heyrman, *Commerce and Culture,* p. 105 n11.

the house."[92] Yet another accused witch, John Proctor, had been fined in 1678 "for selling cider and strong waters to Indians."[93] One of John Alden's accusers charged that he "[sold] Powder and Shot to the Indians and French, and [lay] with the Indian Squa[w]es, and ha[d] Indian Papooses."[94]

In addition to these specific fears relating to Quakers and native Americans, the witchcraft accusations expressed a general hostility toward outsiders. Not only did most of the accused witches from Salem Village live on the side of the village closest to Salem Town, but some of them were only formally resident within the village. John Proctor had become a resident in 1666, but actually lived on a farm southeast of the village boundary. Martha and Giles Corey lived just over the village line in Salem Town.[95] Bridget Bishop had lived within the village boundary for seven years, but had rarely ventured into the village itself. Nobody contradicted Bishop at her examination when she said, "I never was in this place before . . . I know no man, woman or child here."[96] Sarah and Edward Bishop were outsiders in a figurative sense. Sarah Bishop had turned her house into an unlicensed tavern and exercised a disruptive influence over younger members of the community. According to John Hale, Bishop "did entertaine people in her house at unseasonable houres in the night to keep drinking and playing at shovel-board, whereby discord did arise in other families and young people were in danger to bee corrupted."[97] Long before Sarah Bishop sought to intrude her alien and evil ways into the minds of innocent young villagers, Martha Corey had become an outsider by giving birth to an illegitimate mulatto son who still lived in the Corey household.[98] Sarah Osborne had caused scandal after the death of her first husband, Robert Prince, by committing fornication with her indentured servant, a young Irish immigrant named Alexander Osborne, whom she later married. The Osbornes now threatened traditional patterns of inheritance by conspiring to subvert Robert Prince's will so as to gain full control over his land, which Sarah Osborne was holding in trust for Prince's two sons.[99]

The same pattern of hostility toward outsiders characterized Andover accusations. Eight of the suspects were marginalized by ethnic

92 *Salem Witchcraft Papers,* II: 611.
93 *Records and Files of the Quarterly Courts of Essex County,* VII: 135, 26 November 1678.
94 *Salem Witchcraft Papers,* I: 52.
95 Paul Boyer and Stephen Nissenbaum, *Salem Possessed,* pp. 146, 200.
96 *Salem Witchcraft Papers,* I: 83, 86.
97 Ibid., I: 95.
98 Paul Boyer and Stephen Nissenbaum, *Salem Possessed,* p. 146.
99 Ibid., pp. 193–4.

affiliation. Martha Carrier was Scottish and had married a Welshman: she and four of her children were accused. The Carrier family had been further ostracized as carriers of smallpox and were warned out of Andover in 1690.[100] Ann Foster's husband Andrew was Scottish; her own ethnic background is unclear, but she was accused in 1692 along with a daughter and granddaughter.[101] In 1689, Hannah Foster had been killed by her husband, Hugh Stone, the first case of murder in Andover. The taint of this shocking event may well have stuck to the Foster family and strengthened their marginal status.[102] The Wardwell family's reputation was tarnished by connection with heresy: Samuel Wardwell's father and uncle accompanied the Reverend John Wheelwright into New Hampshire when he was banished from Massachusetts as an Antinomian. His uncle, William Wardwell, became a Quaker, as did his brother Eliakim.[103]

In *Wonders of the Invisible World,* a commentary on the events of 1692, Cotton Mather argued that the various threats that faced New Englanders during these years were not discrete, but constituted a vast, interlocking assault. Mather argued that the witch conspiracy was the latest in a series of diabolical offensives against New England: native American sorceries and raids, the revocation of the charter, the French war, and a succession of heresies. Each of these, wrote Mather, should be understood as part of a larger pattern. Mather described the witch conspiracy itself as an outright invasion:

> such is the descent of the Devil at this day upon our selves, that I may truly tell you, The Walls of the whole World are broken down! The usual Walls of defence about mankind have such a Gap made in them that the very Devils are broken in upon us . . . [104]

By no means everybody saw their predicament in diabolical terms, but Mather had captured effectively the general state of mind in

100 Sarah Loring Bailey, *Historical Sketches of Andover,* p. 202; Charlotte Helen Abbott, "Early Records of the Allen Families of Andover" (Andover Historical Society, Andover, Mass.), p. 1.

101 Charlotte Helen Abbott, "Early Records of the Foster Families of Andover" (Andover Historical Society, Andover, Mass.), p. 1; Frederick Clifton Pierce, *Foster Genealogy* (Chicago, 1899), p. 1032.

102 John Noble and John F. Cronin, eds., *Records of the Court of Assistants of the Colony of Massachusetts Bay, 1630–1692,* 3 vols. (Boston, 1901–28), I: 303–4.

103 Anders Robinson, "Wardwell and Barker Families of Andover in the Seventeenth Century" (Andover Historical Society, Andover, Mass.), 3.10–3.12, 4.10.

104 Cotton Mather, *Wonders of the Invisible World,* pp. 74–5, 80.

Massachusetts. Royal officials, native Americans, and dissenters had all threatened the well-being of the community in much the same way that a witch threatened the well-being of an individual; many people believed that native Americans and Quakers were witches. Alien, invasive, and oppressive: these associations provided the context for witch hysteria.

In the light of their experience since 1675, the people of Essex County were only too willing to blame misfortune on alien malefactors. This predisposition, under the pressure of recent events, to locate evil outside the self is the key to understanding what happened in 1692. An accusation of witchcraft involved a decision to blame suffering on a malevolent, external force. There were alternatives: victims could interpret suffering as divine punishment for their own sinfulness, or they could just accept it as an inexplicable misfortune. Ministers urged their congregations to look inward for the source of their troubles, yet clerical descriptions of the ordeals that faced New England in the late seventeenth century magnified the threat from without and so reinforced the literal impact of native American warriors and other invasive forces. Furthermore, ambiguity within Puritan theology enabled even godly colonists to displace responsibility for sin and suffering, should they be inclined to do so, without any clear sense of violating orthodoxy. The likelihood of individuals deciding to blame their troubles on witchcraft would depend on their own psychological inclinations, their mood at the time of misfortune, and the broader influences being exerted upon them by their cultural environment. The latter was crucial in 1692.[105] The Andros regime, the renewal of native American attacks, and the imposition of religious toleration each encouraged the people of Massachusetts to associate external forces with some kind of threat. Andover and Salem Village, where over half of the 1692 cases originated, underwent additional and analogous ordeals that accentuated this cast of mind. When Samuel Parris decided to pursue those responsible for the mysterious "distempers" in Salem Village and so began the witch panic, townsfolk in nearby communities recalled recent misfortunes and readily blamed them on witch suspects. The torments undergone by the afflicted girls in Salem Village touched a raw nerve exposed and sensitized by the ordeals of the last decade. The psychological impact of these ordeals spawned the witch hunt of 1692.

105 As John Demos points out, it was because "the social climate of New England as a whole was then unusually strained" that fears of witchcraft "spread well beyond Salem, and adjacent communities produced responsive accusations of their own" (John Demos, *Entertaining Satan*, p. 385).

The traumatic events of the previous two decades had affected the entire community, clerical and lay, Puritan and non-Puritan. The witch hunt provided an opportunity to release pent-up fears and to root out persons who seemed threatening to the community. Ministers and magistrates sought to locate this process within a religious context. The Salem judges saw themselves as fulfilling an almost priestly function: under their guidance, the accused were to confess their sins, renounce the Devil, and rejoin the church of God. The New-English Israel would emerge from that process cleansed and spiritually reinvigorated. Yet most of those who gave testimony against witch suspects in 1692 had no desire to locate their experience within a theological framework. Just as invasions by native Americans, imperial officials, and iconoclastic dissenters were not perceived by all those who feared them as diabolical, so witchcraft itself impinged upon many people's lives as maleficium rather than as diabolical heresy. Thus, problems of evidence plagued the Salem trials just as they had plagued other New England witch prosecutions. Court officials demanded proof of a direct link between the accused and the Devil, but most witnesses did not interpret witchcraft in diabolical terms and saw no reason to mention the Devil in their testimony. The trials of 1692, although atypical in their scale and intensity, were consistent with other seventeenth-century New England trials in embodying the tension between magical and theological perceptions of witchcraft.

On first inspection, the court records from Salem give the impression that Satan had gripped the imagination of Essex County. Take, for example, the confession of William Barker. On 29 August 1692, Barker, an Andover man, appeared before the special court appointed to deal with the witch crisis. He was accused of having used diabolical witchcraft to afflict three women, Abigail Martin and Rose Foster of Andover, and Martha Sprague of Boxford. During the course of his examination, Barker made a lengthy confession. He admitted that he was a witch and that he had been "in the Snare of the Divel" for about three years. He told the court that he had a large family and was in debt; the Devil had promised to pay off his debts, and so he had made a covenant with him. Since then, Barker confessed, he had indeed afflicted the three women who accused him of witchcraft. He had also attended a recent witch meeting at Salem Village and gave a detailed description of what happened there. George Burroughs, former minister of Salem Village and now "Ring Leader" at the witch gatherings, had blown a trumpet to summon the witches from far and wide. Barker had heard that there were over three hundred witches in New England; about one hundred attended this particular meeting. The Devil himself appeared at the gathering and gave a speech. "Satan's desire," reported Barker, "was to Sett up his own worship, abolish all the Churches in the land, to fall next upon Salem and Soe goe through the Country." The Devil exhorted his followers to recruit new witches and "to pull downe the Kingdom of Christ and Sett Up the kingdome of the Divel." The witches then joined together in a sacrament with bread and wine. Barker told the court that he was "hartyly sorry for W[ha]t he ha[d] done." He promised to renounce the Devil and asked for prayers on his own behalf.[106]

Barker's confession was not an isolated incident. Between February and October 1692, at least forty-three people confessed to diabolical witchcraft, many of them giving graphic descriptions of their dealings with Satan. This made the magistrates' job much easier, since confession was by far the most satisfactory form of evidence for an association with the Devil. When placed in the context of previous New England witch trials, these confessions are, to say the least, surprising. Before 1692, only four New Englanders had confessed to diabolical witchcraft, yet the crowded courtroom at Salem witnessed at least forty-three confessions.[107] Evidence offered against the accused witches also seems to depart radically from that which characterized earlier trials. The depositions seem to be saturated with references to the Devil, his physical appearance, his presentation of the diabolical covenant to initiates, his rites of baptism and sacrament, and his coordination of the witch conspiracy. The usual tension between evidence of maleficium and legal demands for proof of diabolical witchcraft seems to have evaporated.

Yet this initial impression is misleading. Almost all evidence relating to the Devil came from two groups: confessors and the afflicted girls whose torments dominated the court proceedings. The most striking characteristic of other depositions placed before the court is the lack of references to the Devil. Most of these deponents gave no indication whatsoever that they associated witchcraft with a diabolical agency.[108] The evidence they offered against the accused was much more characteristic of earlier trials: misfortune preceded by an argument with the accused witch, generally suspicious be-

106 *Salem Witchcraft Papers,* I: 67–8.

107 For a listing of those who confessed in 1692, see Appendix B. For other confessions, see Appendix A.

108 In all these depositions, I have found only sixteen references to the Devil (*Salem Witchcraft Papers,* I: 112, 177, 231, 261–2; II: 413, 415, 457, 572–3, 606, 633, 683; III: 731, 760, 810, 844). Only six of these references would have been useful to the court as possible grounds for conviction (I: 112; II: 413, 415, 457; III: 731, 760).

havior, and magical activity. The nature of this evidence did not change as the year wore on. By late summer, devil-related testimony given by confessors and afflicted girls must have been common knowledge, yet other deponents continued to describe witchcraft in non-diabolical terms. Their depositions bore eloquent testimony to a widespread popular fear of witchcraft, but such fear was of little use to the magistrates unless deponents provided evidence of a direct link between the accused and the Devil. This they conspicuously failed to do. Only the afflicted girls and those who actually confessed to witchcraft gave evidence that could justify legal conviction. They made constant reference to the Devil and described witchcraft in explicitly diabolical terms. Why was their testimony so different from the other evidence presented to the court?

Officials used both physical torture and psychological pressure to extract evidence of the Devil's involvement from the accused. Most of those who confessed did so under duress and later recanted. John Proctor complained that the authorities had tortured Richard Carrier, Andrew Carrier, and his own son William. According to Proctor, "they tyed them Neck and Heels till the Blood was ready to come out of their Noses and 'tis credibly believed and reported this was the occasion of making them confess that [which] they never did." William Proctor was kept in this position until "the Blood gushed out at his Nose" and they "would have kept him so 24 Hours, if one more Merciful than the rest, had not taken pity on him and caused him to be unbound."[109] Thomas Brattle, a Boston merchant, claimed that "most violent, distracting and draggooning methods" were "used with them, to make them confesse."

> You may possibly think that my terms are too severe; but should I tell you what a kind of blade was employed in bringing these women to their confession; what methods from damnation were taken; with what violence urged; how unseasonably they were kept up; what buzzings and chuckings of the hand were used, and the like, I am sure that you would call them (as I do) rude and barbarous methods.[110]

Samuel Willard also complained that many of the confessions were "Extorted." "And let me tell you," he wrote, "there are other ways of undue force and fright, besides Racks, Strapadoes, and such like things as Spanish Inquisitions use."[111] In most cases, threats sufficed

109 Ibid., II: 689–90.

110 Thomas Brattle, letter to a clergyman, in George L. Burr, ed., *Narratives of the Witchcraft Cases,* pp. 181, 189.

111 Samuel Willard, *Some Miscellany Observations on Our Present Debates Respecting Witchcrafts* (Philadelphia, 1692), p. 6.

to overcome the initial resistance of the accused. Sarah Churchill came to Sarah Ingersoll after her examination and broke down, "Crieng and wringing hur hands se[e]ming to be mutch trobeled in Sparet [spirit]." She told Ingersoll that her confession was false and that she had lied "because they thr[e]atened hur: and told hur thay would put hur in to the dongin [dungeon] and put hur along with mr Borows [George Burroughs]."[112]

Thomas Brattle complained that William Stoughton, chief justice of the court, assumed the guilt of the accused until convinced otherwise and was "very impatient in hearing any thing which look[ed] another way."[113] Samuel Wardwell, for example, confessed that "he was in the snare of the devil" only "after the returneing of negative answers to severall questions." His "negative answers" were unacceptable to the court.[114] John Hathorne's examination of Sarah Good will serve as an illustration of the bullying and leading questions to which the accused were subjected.

Hathorne: Sarah Good, what evil spirit have you familiarity with?
Good: None.
Hathorne: Have you made no contract with the Devil?
Good: No.
Hathorne: Why doe you hurt these children?
Good: I doe not hurt them. I scorn it.
Hathorne: Who doe you imploy then to doe it?
Good: I imploy nobody.
Hathorne: What creature do you imploy then?
Good: No creature but I am falsely accused.[115]

Sarah Good was stubborn and persisted in her refusal to confess, but Deliverance Hobbs of Topsfield eventually gave way. At first, Hobbs denied any responsibility for the torments of the afflicted.

Hathorne: Why do you hurt these persons?
Hobbs: It is unknown to me.
Hathorne: How come you to commit acts of Witchcraft?
Hobbs: I know nothing of it.
Hathorne: It is you, or your appearance, how comes this about? Tell us the truth.
Hobbs: I cannot tell.
Hathorne: Tell us what you know in this case. Who hurts them if you do not?

112 *Salem Witchcraft Papers,* I: 211–12.
113 Thomas Brattle, letter to a clergyman, p. 184.
114 *Salem Witchcraft Papers,* III: 783.
115 Ibid., II: 356.

Hobbs: There are a great many persons hurts us all.
Hathorne: But it is your appearance.
Hobbs: I do not know it.
Hathorne: Have you not consented to it, that they should be hurt?
Hobbs: No in the sight of God, and man, as I shall answere another day.

Hobbs told the court that she herself had been afflicted recently and that she had seen the specters of two witches, but denied that she had been tempted by them. Abigail Williams and Ann Putnam, two of the afflicted girls, now cried out that Goody Hobbs's specter was on the roof beam. They could no longer see her at the bar, even though she stood there.

Hathorne: What do you say to this, that tho[ugh] you are at the bar in person, yet they see your appearance upon the beam, and whereas a few dayes past you were tormented, now you are become a Tormentor? Tell us how this change comes. Tell true.
Hobbs: I have done nothing.
Hathorne: What, have you resolved you shall not confess? Hath any body threatened you if you do confess? You can tell how this change comes.

Hobbs looked over at the afflicted, who promptly fell into fits. It was at this point that her resistance began to crumble.

Hathorne: Tell us the reason of this change: Tell us the truth what have you done?
Hobbs: I cannot speak.
Hathorne: What do you say? What have you done?
Hobbs: I cannot tell.
Hathorne: Have you signed to any book?
Hobbs: It is very lately then.
Hathorne: When was it?
Hobbs: The night before the last.
Hathorne: Well the Lord open your heart to confesse the truth. Who brought the book to you?
Hobbs: It was Goody Wilds.

Hobbs then proceeded to give the magistrates all the information they wanted about her dealings with other witch confederates.[116]

The process of interrogation reduced some of the prisoners to state in which they lost all independence of thought and expres-

116 Ibid., II: 419–21.

sion. Six confessing women later submitted a joint petition in which they claimed that their interrogators had "rendered [them] incapable of making [a] defense."

> And indeed that confession, that it is said we made, was no other than what was suggested to us by some gentlemen, they telling us that we were witches, and they knew it, and we knew it, which made us think that it was so; and our understandings, our reason, our faculties, almost gone, we were not capable of judging of our condition; as also the hard measures they used with us rendered us incapable of making our defense, but said any thing and every thing which they desired, and most of what we said, was but, in effect, a consenting to what they said.[117]

These particular women seem to have been influenced by the social status of the "gentlemen" interrogating them. Deference to the magistracy may have influenced other confessors. The magistrates sometimes began their examinations by reminding suspects that they were now "before Authority" or "in the hands of Authority."[118] Other suspects also came to doubt their own innocence and so confessed, only to recant soon afterward. Sarah Wilson said that "the afflicted persons crying out of her as afflicting them made her fearful of herself."[119] Mary Bridges, Sr., told Increase Mather "that she was brought to her confession by being told that she certainly was a witch, and so made to believe it, although she had no other grounds so to believe."[120]

Several of the accused later admitted that they had confessed in order to save their lives. The court's primary objective was to secure the repentance of those who had become witches, to rescue them from the Devil's clutches, and to enable their reintegration as members of the godly community. Only the recalcitrant would be executed. Under such circumstances, confession was an attractive option. When the magistrates told Margaret Jacobs that she would live if she confessed, her "vile wicked heart" could not resist.[121] In a petition from prison, Rebecca Eames also claimed her confession to have been motivated by fear of execution:

> Abigaill Hobbs and Mary Lacye . . . both of them cryed out against me charging me with witchcraft the space of four dayes

117 Ibid., III: 971.
118 See, for example, ibid., I: 83, 248.
119 Ibid., III: 855.
120 Ibid., I: 132.
121 Ibid., II: 491.

> mocking of me and spitting in my face saying they knew me to be an old witch and If I would not confesse it I should very Spedily be hanged for there was some such as my selfe gone before and it would not be long before I would follow them, w[hi]ch was the Occasion with my owne wicked heart of my saying what I did say.[122]

Relatives often urged the accused to confess, understanding that this might be the only way to save their lives. Martha Tyler of Andover told Increase Mather that when she was brought to Salem, her brother rode with her and "kept telling her that she must needs be a witch, since the afflicted accused her . . . and urging her to confess herself a witch." In the courtroom, her brother and John Emerson, the minister at Gloucester, stood on either side of her, assuring her "that she was certainly a witch, and that she saw the Devil before her eyes at that time (and, accordingly, the said Emerson would attempt with his hand to beat him away from her eyes); and they so urged her to confess, that she wished herself in any dungeon, rather than be so treated." Despite her continued resistance, Martha's brother "still asserted it . . . and that she would be hanged if she would not confess; and continued so long and so violently to urge and press her to confess, that she thought, verily, that her life would have gone from her, and became so terrified in her mind that she owned, at length, almost anything that they propounded to her."[123]

Physical torture and psychological pressure were crucial to the court's success in extracting confessions from accused witches. But some of the accused may also have had their own reasons for confessing. Several claimed that fear of damnation played a prominent role in their recruitment to the Devil's service. Mary Barker signed a covenant with the Devil after he "promesed to perdone her sins."[124] According to William Barker, Satan assured his followers "that their should be no day of resurection or of judgement, and neither punishment nor shame for sin."[125] Elizabeth Johnson, Jr., entered the Devil's service after another witch "told her she Should be Saved if she would be[come] a witch."[126] Testimonies such as these suggest that some confessions sprang from religious anxiety. Under pressure from the court, accused witches who were

122 Ibid., I: 284.
123 Ibid., III: 777–8. See also III: 971.
124 Ibid., I: 59.
125 Ibid., I: 66.
126 Ibid., II: 503.

already worried about their sins may have found considerable relief in the notion of escape from the rigors of Christian fellowship.

A number of confessors, convinced of their spiritual inadequacy, sought to implicate Satan in their failings. Ann Foster had "formerly frequented the publique metting to worship god, but the divill had such power over her that she could not profit there, and that was her undoeing."[127] Mary Toothaker "wished she had not been baptised because she had not improved it as she ought to have done." Toothaker was a "halfway" church member; that is, she had been baptized but was not yet admitted to the Lord's Supper. Toothaker was clearly concerned about her lack of spiritual progress and probably wondered if she would ever become eligible for full membership. She often tried to pray and "sometymes... had been helped to say, Lord be merce full to me a sinner," but usually "she was the worse for praying." Like Ann Foster, she suspected that "the Devil... tempted her not to pray."[128] Individuals who were inclined to blame their spiritual failings on the Devil might well respond positively to the court's insistence that they were enslaved to him. Since ministers taught that the Devil approached those who were fit for his service, accused witches who were doubtful of their own moral worth might well come to believe, at least temporarily, that they had been approached and that they had succumbed.[129]

Apart from confessions, the only other substantial body of evidence before the court that could be used to prove diabolical witchcraft came from the afflicted girls, who claimed to be tormented by the specters of accused witches. These specters were devils whom Satan delegated to take on the likeness of witches and then act on their behalf. According to demonological tradition, witches were themselves powerless and needed devils to carry out their bidding. But why did the afflicted see witchcraft in diabolical terms?

The two girls who became afflicted first and whose behavior set the example for those who followed came from the household of Samuel Parris. Nine-year-old Elizabeth Parris was the minister's daughter; eleven-year-old Abigail Williams was his niece. Living under Parris's parental and pastoral care, it is hardly surprising that Elizabeth and Abigail saw witchcraft in diabolical terms. Once physician William Griggs concluded that the two girls were be-

127 Ibid., II: 343.

128 Ibid., III: 767. See also David D. Hall, *Worlds of Wonder, Days of Judgment: Popular Religious Belief in Early New England* (New York, 1989), pp. 144–45.

129 This paragraph is much indebted to David D. Hall, *Worlds of Wonder, Days of Judgment*, pp. 144–47.

witched, Parris surely talked with Abigail and Elizabeth about their condition; he doubtless reminded them, if reminder was necessary, that their tormentors were in league with the Devil. Three other afflicted girls came from the household of Thomas Putnam Jr.: Ann Putnam, a daughter; Mary Walcott, a niece; and Mercy Lewis, a servant girl. Putnam, whose young wife also fell ill, was a close ally of Parris. He interpreted events along the same lines as his pastor and made sure that those under his authority did likewise.

In late March, Parris sent his daughter Elizabeth to live with Stephen Sewall in nearby Salem Town, but Abigail Williams remained in the village. She and the other afflicted girls claimed to be possessed as well as bewitched. During their fits, the girls seemed to lose control over their words and actions: they uttered blasphemies; they interrupted church meetings; they refused to pray. Their irreligious behavior whilst under diabolical influence suggests that they were using possession to express impulses that were otherwise inadmissible; this was, as noted above, a common feature of possession cases. Just as religious anxiety may have prompted some of the accused witches to confess, so the afflicted girls may have used possession to resolve their own spiritual doubts and fears. During the winter of 1691–2, several of the girls who later became possessed had experimented with divination. The members of this fortune-telling group may have realized that such activities were illicit. If so, the unexpected appearance in a divining glass of "a Spectre in likeness of a Coffin" must have been particularly frightening; it was shortly after this "Spectre" appeared that the fits began.[130] Through possession, the girls were able to shift responsibility for their wickedness onto demons within them.[131] Possession must have reinforced the girls' conviction that the witches afflicting them were diabolical: after all, if they were possessed by devils, then the witches willing their possession must be in league with devils.[132]

In general, it was fear of human witches, and not of witches as the servants of Satan, that obsessed the people of Essex County in 1692. Magistrates, ministers, and the possessed girls were convinced that Satan had inspired and coordinated the witches' activities; some of

130 John Hale, *A Modest Enquiry,* pp. 132–33.

131 Joseph Klaits also argues that "the girls' feelings of guilt for having engaged in forbidden behavior" paved the way for their subsequent possession (Joseph Klaits, *Servants of Satan: The Age of the Witch Hunts* [Bloomington, Ind., 1985], pp. 119–20).

132 See Chapter 3 for a more detailed discussion of possession and its spiritual context.

the confessors also believed, at least temporarily, that they were in league with the Devil. But other witnesses against the accused rarely mentioned the Devil in their testimony and gave little indication that they believed witchcraft to involve diabolical allegiance, despite the fact that this would have facilitated conviction. These witnesses focused instead on their arguments with the accused and the misfortunes that followed, the mysterious behavior that led them to believe the accused had supernatural power, and the magical skills the accused apparently possessed. The one common link between confessors, the possessed, and other hostile witnesses was that all three groups made frequent reference to the practice of magic in their local communities: they spoke of divination, image magic, and countermagic. The Devil appeared in only specific kinds of testimony, but magic was ubiquitous.

During the course of the trials, it became clear that several of the accused either claimed to have expertise in divination, or had at least experimented with divining techniques. Dorcas Hoar of Beverly was widely reputed to be a fortune-teller. Joseph and Deborah Morgan, for example, testified that Hoar "did pretend sum thing of fort[une] telling."[133] John Hale told the court that Hoar "had borrowed a book of Palmistry" and later acquired another "book of fortune telling."[134] Samuel Wardwell of Andover, another of the accused, admitted that "he had been foolishly Led along with telling of fortunes, which sometymes came to pass." Several of Wardwell's neighbors testified that he had indeed told fortunes.[135] Sarah Hawkes of Andover confessed to having used the sieve and scissors, as did Rebecca Johnson, also of Andover. Johnson "acknowledged the turneing of the sieve, in her house by hir daughter, whom she Desyred to no [know] if her brother Moses Haggat was alive or dead."[136] The afflicted girls had themselves been experimenting with divination during the winter of 1691–2: one of them had used "an egg and a glass" to identify her "future Husbands Calling."[137]

Divination was not the only form of magic being used by people in Essex County. Many of the accused were evidently familiar with image magic. Mary Lacey, Sr., testified as follows:

> that if she doe take a ragg, clout or any such thing and Roll it up together And Imagine it to represent such and such a

133 *Salem Witchcraft Papers,* II: 400.
134 Ibid., II: 397–8.
135 Ibid., III: 783, 787–8.
136 Ibid., II: 387, 507.
137 John Hale, *A Modest Enquiry,* pp. 132–3.

> persone; Then whatsoever she doth to that Ragg or clout so rouled up, The persone represented thereby will be in lyke manner afflicted.[138]

Mary Bridges, Sr., said that she afflicted people "by sticking pins into things and Clothes and think[ing] of hurting them."[139] Elizabeth Johnson actually produced three poppets in court, two "made of rags" and a third "made of a birch Rhine." One of them had "four peices or stripes of cloth rapt [wrapped] one upon another which she s[ai]d was to afflict four persons with." Another had "two such peices of rags rolld up together and 3 pins stuck into it."[140] John and William Bly, employed by Bridget Bishop to take down a wall in her cellar, testified that they found there several poppets made of cloth with pins stuck into them. Samuel Shattuck testified that Bishop once asked him to dye "Sundry peeces of lace, Some of w[hi]ch were Soe Short that [he] could not judge them fit for any uce." The implication was that these were intended for a poppet.[141]

Some of the images suspects had apparently used were much less anthropomorphic than others. Mary Lacey, Jr., testified that she "lay on a forme yesterday and squesed that."[142] Ann Foster claimed that "she tyed a knot in a Rage and thre[w] it into the fire to hurt a woeman at Salem Village and that she was hurt by her."[143] Image magic did not necessarily require the use of any intermediary tool. When the magistrates asked Mary Marston what method she used to afflict her victims, she "Answered to pinch and Squeeze her hands together and so to think upon the persones to be afflicted."[144] In the courtroom, the movements of accused witches produced corresponding torments in the afflicted: when suspect Mary Easty clenched her hands together, Mercy Lewis's hands also clenched; when Easty bowed her head, the necks of the afflicted girls were wrenched out of their natural position.[145] "Natural Actions in them produced Preternatural actions in the Afflicted," related Deodat Lawson, "so that they are their own Image without any Poppits of Wax or otherwise."[146]

138 *Salem Witchcraft Papers,* II: 514.
139 Ibid., I: 135. See also II: 529; III: 768.
140 Ibid., II: 504–5.
141 Ibid., I: 97, 101. For other references to poppets, see I: 211; II, 342, 410, 523, 627–8; III: 741, 762.
142 Ibid., II: 521.
143 Ibid., II: 343.
144 Ibid., II: 545. See also I: 139.
145 Ibid., I: 289.
146 Deodat Lawson, "A True Narrative," in Cotton Mather, *Wonders of the Invisible World,* p. 213.

A third form of magic, countermagic, also appeared in court testimony. Samuel Shattock, a Quaker of Salem Village, told the court that in 1685, when one of his children fell ill, neighbors had cut off some of the child's hair and boiled it over a fire. While the hair was boiling, Mary Parker arrived at Shattock's door. The neighbors concluded that Parker had caused the child's illness and Shattock now related the incident as evidence against her.[147] Tituba, the slave in Parris's household whom Mary Sibley had commissioned to make a urine-cake, told the court that she was acquainted with "means to be used for the discovery of a Witch."[148] Martha Emerson of Haverhill admitted to having used a witch-bottle. Roger Toothaker, Martha's father and another witch suspect, had taught Martha "to take the afflicted persons water and put [it] in a glass or bottle: and sett it into an oven" as a measure against witchcraft. Martha "owned she had [kept] a womans urin: in a glass." But Toothaker went further and told Thomas Gage that his daughter had actually killed a witch: "his s[ai]d Daughter gott some of the afflicted persons Urine and put it into an Earthen pott and stopt s[ai]d pott very Close and putt s[ai]d pott [very Close] [in] to a hott oven and stopt up s[ai]d oven and the next morning s[ai]d [witch] was Dead."[149]

There is no surviving record of how the magistrates reacted to this evidence of widespread magical activity. Ministers argued that all forms of magic relied upon a diabolical agency, but what did those giving the evidence believe? The afflicted girls presented testimony relating to magic within the framework of their diabolical narratives. Two confessors also associated magic with devil-worship in their testimony: Abigail Hobbs claimed to have seen poppets in the hands of the Devil himself; Sarah Hawkes testified that the Devil first came to her after she had been using the sieve and scissors, implying that the two incidents were connected.[150] Yet when the court examined Rebecca Johnson, she denied that she was a witch, even though she admitted to having used the sieve and scissors: as far as Johnson was concerned, there was a clear distinction between magic and witchcraft.[151] Hostile witnesses other than the possessed made no mention of any connection between magical practices and the Devil. These people gave no indication that they believed fortune-telling, image magic, or countermagic to depend upon a diabolical agency. Court officials and ministers

147 *Salem Witchcraft Papers,* II: 635–6.
148 John Hale, *A Modest Enquiry,* p. 25.
149 *Salem Witchcraft Papers,* I: 308; III: 772–3.
150 Ibid., II: 387, 410.
151 Ibid., II: 507.

observing the proceedings would have had to infer any such dependence. When deponents claimed that Dorcas Hoar, Samuel Wardwell, and other accused witches could tell fortunes, they sought to establish only that the accused had occult powers: such powers might well be used for malevolent as well as benevolent purposes and were cause for fear and distrust, but there is no evidence to suggest that witnesses saw these powers as being inherently evil, let alone diabolical.

Two kinds of witchcraft were under attack at the Salem trials. The afflicted girls insisted that the accused had convenanted with Satan. But hostile witnesses other than the afflicted did not seem to believe that witchcraft involved diabolical allegiance. Because these witnesses did not interpret witch incidents in diabolical terms, their evidence was of little use to the court. Indeed, were it not for confessions and the afflicted girls' testimony, there would have been very few, if any, convictions in 1692. By mid-fall, not only had a number of confessors recanted, but critics succeeded in discrediting evidence given by the afflicted. The magistrates now found themselves in an untenable position and the trials collapsed amid what Cotton Mather described as "most agitated Controversie."[152]

That controversy focused on the issue of spectral evidence. Apart from confessions, the only direct evidence of diabolical witchcraft before the court was spectral testimony provided by the afflicted girls. The magistrates relied heavily on that testimony: when the possessed girls announced that a specter resembling one of the accused had appeared and attacked them, the judges treated this as proof that the accused was a witch. In other words, they assumed that devils representing specific individuals must operate by consent of those individuals. Furthermore, court officials noted that the afflicted girls suffered terrible pains whenever accused witches either moved or glanced in their direction; the magistrates believed that the witches were willfully tormenting the girls and treated such incidents as damning evidence. Critics warned that both of these assumptions were dangerous: spectral devils afflicting the girls might adopt the guise of innocent people in order to mislead the court; seeming connections between the movements of the accused and the torments of the afflicted might be equally specious.

The magistrates' assumptions bore a close resemblance to those which underpinned image magic. Ironically, they sought to convict suspects of diabolical witchcraft by a reasoning that ministers had rejected in their attacks on magical belief. As opposition to spectral

152 Cotton Mather, *Wonders of the Invisible World*, p. 83.

testimony grew, the trials were crippled by what was, in effect, a clash between magical and theological principles. On the one side, the magistrates and their supporters presumed a direct correspondence between appearance and reality in the courtroom. Just as users of magic believed that the mutilation of an effigy actually caused an injury in the enemy represented, so the judges assumed that the movements of the accused actually caused the agonies of the afflicted. On the other side, critics warned that appearance and reality did not necessarily correspond. Just as magic seemed to work only because devils intervened to bring about the desired effect, so spectral devils rather than the witches themselves were tormenting the afflicted; devils might choose to incriminate the innocent by appearing in their form.[153] These parallels did not elude contemporary observers. According to Thomas Brattle, the magistrates were using implicitly magical tests and so were themselves guilty of "sorcery."[154]

"The Return of Several Ministers," a brief document submitted to Governor Phips and his council by twelve clergymen, rejected spectral evidence as a sound basis even for committing suspects, let alone convicting them, "inasmuch as 'tis an undoubted and a notorious thing that a Daemon may, by God's Permission, appear even to ill purposes, in the Shape of an innocent, yea, and a vertuous Man."[155] In a pamphlet entitled *Some Miscellany Observations on Our Present Debates Respecting Witchcrafts,* Samuel Willard also rejected spectral evidence on the grounds that a devil might represent people without their consent.[156] The clergy were by no means alone in objecting to spectral testimony. A petition for John and Elizabeth Proctor, signed by thirty-one laymen, also questioned the legitimacy of such evidence:

> We do at present Suppose that it may be A Method w[i]thin the Severer But Just Transaction of the Infinite Majestie of God: that he some times may p[e]rmitt Sathan to p[e]rsonate, Dissemble, and ther[e]by abuse Inocents, and Such as Do in the fear of God Defie the Devill and all his works.[157]

153 See Robert Middlekauff, *The Mathers: Three Generations of Puritan Intellectuals, 1596–1728* (New York, 1971), pp. 154–5, and Perry Miller, *The New England Mind: From Colony to Province* (Cambridge, Mass., 1953), chap. 13.
154 Thomas Brattle, letter to a clergyman, in George L. Burr, ed., *Narratives of the Witchcraft Cases,* p. 171.
155 "The Return of Several Ministers," 15 June 1692, in Cotton Mather, *Wonders of the Invisible World,* p. 290.
156 Samuel Willard, *Some Miscellany Observations,* pp. 10–12.
157 *Salem Witchcraft Papers,* II: 681.

Thomas Brattle ridiculed the notion that individuals represented by spectral demons were necessarily responsible for the specters' actions.[158]

Cotton Mather warned repeatedly against a reliance upon spectral testimony.[159] He urged Margaret Rule, an afflicted young woman in his care, "to forbear blazing the Names" of her spectral tormentors, "lest any good Person should come to suffer any blast of Reputation thro[ugh] the cunning Malice of the great Accuser."[160] Mather believed that God usually provided "a way for the Speedy vindication of the persons thus abused" and that many who had been wrongly represented were sinners whose conduct made them deserving of such judgment.[161] Cotton's father, Increase, suggested that some of those falsely represented may "have been tampering with some foolish and wicked Sorceries, tho[ugh] not to that degree which is Criminal and Capital by the Laws both of God and Men." In other words, they had been experimenting with beneficent magic. For that reason, Increase argued, God had permitted Satan "so to scourge them."[162] Cotton Mather maintained that the magistrates should exercise extreme caution in considering spectral evidence. Mather suggested that those represented by specters should be exiled, so as to "cleanse the land of witchcrafts and yet also prevent the shedding of innocent blood." Mather declared that he himself would "very patiently submit unto a judgement of transportation" if a specter in his shape were to torment anybody.[163]

Critics of the proceedings at Salem were equally insistent that the magistrates should not be misled by courtroom fits apparently brought on by the movements or glances of accused witches. The ministers warned Phips that "Alterations made in the Sufferers, by

158 Thomas Brattle, letter to a clergyman, in George L. Burr, ed., *Narratives of the Witchcraft Cases,* pp. 174–5. See also Robert Pike, letter to Jonathan Corwin, 9 August 1692, in Charles Upham, *Salem Witchcraft,* 2 vols. (Boston, 1867), II: 538–9.

159 See, for example, *Wonders of the Invisible World,* pp. 17–18; Cotton Mather to John Richards, 31d 3m 1692, in *Collections of the Massachusetts Historical Society,* 4th ser., 8 (1868), 392; Mather, "Another Brand Pluck't Out of the Burning," in George L. Burr, ed., *Narratives of the Witchcraft Cases,* pp. 320–1; and Mather, *Diary,* ed., Worthington C. Ford, 2 vols. (1911; New York, 1957), I: 150.

160 Cotton Mather, "Another Brand Pluck't Out of the Burning," p. 311.

161 Cotton Mather to John Richards, pp. 392–3.

162 Increase Mather, "Cases of Conscience," in Cotton Mather, *Wonders of the Invisible World,* p. 233.

163 Cotton Mather to John Foster, 17 August 1692, in Paul Boyer and Stephen Nissenbaum, eds., *Salem-Village Witchcraft: A Documentary Record of Local Conflict in Colonial New England* (Belmont, Calif., 1972), pp. 118–19. For a detailed discussion of Cotton Mather's involvement in the crisis of 1692 and his ambivalent attitude toward the trials, see Kenneth Silverman, *The Life and Times of Cotton Mather,* chap. 4.

a Look or Touch of the Accused" were not "infallible Evidence of Guilt; but frequently liable to be abused by the Devil's Legerdemains."[164] Cotton Mather considered these "odd effects" to be just as untrustworthy as spectral evidence.[165] "The effect," wrote Samuel Willard, "is preternatural, and the thing unaccountable: and men's wild guesses in such an affair, ought not to pass for Maxims, where life is concerned."[166] Witch suspects who were supposedly responsible for fits and torments in the courtroom often calmed the afflicted girls by touching them. They did so at the request of the magistrates, who then used their healing power as further proof of guilt.[167] Critics were well aware of the parallels between this and countermagic. Increase Mather pointed out that proving a witch by her ability to heal was "no better than . . . putting the Urine of the afflicted Person into a Bottle, that so the Witch may be tormented and discovered."[168] Thomas Brattle condemned the magistrates' strategy as "sorcery, and a superstitious method."[169]

The magistrates, wrote Cotton Mather, were convinced that unless these tests were admitted as incriminating evidence, "it would scarce be possible ever to Convict a Witch." Indeed, "they had some Philosophical Schemes of Witchcraft, and of the Method and Manner wherein Magical Poisons operate, which further supported them in their Opinion."[170] According to Brattle, the magistrates argued from Cartesian philosophy and the doctrine of effluvia, reasoning "that by this touch, the venemous and malignant particles, that were ejected from the eye, do, by this means, return to the body whence they came, and so leave the afflicted persons pure and whole."[171] Yet for all the magistrates' attempts to give such evidence

164 "The Return of Several Ministers," in Cotton Mather, *Wonders of the Invisible World,* p. 290.

165 Cotton Mather to John Foster, in Paul Boyer and Stephen Nissenbaum, *Salem-Village Witchcraft,* p. 119.

166 Samuel Willard, *Some Miscellany Observations,* p. 15.

167 See Governor Phips to the Earl of Nottingham, 21 February 1692/3, in George L. Burr, ed., *Narratives of the Witchcraft Cases,* p. 199: "When touched by them upon the arme or some other part of their flesh they immediately revived and came to themselves."

168 Increase Mather, "Cases of Conscience," p. 265.

169 Thomas Brattle, letter to a clergyman, in George L. Burr, ed., *Narratives of the Witchcraft Cases,* p. 171.

170 Cotton Mather, *Magnalia Christi Americana,* p. 331.

171 Thomas Brattle, letter to a clergyman, in George L. Burr, ed., *Narratives of the Witchcraft Cases,* p. 171. According to Cartesian physics, the universe was completely filled with matter, which separated into the subtle matter of space and the denser matter of bodies. The doctrine of "effluvia," or "subtle matter," held that "empty" space consisted of material particles too subtle to be perceived by touch or sight; these particles were adaptable and could conduct from one dense concentration of matter to another. The judges argued that streams of "venemous and malignant particles" were passing between the accused witches and their victims.

a respectable intellectual basis, fundamental problems remained. Did the correspondence between the movements of the accused and the torments of the afflicted establish guilt? Did the cessation of the torment by the touch of the accused further corroborate that guilt? Did the appearance of a specter prove that the person represented was a witch? Or was the court being duped by the Devil?

Critics warned that the court was relying on evidence "received only upon the Devil's Authority."[172] Willard pointed out that the afflicted were either possessed by the Devil, or involved in "some unlawful commerce with the Devil." "What Credit," he asked, "is legally to be given to a thing which an Humane Person swears, meerly upon the Devil's Information?"[173] Brattle was appalled that people from neighboring towns had consulted the afflicted girls in order to discover the origin of various afflictions, thus relying upon "a supernatural knowledge; a knowledge which they obtain by holding correspondence with spectres or evil spirits, as they themselves grant." Increase Mather, Brattle related, had reproved one of his parishioners who consulted the girls, "asking him whether there was not a God in Boston, that he should go to the Devill in Salem for advice." Brattle himself condemned this practice as "a very grosse evill, a real abomination."[174]

Testimony given by confessors was no more trustworthy, even if the confessors really were witches. As Robert Pike, a pious magistrate of Salisbury, pointed out, "If the root of all their knowledge be the Devil, what must their testimony be?"[175] When confessors contradicted themselves, the judges argued that Satan took away their memory. If so, argued Brattle, "the Devill, at other times, may very reasonably be thought to affect their fancyes, and to represent false ideas to their imagination." Brattle suspected that much of the evidence offered by confessing witches was "the effect of their fancye, depraved and deluded by the Devill, and not a Reality to be regarded or minded by any wise man."[176] Cotton Mather argued that many of those who seemed to be witches were really possessed: "under a Satanical Energy ... [they] Ignorantly used the Speeches and Actions, which according to the common Rules of Judging ... brought them under the Praesumptions of

172 "The Return of Several Ministers," p. 289.
173 Samuel Willard, *Some Miscellany Observations,* pp. 7–9.
174 Thomas Brattle, letter to a clergyman, in George L. Burr, ed., *Narratives of the Witchcraft Cases,* pp. 179–80.
175 Robert Pike to Jonathan Corwin, in Charles Upham, *Salem Witchcraft,* II: 544.
176 Thomas Brattle, letter to a clergyman, in George L. Burr, ed., *Narratives of the Witchcraft Cases,* pp. 173–4, 189.

criminal Familiarities."[177] English medical authorities such as John Cotta had argued that persons who confessed to witchcraft might be hallucinating as a result of natural illness.[178] Mather and Brattle, on the other hand, doubted confessions because they believed that the Devil had taken control of the confessors' minds. Like other critics of the proceedings at Salem, they challenged court testimony *because* they were convinced that Satan had come among them.[179]

None of these critics questioned the appalling reality of witchcraft. What did stand in doubt was the possibility of showing exactly who was responsible for witchcraft. The magistrates, critics argued, had made the mistake of assuming that they could understand supernatural operations; yet all such phenomena lay beyond human comprehension. According to Willard, the court should not accept any evidence provided "by extraordinary Revelation from God, or by the insinuation of the Devil." Testimony should be based on "that which one man can know concerning another by his Senses, and that according to the true nature, and use of them."[180] The magistrates might well have asked how they were supposed to find such evidence when dealing with matters intrinsically supernatural. In fact, the ministers and their allies were groping toward the view that legal prosecution for witchcraft was inherently impracticable.

By early fall, the court at Salem was under heavy attack. In October 1692, Thomas Brattle wrote a letter to an unnamed clergyman in which he gave an impressive list of those opposed to the trials. These critics included ex-governor Simon Bradstreet and ex-deputy-governor Thomas Danforth; all the ministers "throughout the whole Country" except Samuel Parris, Nicholas Noyes, and John Hale; a number of ex-judges; and "the principal Gentlemen in Boston, and thereabout."[181] But not everybody was dissatified with the court's handling of the witch crisis. In mid-October, Samuel Sewall, one of the court magistrates, visited Thomas Danforth "and discoursed with Him about the Witchcraft." Danforth told Sewall that the trials could not proceed "except there be some better consent of [agreement between] Ministers and People."[182] The "People" to whom Danforth referred did not agree that the evi-

177 Cotton Mather, "Paper on Witchcraft," in *Proceedings of the Massachusetts Historical Society*, 47 (1914): 244–5.
178 John Cotta, *The Triall of Witchcraft* (London, 1616).
179 See Robert Middlekauff, *The Mathers*, p. 157.
180 Samuel Willard, *Some Miscellany Observations*, p. 7.
181 Thomas Brattle, letter to a clergyman, in George L. Burr, ed., *Narratives of the Witchcraft Cases*, pp. 184–5.
182 Samuel Sewall, *Diary*, I: 298, 15 October 1692.

dence before the court was inadequate. Subsequent events suggest that a significant proportion of the community had wanted the trials to continue. Every judge from the witch court was elected to the governor's council in 1693. Samuel Sewall received more votes than Nathaniel Saltonstall, who was "very much dissatisfyed with the proceedings" and had resigned from the court in protest.[183] The General Court itself had voted by only a narrow margin to dissolve the Salem court; that the vote was carried at all was probably due to the fact that a number of the representatives had relatives among the accused.[184]

It is not surprising that the witch trials were popular. The mass of depositions placed before the court expressed an intense fear of witchcraft in and around Salem Village. The ordeals of the last decade had raised that fear to an almost pathological level: the people of Essex County needed and welcomed a witch hunt. Yet two problems of evidence undermined the court proceedings. First, most hostile deponents presented witchcraft simply as maleficium and so did not provide the kind of evidence required by law. Apart from testimony given by confessors and the afflicted, there was hardly any direct evidence of diabolical witchcraft before the court. Second, a growing number of critics attacked the magistrates for their credulous and mechanistic response to spectral events in the courtroom. That response, they argued, not only denied the inscrutability of supernatural phenomena, but also bore an alarming resemblance to those very magical beliefs that threatened to deliver New Englanders into the Devil's clutches. Once critics discredited spectral evidence and confessors began to recant, the collapse of the trials was inevitable. Religious doctrine as embodied in the law against witchcraft had once again failed to accommodate public hostility toward witches. As Thomas Danforth pointed out in his conversation with Samuel Sewall, there was no "consent of Ministers and People" on this issue.

183 Thomas Brattle, letter to a clergyman, in George L. Burr, ed., *Narratives of the Witchcraft Cases*, p. 184, and Chadwick Hansen, *Witchcraft at Salem*, p. 205.

184 For an example of growing concern within the elite about the social status of some witch suspects, see Governor Phips to the Earl of Nottingham, in Paul Boyer and Stephen Nissenbaum, *Salem-Village Witchcraft*, p. 121.

EPILOGUE

John Hale, the minister at Beverly in Essex County, had been a close observer of the Salem witch crisis and supported the court's literal interpretation of spectral testimony into the fall of 1692.[1] However, when seventeen-year-old Mary Herrick accused Hale's own wife of afflicting her in spectral form, he began to rethink his position.[2] Hale came to realize that spectral evidence was indeed unreliable and that innocent blood had been shed; he blamed himself for "unwittingly encouraging . . . the Sufferings of the innocent."[3] In the aftermath of the witch hunt, a number of figures involved in the trials acknowledged in public their sense of personal guilt. Twelve jurymen signed an open letter of apology in which they admitted that they had been "sadly deluded and mistaken."[4] In early 1697, on a fast day commemorating "the late tragedy," Samuel Sewall, one of the court magistrates, had his minister Samuel Willard read from the pulpit a statement in which Sewall accepted "blame and shame" for his role in the proceedings, "Asking pardon of men, And especially desiring prayers that God . . . would pardon that sin and all other his sins."[5] John Hale decided to express his contrition rather differently. By the end of 1697, he had decided to write a treatise on witch trials, the purpose of which was to ascertain "How Persons Guilty of that Crime may be Convicted." Hale wrote in the hope that future generations would "shun those Rocks by which we were bruised, and narrowly escaped Shipwrack

1 Thomas Brattle, letter to a clergyman, in George L. Burr, ed., *Narratives of the Witchcraft Cases* (1914; New York, 1952), p. 184.

2 *New England Historical and Genealogical Register,* 27 (1873): 55.

3 John Hale, *A Modest Enquiry into the Nature of Witchcraft* (1702; Bainbridge, N.Y., 1973), p. 11.

4 Apology, in Robert Calef, "More Wonders of the Invisible World," in George L. Burr, ed., *Narratives of the Witchcraft Cases,* p. 387.

5 Proclamation, 17 December 1696, in Robert Calef, "More Wonders of the Invisible World," p. 386; Samuel Sewall, *Diary*, ed. M. Halsey Thomas, 2 vols. (New York, 1973), I:367.

upon."[6] The resulting book, *A Modest Enquiry into the Nature of Witchcraft,* was first published in 1702.

A Modest Enquiry embodied Hale's full conversion to the position developed by critics of the court during the summer and fall of 1692. John Higginson, pastor at neighboring Salem Town, captured the central theme of Hale's work when he declared in the preface that witchcraft was "one of the most hidden Works of Darkness."[7] Hale emphasized that Satan's actions, like those of God, were utterly inscrutable:

> And among Satans Mysteries of Iniquity, this of Witchcraft is one of the most difficult to be searched out by the Sons of men.[8]

It was now generally agreed, wrote Hale, that the court at Salem had proceeded on the basis of false suppositions. Hale insisted that acts of witchcraft should be proven "in the same way that Murder, Theft, and such like crimes are provable." He posited four acceptable grounds for conviction: confession; the testimony of two witnesses that the accused had committed an act unquestionably dependent upon diabolical assistance; the testimony of partners in the crime; or "Circumstances antecedent to, concomitant with, or suddenly consequent upon such acts of Sorcery" that had "like force to fasten a suspicion of this crime upon this or that person." On first reading, these criteria seem fairly inclusive, but Hale hedged each of them with so many conditions and precautions that conviction on such terms would be all but impossible. Hale recognized this difficulty, but reminded his audience that "the Lord can and doth discover Sorcerers, Magicians, and all sorts of Witches, when, and as oft as he pleaseth." This was not necessarily reassuring to those who favored legal action against witches, nor could it disguise the radical implications of Hale's proposed criteria: unless suspects confessed or God himself intervened to expose the guilty, witches would almost certainly elude judicial punishment.[9]

In common with earlier critics of the court, Hale stopped short of declaring explicitly that the very concept of witchcraft was irreconcilable with legal proof; refusing to take that final step, he invoked the possibility of exposure by God. Yet in practice, the train of thought that received its fullest and most eloquent expression in Hale's *Modest Enquiry* did effectively preclude legal convic-

6 John Hale, *A Modest Enquiry*, title page, p. 9. Hale discussed his plans with Samuel Sewall in November of 1697 (Samuel Sewall, *Diary,* I:382).

7 John Hale, *A Modest Enquiry,* p. 3.

8 Ibid., pp. 8–9.

9 Ibid., pp. 162–4.

tion for witchcraft, barring a voluntary and explicit confession. During the decades that preceded the crisis at Salem, problems of evidence in witchcraft cases had undermined popular confidence in the legal process, so that the number of witch prosecutions declined dramatically during the 1670s and 1680s. The legislative revival of 1692, sparked by the convergence of extraordinary strains and fears in Essex County, was no less problematic in evidentiary terms. Moreover, the sheer scale of the witch crisis prompted a public debate that challenged, albeit obliquely, the very possibility of a witch trial. The impact of that debate combined with popular frustration in the face of yet another legal debacle to bring about the end of witch prosecutions in New England. The last occasion on which a Massachusetts court addressed an accusation of witchcraft was in 1693, when a servant, Mary Watkins, accused herself of witchcraft after attempting to commit suicide: the jury appointed to consider her case rejected the bill of indictment, probably on the grounds that Watkins was not in a fit state to offer credible evidence.[10] Four years later, in Wallingford, Connecticut, a mother and daughter, both named Winifred Benham, appeared in court on charges of witchcraft and were duly acquitted.[11] Thereafter, witchcraft vanished from the official records of New England.

The cessation of witch prosecutions did not originate in skepticism or "enlightened" attitudes, either within the New England elite or in the community at large. The ministers and their lay allies had called for an end to the Salem trials not because they doubted the reality of witchcraft, but because they now realized that witch trials were incompatible with belief in the inherent mystery of supernatural operations. In other words, it was the internal logic of Puritanism itself that finally mobilized them against witch proceedings. Throughout the seventeenth century, magistrates and ministers had struggled to determine how a court of law could prove a crime that was inherently occult. In 1692, prompted by the Salem court's extraordinary reliance upon spectral testimony and the prospect of bloodshed on a horrific scale, New England clergymen finally confronted the contradiction between witch trials and the doctrine of inscrutability. It now transpired that providential theology was a double-edged sword: on the one hand, it condemned diabolical witchcraft and, through scriptural injunction, seemed to justify the prosecution of witches; on the other, it invalidated almost all the evidence likely to be offered against

10 Robert Calef, "More Wonders of the Invisible World," pp. 383–4.

11 C. Bancroft Gillespie and George Munson Curtis, *A Century of Meriden* (Meriden, Conn., 1906), pp. 254–9; *New Haven Genealogical Magazine,* IV: 955–8.

witches in a court of law and so left the children of God powerless to act on their own behalf against the servants of Satan.

As the eighteenth century unfolded, a degree of skepticism did begin to take hold within educated circles, although the same cannot be said of the population at large. Those people who were exposed to Enlightenment thought gradually absorbed the new scientific ethos, which shifted attention away from a world of wonders to a universe characterized by mechanical order and natural process. As the realm of natural causation encroached onto territory formerly designated as supernatural, commentators began to explain seemingly occult phenomena in rationalist terms; a growing number of educated people became less willing to categorize particular incidents as supernatural.[12] Few were willing to deny outright the possibility of witchcraft, since to do so was to reject both holy scripture and historical experience; but a growing number did question the authenticity of specific instances. This ambivalent, semiskeptical attitude is captured in a personal testimony written by Ebenezer Turell, a Massachusetts clergyman, in 1728:

> Although I ... firmly believe [in] the existence of spirits, an invisible world, and particularly the agency of Satan, and his instruments, in afflicting and tormenting the children of men ... yet I fear the world has been wretchedly imposed upon by relations of such matters.... Many things have been dubb[e]d witchcraft, and called the works of the devil, which were nothing more than the contrivance of the children of men.... Where one relation is exactly according to truth, there are two, at least, that are wholly the fruit of wild imagination, or intolerably mixt with deceit and falsehood.[13]

Critics in 1692 had warned that Satan might incriminate the innocent; Turell now emphasized human "deceit and falsehood." Seventeenth-century commentators had recognized the possibility of fabrication, but usually defended the authenticity of specific incidents.[14] Turell reversed the emphasis by acknowledging the reality of witchcraft but doubting the veracity of most accusations.[15]

12 David D. Hall describes the beginning of this process in *Worlds of Wonder, Days of Judgment: Popular Religious Belief in Early New England* (New York, 1989), pp. 106–10.

13 Ebenezer Turell, "Detection of Witchcraft," *Collections of the Massachusetts Historical Society,* 2nd ser., 10 (1823): 6–7.

14 In the cases of Elizabeth Clawson and Mercy Disborough, discussed in Chapter 5, a number of people questioned the veracity of Katherine Branch's accusations, but they did so because she was known to be a liar, not because they automatically suspected such accusations.

15 For a similar expression of ambivalence, written at midcentury, see Josiah Cot-

We should not exaggerate either the rate or the degree of change in eighteenth-century attitudes. Ebenezer Turell had been pastor of Littleton, Massachusetts, in 1720 when an eleven-year-old girl and her two younger sisters accused a neighbor's specter of afflicting them and plunged the town into crisis. One of the girls later admitted in private conversation with Turell that she and her sisters had feigned their illness and falsely accused their neighbor. Some of the townsfolk had suspected from the start that the girls were either sick from some natural cause or "perverse and wicked," but "the general cry of the town ... plumply pronounced it witchcraft as much as that which was formerly acted at Salem." It is instructive that most people not only believed the girls to be bewitched, but also considered the bewitchments at Salem to have been genuine. On the other hand, the townsfolk were less willing than before to accept spectral evidence: some were convinced that the accused neighbor was a witch, but others saw "sufficient reason to believe [that] the accused are not always the guilty persons."[16]

Even within intellectual circles, older ideas and traditions survived alongside Lockean psychology and Newtonian science.[17] Newton himself had been a committed alchemist and a number of eighteenth-century American intellectuals attempted alchemical experiments; others at least read alchemical texts and corresponded with other devotees.[18] Students of medicine and chemistry continued to believe in the four elements and four humors, incorporating these ancient schemata into new theories and procedures.[19] Enlightenment thought, then, brought about no sudden transformation of attitudes, but rather a gradual shift in emphasis.

Humbler folk were largely unaffected by these new intellectual currents and continued to see the world as an enchanted place, filled with occult forces that could be harnessed for good or evil purposes.[20] Scattered references in clerical writings testify to the

ton, "Some Observations Concerning Witches, Spirits, and Apparitions, Collected from Diverse Authors" (Houghton Library, Harvard University, Cambridge, Mass.), p. 53. Leventhal discusses this trend in the broader context of trans-Atlantic discourse (Herbert Leventhal, *In the Shadow of the Enlightenment: Occultism and Renaissance Science in Eighteenth-Century America* [New York, 1976], pp. 91–5). See also John Demos, *Entertaining Satan: Witchcraft and the Culture of Early New England* (New York, 1982), pp. 392–3.

16 Ebenezer Turell, "Detection of Witchcraft," p. 11.

17 Herbert Leventhal's *In the Shadow of the Enlightenment* examines the persistence of these older concepts and beliefs.

18 Ronald Sterne Wilkinson, "New England's Last Alchemists," *Ambix*, 10 (1962): 128–38; Herbert Leventhal, *In the Shadow of the Enlightenment*, chap. 4.

19 Herbert Leventhal, *In the Shadow of the Enlightenment*, chap. 7.

20 Jon Butler discusses "the folklorization of magic" in *Awash in a Sea of Faith: Christianizing the American People* (Cambridge, Mass., 1990), pp. 83–97. See also John Demos, *Entertaining Satan*, pp. 393–4.

persistence of magical tradition even among godly layfolk. In 1728, Ebenezer Turell, now pastor at Medford, Massachusetts, condemned young people for their use of "sieve-turning," "senseless palmistry and groundless astrology."[21] At a meeting of the Salem Village Church in 1746, several members of the congregation were reported to have "resorted to a woman of very ill reputation, pretending to the art of Divination and fortune-telling." The meeting expressed its "disapprobation and abhorrence of this infamous and ungodly practice."[22] The village minister, Joseph Green, had "preached against Divination" in 1702, as had Deodat Lawson in 1692, both apparently without any lasting effect.[23] In 1755, Ebenezer Parkman wrote that one of his parishioners, Thomas Smith, "went to a Wise-Man . . . to know where Mr. Keys's lost Child might be found." Parkman had "Discourse" with Smith and later preached to his congregation "against the foolish and wicked practice of going to Cunning Men to enquire for lost Things."[24] Ezra Stiles, pastor at Newport, Rhode Island, and later president of Yale College, noted in a diary entry for June 1773 the recent death of "Mr. Stafford of Tiverton . . . who was wont to tell where lost things might be found and what day, hour and minute was fortunate for vessels to sail." Stiles mentioned in the same entry an elderly woman of Newport, Rhode Island, "old Granny Morgan," who was well known for "making Cakes of flour and her own Urine and sticking them full of pins and divining by them." Stiles saw these practices as relics of an "Antient System" which had involved "a direct seeking to Satan." Now, he wrote, the "System" was "broken up, the Vessel of Sorcery shipwreckt and only some shattered planks and pieces disjoyned floating and scattered on the Ocean of the human Activity and Bustle." Stiles was right to emphasize the disorganized nature of magical practice, but wrong in his supposition that it had once been a structured system. Magic was inherently "disjoyned[,] floating and scattered."[25]

21 Ebenezer Turell, "Detection of Witchcraft," pp. 19–20.

22 "Danvers First Church Records," *New England Historical and Genealogical Register*, 13 (1859): 55.

23 "Diary of the Reverend Joseph Green," *Essex Institute Historical Collections*, 8 (1866): 221; Deodat Lawson, *Christ's Fidelity the Only Shield against Satan's Malignity* (Boston, 1692), p. 65.

24 Francis Wallett, ed., *The Diary of Ebenezer Parkman* (Worcester, Mass., 1982), p. 218.

25 Franklin Dexter, ed., *The Literary Diary of Ezra Stiles*, 3 vols. (New York, 1910), I: 385–6. See also Josiah Cotton, "Some Observations," p. 53. Magical healing seems also to have continued into the eighteenth century. In a medical treatise written around 1720, Cotton Mather lamented that people still used "Sorceries" and "Charms" to "help them to some Ease of their Distempers." According to Mather, such techniques were "commonly . . . practised: even among those who

Local histories compiled during the nineteenth century confirm the impression given by other fragments of evidence that magical tradition lived on in popular culture. These town histories include numerous accounts of magical practice in New England towns and villages throughout the preceding century.[26] Many of these stories involve retaliation against witchcraft. The cessation of witch prosecutions at the end of the seventeenth century neither reflected nor caused a decline in popular fear of witchcraft. Local histories suggest that people continued to blame their misfortunes on witchcraft and, furthermore, that they showed no hesitation in acting against suspect witches. Countermagic remained a popular weapon against occult attack. Take, for example, problems with butter-making: if the cream refused to thicken, the churner might suspect witchcraft and plunge a rod of hot metal into the churn so as to burn the witch and undo the bewitchment. Heat from the metal would have aided the churning process, encouraging belief that the technique worked. When Jabez Hall of Wentworth, New Hampshire, dipped a hot poker in her apparently bewitched cream, not only did the cream begin to thicken, but soon afterward a suspected neighbor, Page Kimball, was found to have a severe burn on one of her legs; Hall was doubtless gratified by the latter as well as former turn of events.[27]

New Englanders continued to injure bewitched animals and to heat the blood or urine of human victims, trusting that the witch responsible would be wounded or burned as a result. In Warren, New Hampshire, soon after the War of Independence, Steven Merrill's deaf son Caleb began to suffer strange fits and pains. One of Merrill's neighbors suggested that the boy might be bewitched. Merrill was "incredulous as to believing in witches," but eventually agreed to put some of the boy's urine in a bottle and place it by the fireplace. It later transpired that Simeon Smith, a neighbor who

have been Baptised for God, and in their Baptism have renounced all Dependence on the Devil" (Cotton Mather, *The Angel of Bethesda,* ed. Gordon Jones [Barre, Mass., 1972], p. 294).

26 Some of the anecdotes contained in these nineteenth-century histories must have been embellished in the telling and retelling; in many cases, they had been passed down through two or three generations. Yet the beliefs and practices recorded show a remarkable consistency. They should be treated with caution, but, as Herbert Leventhal points out, "their prevalence at least indicates that the examples . . . found in more reliable sources are not isolated archaisms, but rather are the tip of the iceberg extending above the waterline of literacy" (Herbert Leventhal, *In the Shadow of the Enlightenment,* p. 78).

27 George Plummer, *History of Wentworth* (Concord, N.H., 1930), p. 345. See also Warren Cochrane, *History of the Town of Antrim, New Hampshire* (Manchester, N.H., 1880), p. 315; Charles Smith, *Annals of the Town of Hillsborough, Hillsborough County, New Hampshire* (Sandbornton, N.H., 1841), p. 29; and Lucy Cross, *History of Northfield, New Hampshire* (Concord, N.H., 1905), pp. 221–2.

was reputed to be a witch, had bled violently at his nose that same day. When the cork repeatedly popped out from the bottleneck, releasing the urine, Merrill and his neighbor decided to use the boy's blood instead and placed a small dagger in the cork to prevent its escape. That night, Simeon Smith died suddenly. When Merrill heard about Simeon's death the next morning, he examined the bottle and discovered that the dagger blade had penetrated through to the blood.[28]

At midcentury, the Reverend Josiah Cotton wrote: "There are but few towns, if any, but at one time or other have not had one or more in suspicion for witchcraft."[29] Popular fear of witchcraft not only remained potent, but occasionally erupted in direct physical violence. In 1660, a Pennsylvanian woman was attacked and forced from her home by townsfolk who believed that she had bewitched a child in the neighborhood.[30] Another woman who was suspected of witchcraft died from injuries inflicted by a mob in Philadelphia. This incident took place in July 1787, just outside the meeting place of the Constitutional Convention. The convention is often described as the apogee of Enlightenment in America, yet outside in the streets Americans were lynching a witch, a telling juxtaposition.[31] Fifteen years later, in 1802, a young man was tried and convicted in New York for assaulting an elderly woman: the man believed that the woman had bewitched him and that he could escape her powers only by cutting her three times across the forehead.[32]

28 William Little, *History of Warren* (Manchester, N.H., 1870), p. 438. See also William Little, *History of Weare, New Hampshire* (Lowell, Mass., 1888), p.414; and Silvanus Hayward, *History of the Town of Gilsum* (Manchester, N.H., 1881), p. 162. For the use of countermagic in cases of animal bewitchment, see Edgar Gilbert, *History of Salem, New Hampshire* (Concord, N.H., 1907), p. 349; Ephraim Jameson, *History of Medway, Massachusetts* (Providence, R.I., 1886), p. 16; Daniel Secomb, *History of the Town of Amherst, Hillsborough County, New Hampshire* (Concord, N.H., 1883), p. 471; John Sibley, *History of the Town of Union in the County of Lincoln, Maine* (Boston, 1851), pp. 228–9; and John Greenleaf Whittier, *Supernaturalism of New England* (1847; Norman, Okla., 1969), p. 92.

29 Josiah Cotton, "Some Observations," p. 49.

30 J. Smith Furthey and Gilbert Cope, *History of Chester County, Pennsylvania* (Philadelphia, 1881), p. 413.

31 *Independent Journal* (New York, N.Y.), 18 July 1787; *Massachusetts Centinel,* 1 August 1787.

32 *Boston Weekly Magazine,* I (18 December 1802). For further discussion of witch beliefs and witchcraft incidents in the eighteenth century, see Herbert Leventhal, *In the Shadow of the Enlightenment,* chap. 3, and John Demos, *Entertaining Satan,* pp. 387–400. Demos argues that the "ideational, social and psychological structures which had traditionally supported the belief in witchcraft" gradually weakened during the late eighteenth and early nineteenth centuries so as to bring about an eventual decline in witch accusations (p. 399). I would argue that the "ideational" component was extremely resilient. Jon Butler demonstrates "the tenacity of popular belief in magic, the occult, and other forms of supernatural

Alongside countermagic and divination, astrology also retained its popular appeal. Almanacs continued to attract an enormous readership, despite the fact that astrology had ceased to be respected as a scientific discipline by midcentury.[33] Almanac compiler Nathaniel Low admitted in his 1786 edition that "no books or pamphlets [were] so much the objects of ridicule and contempt as Almanacks." Yet, Low continued, "it is easy to prove that no book we read (except the Bible) is so much valued, and so serviceable to the community."[34] Many almanacs still included the Anatomy, which enabled even the semiliterate to correlate medical treatment with astral movement.[35] Those almanacs that did not include an Anatomy usually provided equivalent information, requiring no intermediary calculation on the reader's part, in the month-by-month tabulations. Some editors were clearly embarrassed about including the diagram and assured the more skeptical of their readers that they did so only in response to popular demand. Samuel Stearns wrote in 1773:

> Should we omit to place this Figure here,
> The Book would hardly sell another Year;
> What (quoth our Country Friend) D'ye think I'll buy
> An Almanack without th'Anatomy?[36]

In 1800, Isaiah Thomas declared that his almanac would henceforth omit the Anatomy, which he denounced as "of use only to those who deal in the marvellous." Yet Thomas had to restore it the following year. Stearns was evidently correct in his assessment of the market.[37]

Eighteenth-century agricultural writers also advised their readers

intervention" throughout the post-revolutionary and ante-bellum periods (Jon Butler, *Awash in a Sea of Faith,* pp. 228–36). See also Alan Taylor, "The Early Republic's Supernatural Economy: Treasure Seeking in the American Northeast, 1780–1830," *American Quarterly,* 38 (1986): 6–34.

33 In the early eighteenth century, students at William and Mary, Yale, and Harvard were still taught natural astrology (Herbert Leventhal, *In the Shadow of the Enlightenment,* pp. 14–20).

34 Nathaniel Low, *An Astronomical Diary, or Almanack for the Year of the Christian Aera 1786* (Boston, 1785).

35 Herbert Leventhal estimates that "about seventy-five percent of the almanacs published in 1760" still included the anatomy (Herbert Leventhal, *In the Shadow of the Enlightenment,* p. 32).

36 Samuel Stearns, *The North-American's Calendar and Gentlemen and Ladies' Diary, Being an Almanack for the Year of the Christian Aera 1773* (Boston, 1772).

37 Isaiah Thomas, *Isaiah Thomas' Massachusetts, Connecticut, Rhode Island, New Hampshire and Vermont Almanack, with an Ephemeris, for the Year of Our Lord 1800* (Worcester, Mass., 1799); *Isaiah Thomas' Massachusetts, Connecticut, Rhode Island, New Hampshire and Vermont Almanack, with an Ephemeris, for the Year of Our Lord 1801* (Worcester, Mass. 1800).

to take notice of the planets and signs. *The Husband-Man's Guide*, published in 1712, recommended that herbs be picked at full moon during June or July. Six years later, *The Husbandman's Magazine* claimed that fruit trees should be planted and grafted in the increase of the moon. In 1797, Samuel Deane's *New England Farmer* urged readers to cut their bushes in careful coordination with astral movement.[38] Many New Englanders were still wedded to a traditional moon-lore: hair cut in the increase of the moon was supposed to grow more luxuriantly; pigs killed in the increase of the moon were said to expand in the barrel.[39] Almanac compilers and farming manuals alike recommended that cattle be gelded when the moon was increasing in Aries, Sagittarius, or Capricorn; sheep were to be shorn when the moon was in Taurus, Virgo, or Libra.[40]

The "Country Friend[s]" to whom Samuel Stearns condescended in his 1773 ditty were not alone in paying attention to astrological information. The owners of trading ships often employed astrologers and fortune-tellers to ascertain the most propitious moment for leaving port. George Mason, a nineteenth-century historian, claimed to have seen hundreds of eighteenth-century horoscopes drawn up for ships departing from Rhode Island.[41] "Mr. Stafford of Tiverton," mentioned by Ezra Stiles in his diary, estimated "what day, hour and minute was fortunate for vessels to sail." Moll Pitcher, a fortune-teller who lived in Lynn, Massachusetts, until her death in 1813, had many clients from nearby seaports.[42] This aspect of mercantile activity serves as a reminder that traditional beliefs were not limited to rural backwaters. Magical divination and astrological prediction remained vitally important in the personal and business affairs of many people throughout the northern colonies.

The leaders of New England's "Errand into the Wilderness" had hoped to build a community in which godly men and women would be "better preserved from the common corruptions of this evil world." Liberated from the vortex of sin that was Stuart England, New Englanders would "serve the Lord and work out [their] sal-

38 *The Husband-Man's Guide* (Boston, 1712), p. 9; *The Husbandman's Magazine* (Boston, 1718), p. 117; Samuel Deane, *The New England Farmer* (Worcester, Mass., 1797), p. 12.

39 William Bliss, *Old Colony Town and Other Sketches* (Boston, 1893), p. 104.

40 Daniel Leeds, *The American Almanack for the Year of Christian Account 1713* (New York, 1713); Titan Leeds, *The American Almanack for the Year of Christian Account 1722* (Philadelphia, 1721); *The Husband-Man's Guide*, pp. 7–8.

41 George Mason, "African Slave Trade in Colonial Times," *American Historical Record and Repository of Notes and Queries*, 1 (1872): 319.

42 Samuel Drake, *New England Legends and Folklore* (New York, 1967), p. 119.

vation under the power and purity of His holy ordinances."[43] One hundred and fifty years later, the rhetoric with which New England ministers justified resistance, rebellion, and then independence emphasized continuity with that earlier vision. Clergymen compared the break with Great Britain to the Israelites' flight from Egypt and the Puritans' departure from England in the early seventeenth century: each of these providential events signaled the triumph of liberty and piety over despotism and sin. The new republic was to preserve unsullied the faith that Puritan leaders had sought to embody in their New-English Israel. These revolutionary sermons used the same texts, the same themes, and the same language that characterized sermonic literature in early New England.[44] Indeed, ministers urged Americans to emulate the faith of earlier founding fathers:

> Let us be careful to keep up among us, the religion of Jesus Christ pure and uncorrupted by human additions and mixtures, and the worship of God unadulterated, and then God in whom our fathers trusted and were delivered, will delight to build us up, and to plant us.[45]

Yet underlying that rhetoric of uncorrupted faith, the reality of supernatural culture in New England was just as complex and confused as ever.

As the eighteenth century drew to a close, magical belief and practice persisted in the popular culture of New England. Not only the inhabitants of isolated rural communities but even the merchants and sea captains of coastal ports consulted cunning folk and astrologers. People also wielded magical power on their own behalf as occasion demanded, primarily to defend themselves against occult attack. These New Englanders gave credence to a dazzling array of beliefs and traditions; they drew from a chaotic fund of supernatural resources, rich and colorful in its diversity. The quixotic dream of spiritual purity that overlay that ferment of activity has proven to be extremely resilient, but it was as quixotic then as it is now.

43 John Winthrop, "A Model of Christian Charity," in Perry Miller, ed., *The American Puritans: Their Prose and Poetry* (Garden City, N.Y., 1956), p. 82.

44 Harry Stout examines this rhetoric of continuity in *The New England Soul: Preaching and Religious Culture in Colonial New England* (New York, 1986), chap. 14.

45 Peter Whitney, *American Independence Vindicated* (Boston, 1777), p. 51.

APPENDIX A

WITCHCRAFT TRIALS IN SEVENTEENTH-CENTURY NEW ENGLAND (EXCLUDING PERSONS ACCUSED DURING THE SALEM WITCH HUNT)

The following list includes only cases that went to trial and came to final judgment. For prosecutions that did not reach trial, see John Demos, *Entertaining Satan: Witchcraft and the Culture of Early New England* (New York, 1982), pp. 402–9.

*	=	confession
E	=	executed
?	=	probably, but not certainly
[ ]	=	a trial probably, but not certainly, took place
R	=	verdict reversed

Year	*Accused Person*	*Town, Colony*	*Verdict*	
1647	Alice Young	Windsor, Conn.	convicted	E
1647?	Elizabeth Kendall	Cambridge, Mass.	convicted	E
1648	Margaret Jones	Charlestown, Mass.	convicted	E
1648	Mary Johnson	Wethersfield, Conn.	convicted	E*
1651	Joan Carrington	Wethersfield, Conn.	convicted	E
1651	John Carrington	Wethersfield, Conn.	convicted	E
1651	Mary Parsons	Springfield, Mass.	acquitted	
1651	Hugh Parsons	Springfield, Mass.	convicted	R
1651	Alice Lake	Dorchester, Mass.	convicted	E
1651	Bassett (f)	Fairfield, Conn.	convicted	E*
1652	John Bradstreet	Rowley, Mass.	acquitted	
1653?	Knapp (f)	Fairfield, Conn.	convicted	E
1654	Lydia Gilbert	Windsor, Conn.	convicted	E?
1655	Elizabeth Godman	New Haven, New Haven[a]	acquitted	
1655	Bailey (f)	New Haven, New Haven	acquitted	
1655	Nicholas Bailey	New Haven, New Haven	acquitted	

[a]The colony of New Haven was later incorporated into Connecticut.

Year	Accused Person	Town, Colony	Verdict	
1656	Jane Walford	Portsmouth, Mass.	acquitted?	
1656	Eunice Cole	Hampton, Mass.	acquitted	
1656	Ann Hibbens	Boston, Mass.	convicted	E
1658	Elizabeth Garlick	Easthampton, Conn.	acquitted	
1659	John Godfrey	Andover, Mass.	acquitted	
1659	Mary Holman	Cambridge, Mass.	acquitted?	
1659	Winifred Holman	Cambridge, Mass.	acquitted?	
1659	Elizabeth Bailey	York, Mass.	acquitted	
1661	Margaret Jennings	Saybrook, Conn.	acquitted	
1661	Nicholas Jennings	Saybrook, Conn.	acquitted	
1662	John Godfrey	Haverhill, Mass.	acquitted	
1662	Judith Varlet	Hartford, Conn.	[acquitted?]	
1662	Mary Sanford	Hartford, Conn.	convicted	E?
1662	Andrew Sanford	Hartford, Conn.	acquitted	
1662	Ayers (f)	Hartford, Conn.	escaped	
1662–3	Rebecca Greensmith	Hartford, Conn.	convicted	E*
1662–3	Nathaniel Greensmith	Hartford, Conn.	convicted	E
1663	Mary Barnes	Farmington, Conn.	convicted	E
1663 (Jan)	Elizabeth Seager	Hartford, Conn.	acquitted	
1663 (Jul)	Elizabeth Seager	Hartford, Conn.	acquitted	
1665	John Godfrey	Haverhill, Mass.	acquitted	
1665	Elizabeth Seager	Hartford, Conn.	convicted	R
1665	Mary Hall	Setauket, Conn.	acquitted	
1665	Ralph Hall	Setauket, Conn.	acquitted	
1668–9	Katherine Harrison	Wethersfield, Conn.	acquitted	
1669	Robert Williams	Hadley, Mass.	acquitted	
1669	Susannah Martin	Amesbury, Mass.	[acquitted?]	
1670?	Ann Burt	Lynn, Mass.	[acquitted?]	
1673	Eunice Cole	Hampton, Mass.	acquitted	
1674–5	Mary Parsons	Northampton, Mass.	acquitted	
1676	Mary Ingham	Scituate, Plymouth	acquitted	
1679	Caleb Powell	Newbury, Mass.	acquitted	
1679–80	Elizabeth Morse	Newbury, Mass.	convicted	R
1680	Rachel Fuller	Hampton, N.H.	acquitted	
1680	Isabella Towle	Hampton, N.H.	acquitted	
1680	Eunice Cole	Hampton, N.H.	acquitted	
1680	Bridget Oliver	Salem, Mass.	[acquitted?]	
1681	Mary Hale	Boston, Mass.	acquitted	
1683	James Fuller	Springfield, Mass.	acquitted	
1683	Mary Webster	Hadley, Mass.	acquitted	
1688	Glover (f)	Boston, Mass.	convicted	E*
1692	Elizabeth Clawson	Stamford, Conn.	acquitted	
1692	Mercy Disborough	Fairfield, Conn.	convicted	R

Year	*Accused Person*	*Town, Colony*	*Verdict*
1697	Winifred Benham	Wallingford, Conn.	acquitted
1697	Winifred Benham, Jr.	Wallingford, Conn.	acquitted
	61	28 different communities	16 convictions 4 confessions At least 14 (perhaps 16) executions

[In addition to the cases listed above, Samuel Drake, *Annals of Witchcraft in New England* (1869; New York, 1972), pp. 64 and 117–19 mentions the case of Mary Oliver of Boston, apparently convicted in 1650; and that of Mary Wright, a Quaker of Oyster Bay, Mass., apparently acquitted in 1660. Neither, however, are substantiated by surviving legal records.]

APPENDIX B

PERSONS ACCUSED DURING THE SALEM WITCH HUNT

The information below is taken from Paul Boyer and Stephen Nissenbaum, eds., *The Salem Witchcraft Papers: Verbatim Transcripts of the Legal Documents of the Salem Witchcraft Outbreak*, 3 vols. (New York, 1977). This list includes only persons against whom legal actions were initiated during the Salem prosecutions of 1692. Many others were accused informally.

For those of the accused not given a separate case entry in *The Salem Witchcraft Papers*, the page citation for the complaint, warrant, or other reference to the accused is given after the defendant's name in parentheses. All towns and villages cited were in Massachusetts unless stated otherwise.

* = confession
E = executed

Name	*Town or Village*	*Verdict of Special Court (if any)*	
Arthur Abbot (I, 183)	?		
Nehemiah Abbot, Jr.	Topsfield	released[a]	
John Alden	Boston	escaped	
Daniel Andrew (II, 493)	Salem Village	escaped	
Abigail Barker	Andover	*	
Mary Barker	Andover	*	
William Barker, Sr.	Andover	*	
William Barker, Jr.	Andover	*	
Sarah Bassett	Lynn		
Sarah Bibber	Wenham		
Bridget Bishop	Salem Village	convicted	E
Edward Bishop, Jr. (III, 805)	Salem Village	escaped	
Sarah Bishop	Salem Village	escaped	

[a]accusation withdrawn

Name	*Town or Village*	*Verdict of Special Court (if any)*	
Mary Black	Salem Village		
Mary Bradbury	Salisbury	convicted[b]	
Mary Bridges, Sr.	Andover	*	
Mary Bridges, Jr.	Andover	*	
Sarah Bridges	Andover	*	
Hannah Bromage	Andover		
Sarah Buckley	Salem Village		
George Burroughs	Wells, Maine	convicted	E
Candy (slave)	Salem Town	*	
Andrew Carrier (I, 197)	Andover	*	
Martha Carrier	Andover	convicted	E
Richard Carrier	Andover	*	
Sarah Carrier	Andover	*	
Thomas Carrier, Jr.	Andover	*	
Hannah Carroll (I, 235)	Salem Town		
Bethia Carter, Sr.	Woburn		
Bethia Carter, Jr. (III, 729)	Woburn		
Elizabeth Cary	Salem Town	escaped	
Sarah Churchill	Charlestown		
Mary Clarke	Haverhill		
Rachel Clenton	Ipswich		
Sarah Cloyse	Salem Village		
Sarah Cole	Lynn		
Sarah Cole	Salem Town		
Elizabeth Colson	Reading	escaped?	
Mary Colson (II, 539)	?		
Giles Corey	Salem Village		
Martha Corey	Salem Village	convicted	E
Deliverance Dane	Andover	*	
Sarah Davis (III, 956)	Wenham		
Day (f) (III, 880–881)	?		
Mary DeRich	Salem Village		
Elizabeth Dicer (II, 651)	Piscataqua, Maine		
Rebecca Dike (I, 305)	Gloucester		
Ann Dolliver	Gloucester		
Mehitabel Dowing (III, 880–881)	?		
Joseph Draper (II, 335)	Andover	*	
Lydia Dustin	Reading		
Sarah Dustin	Reading		
Rebecca Eames	Andover	convicted	*[c]
Mary Easty	Salem Village	convicted	E
Esther Elwell	Gloucester		

[b] escaped from prison
[c] reprieved after confession

Name	Town or Village	Verdict of Special Court (if any)
Martha Emerson	Haverhill	*
Joseph Emons	Manchester	
Mary English (III, 805)	Salem Town	escaped
Phillip English	Salem Town	escaped
Thomas Farrer	Lynn	
Edward Farrington	Andover	
Abigail Faulkner, Sr.	Andover	convicted[d]
Abigail Faulkner, Jr. (II, 335)	Andover	*
Dorothy Faulkner	Andover	*
John Flood (I, 183)	Rowley	
Elizabeth Fosdick	Malden	
Ann Foster	Andover	convicted *[c]
Nicholas Frost	Manchester	
Eunice Frye	Andover	
Dorcas Good	Salem Village	
Sarah Good	Salem Village	convicted E
Mary Green	Haverhill	
Thomas Hardy (II, 565)	Piscataqua, Maine	
Elizabeth Hart	Lynn	
Rachel Hatfield (III, 880–881)	?	
Margaret Hawks	Salem Town	
Sarah Hawkes	Andover	*
Dorcas Hoar	Beverly	convicted *[c]
Abigail Hobbs	Topsfield	convicted[e]
Deliverance Hobbs	Topsfield	*
William Hobbs	Topsfield	
Elizabeth How	Topsfield	convicted E
John Howard (II, 465)	Rowley	
Elizabeth Hubbard	Salem Village	
Francis Hutchens	Haverhill	
Mary Ireson	Lynn	
John Jackson, Sr.	Rowley	
John Jackson, Jr.	Rowley	*
George Jacobs, Sr.	Salem Town	convicted E
George Jacobs, Jr.	Salem Village	escaped
Margaret Jacobs	Salem Town	*
Rebecca Jacobs	Salem Village	
Abigail Johnson (II, 499)	Andover	
Elizabeth Johnson, Sr.	?	*
Elizabeth Johnson, Jr.	?	*[f]
Rebecca Johnson	Andover	

[d] reprieved because pregnant
[e] may have saved her life by confessing, although no record of her doing so survives
[f] convicted by Superior Court of Judicature in Jan. 1693; reprieved by governor

Name	Town or Village	Verdict of Special Court (if any)	
Stephen Johnson	Andover	*	
Mary Lacey, Sr.	Andover	convicted	*[c]
Mary Lacey, Jr.	Andover	*	
John Lee	?		
Mercy Lewis	Salem Village		
Jane Lilly	Malden		
Mary Marston	Andover	*	
Susannah Martin	Amesbury	convicted	E
Sarah Morey	Beverly		
Rebecca Nurse	Salem Village	convicted	E
Sarah Osborne	Salem Village		
Mary Osgood	Andover	*	
Elizabeth Paine (II, 339)	Charlestown		
Alice Parker	Salem Town	convicted	E
Mary Parker	Andover	convicted	E
Sarah Parker (III, 1021)	Andover		
Sarah Pease	Salem Town		
Joan Penny	Gloucester		
Hannah Post	Rowley	*	
Mary Post	Rowley	[f]	
Susannah Post	Andover	*	
Margaret Prince	Gloucester		
Benjamin Proctor	Salem Village		
Elizabeth Proctor	Salem Village	convicted[d]	
John Proctor	Salem Village	convicted	E
Sarah Proctor	Salem Village		
William Proctor	Salem Village	*	
Ann Pudeator	Salem Town	convicted	E
Wilmott Reed	Marblehead	convicted	E
Sarah Rice	Reading		
Abigail Roe (I, 305)	Gloucester		
Susannah Roots	Beverly		
Henry Salter	Andover		
John Sawdy	Andover		
Margaret Scott	?	convicted	E
Ann Sears	Woburn		
Susannah Sheldon	?		
Abigail Somes	Salem Town		
Martha Sparks	Chelmsford		
Mary Taylor	Reading		
Tituba (slave)	Salem Village	*	
Job Tookey	Beverly		
Jerson Toothaker	Billerica		
Mary Toothaker	?	*	

Name	Town or Village	Verdict of Special Court (if any)	
Toothaker (f) (I, 183) (daughter of Mary)	?		
Roger Toothaker	Billerica		
Johanna Tyler	Andover	*	
Martha Tyler	Andover	*	
Vincent (f) (III, 880–881)	?		
Mercy Wardwell	Andover	*	
Samuel Wardwell	Andover	convicted	E*[g]
Sarah Wardwell	Andover	*[f]	
Mary Warren	Salem Village	*	
Sarah Wilds	Topsfield	convicted	E
Ruth Wilford (II, 459)	Haverhill		
John Willard	Salem Village	convicted	E
Abigail Williams	Salem Village		
Sarah Wilson, Sr.	Andover	*	
Sarah Wilson, Jr. (I, 335)	Andover	*	
Mary Withridge (II, 493)	Salem Village		
156	24 different communities	30 convictions 44 confessions 19 executions	

[g]withdrew his confession and so was executed

[In addition to the 19 executions, Giles Corey was pressed to death during interrogation. Lydia Dustin, Ann Foster, Sarah Osborne, and Roger Toothaker died in prison.]

NAME INDEX

SUBJECT INDEX